ENVIRONMENTAL MANAGEMENT
Issues in Potable Water in Rural Tamil Nadu

About the Authors

M. Ravichandran is Professor and Head of the Department of Environmental Management, Bharathidasan University, Tiruchirapalli. He received research training in Environmental Economics under the supervision of Prof. M.V. Nadkarni, former Professor of Ecological Economics unit, ISEC, Bangalore and the former Vice-Chancellor of Gulburga University, Karnataka.

Dr. Ravichandran is a Fulbrighte recipient of the Fulbright Award for Indo-American Environmental Leadership Programme (IAELP) and visited the Western Michigan University, USA during September-October 2004. He has several publications of research articles to his credit. And he undertook three major and two minor research projects on various economic aspects of environment.

S. Boopathi is Lecturer, Department of Economics, Bharathiar University, Coimbatore. He received his doctoral degree from the same university Bharathidasan University, Tiruchirappalli.

He rendered assistance to Prof. Haruka Yanagisawa, Institute of Oriental Culture University of Tokyo in completing his research project. Dr. Boopathi is well trained in computer applications to statistical analysis. He offers a course in Environmental Economics at the Post-graduate and M.Phil. Level in Bharathiar University. He has published a number of research papers in referred journals.

ENVIRONMENTAL MANAGEMENT
Issues in Potable Water in Rural Tamil Nadu

M. Ravichandran
S. Boopathi

CONCEPT PUBLISHING COMPANY, NEW DELHI–110 059

Cataloging in Publication Data—DK
Courtesy: D.K. Agencies (P) Ltd. <docinfo@dkagencies.com>

Ravichandran, M.
Environmental management : issues in potable water in rural Tamil Nadu / M. Ravichandran, S. Boopathi.
p. cm.
Study conducted in Tiruchirappalli District.
Includes bibliographical references (p.)
Includes index.
ISBN 8180694100

1. Water-supply, Rural—Environmental aspects—India—Tiruchirappalli (District). 2. Water-supply, Rural—India —Tiruchirappalli (District)—Planning. 3. Drinking water—Prices—Government policy—India—Tiruchirappalli (District). I. Boopathi, S., joint author. II. Title.

DDC 363.610 954 82 22

ISBN -13: 978-81-8069-410-3
ISBN -10: 81-8069-410-0

First Published 2007

Published and Printed by
Ashok Kumar Mittal
Concept Publishing Company
A/15-16, Commercial Block, Mohan Garden
New Delhi-110059 (INDIA)
Phones : 25351460, 25351794 *Fax* : 091-11-25357103
Email : publishing@conceptpub.com

Dr. C. THANGAMUTHU
Vice – Chancellor

BHARATHIDASAN UNIVERSITY
PALKALAIPERUR
TIRUCHIRAPPALLI – 620 024
TAMIL NADU

FOREWORD

There has been a growing concern for environment in the last two decades in the developing countries. Greater responsibilities lie with the academia in fostering scientific treatment in environmental problems. Corollary to this, many a branch on environmental studies, is in the offing, Environmental Management, as a branch has come to reckoning in the reeecent period. As Hare (1970) puts it succintctly that environmental management is concerned with man-environment interface, where the biophysical and socio-economic system interact. There is a need to bridge the gap between physical, natural and social sciences to look for holistic solutions to environmental issues. No single discipline would suffice to bring forth a comprehensive plan for environmental protection. Environmental Management essentially posits to coordinate planning, conservation of resources, environmental legislation and administration.

In this backdrop, this book assumes importance. Actually this is an offshoot of a research study carried out by the authors on environmental and economic aspects of potable water supply at the district level in Tamil Nadu during 1999-2001. The study was sponsored by World Bank under the Capability Building Program in Environmental Eeconomics. This original empirical study brought forth the varius sources of drinking water in rural areaaas, direct and indirect cost involved for the rural households to access water, gender issues, institutional aspects and the environmental factors intervening in sustainable water supply.

Scientific endeavours rest mainly on authentic information on eneivornmental aspects. This book, no doubt, will be immense use to students, researchers and policy-makers as well. In addition, this book is timely that the Millennium Development Goals (MDGs) launched at the Millennium Summit in New York in September 2000, includeee, inter alia, haaving the proportion of people without access to safe water aas one of the targets to be achieved by 2015 from their levels in 1990.

Dr. C . Thangamuthu
Vice Chancellor

PHONE : (Off.) 2407048 (Res.) 2407070 GRAMS : BARD FAX : 91-0431-2407032 E-mail : vc@bdu.ac.in website : www.bdu.ac.in

ACKNOWLEDGEMENTS

At the outset, we express our heartfelt thanks to Dr. C. Thangamuthu, the Vice-Chancellor of Bharathidasan University, for having motivated us to publish this book. We are grateful to him for extending the publishing grant for the same.

We are grateful to the funding agency, viz., the "World Bank Aided India: Environmental Management Capacity Building Technical Assistance Project". We express our gratitude to the Indira Gandhi Institute of Development Research, Mumbai for implementing the program. Our thanks are due to Dr. (Mrs.) Jyothi K. Parikh, Chairperson EERC.

We are obliged to Dr. Chellam Balasundaram, Professor, Department of Animal Science, Bharathidasan University for having served as Assistant Co-ordinator of the Project. We are also thankful to Prof. Paul P. Appasamy, Former Director of Madras School of Economics, Chennai, for his constant encouragement right from the beginning of the project. We thank our research team; Mr. A. Arunachalam (Who worked for one month as Research Associate), Mr. A. Sambanham, Research Associate, and Mr. P. Balamurugan, Research Investigator, for their invaluable service in collection and compilation of data for the study.

The officials of the Tamil Nadu Water and Drainage (TWAD) Board and the Ground Water Board, Tiruchirappalli were kind enough to furnish necessary information from their end. We are grateful to them. We whole-heartedly thank the local body officials of the select village panchayats and the respondents, the rural households for having shared information and their experiences with our research team.

Finally, we wish to record our appreciation to Mr. A. Kannan and Mr. A. Royal Edward Williams for their help in arranging the final manuscript and the soft copy of the same.

M. Ravichandran
S. Boopathi

CONTENTS

ABBREVIATIONS

ARWSP	–	Accelerated Rural Water Supply Progammes
Ca	–	Calcium
CAHEEO	–	Central Public Health and Environmental Engineering Organisation
Cl	–	Chloride
CO_3	–	Carbonate
CSE	–	Centre for Science and Environment
CVM	–	Contingent Valuation Method
CWSS	–	Combined Water Supply Scheme
DRDA	–	District Rural Development Authority
DRP	–	Drought Relief Programme
DW	–	Drinking Water
EC	–	Electrical Conductivity
EEC	–	European Economic Council
F	–	Fluoride
Fe	–	Iron and Feacal Coliform
GLWR	–	Ground Level Water Reservoir
HCO_3	–	Bicarbonate
HHs	–	Households
HP	–	Hand Pump
ITDP	–	Integrated Tribal Development Programme
K	–	Potassium
KIRWS and ES	–	Karnataka Integrated Rural Water Supply and Environmental Schemes
KM	–	Kilometres
LIC	–	Life Insurance Corporation
Lpcd	–	Litre per capita per day
Mg	–	Magnesium
MNP	–	Minimum Need Programmes
NDWM	–	National Drinking Water Mission
NGO	–	Non-Governmental Organization

NO_3	–	Nitrate
NSSO	–	National Sample Survey Organisation
NWP	–	National Water Policy
OHT	–	Over Head Tank
PS	–	Principal Source
PWD	–	Public Works Department
QLPM	–	Quantity Litre Per Minute
RGNDWM	–	Rajiv Gandhi National Drinking Water Mission
Rs.	–	Rupees (Indian currency)
RWS	–	Rural Water Supply
RWSS	–	Rural Water Supply Scheme
SO_4	–	Sulphate
TDS	–	Total Dissolved Solids
TH	–	Total Hardness
TWAD	–	Tamil Nadu Water Supply and Drainage Board
UNCED	–	United Nations Conference on Environment and Development
VWSC	–	Village Water Supply Committee
WB	–	World Bank
WGDP	–	Western Ghats Development Programme
WHO	–	World Health Organisation

LIST OF TABLES

LIST OF FIGURES

LIST OF MAPS

LIST OF COLOUR PLATES

1

ENVIRONMENTAL MANAGEMENT

"We Have To Understand That We Can Never Control Nature.
Nature's Systems Are Far, Far Too Complex.
But We Can Manage Them".

(Charles Secrett, 1998)

It envisages the *modus operandi* of allocation of natural and man-made resources in such a way that it makes optimum use of the environment on a sustainable manner. In this process the aspirations of the present generation are satisfied without jeopardizing the needs the coming generation as well.

> *There is compelling need to clarify one thing. That is, there exist numerous disciplines on environmental studies like environmental science, environmental geography, environmental history, environmental economics and environmental engineering and so on, however environmental management does differ from the above-listed branches of environmental studies. Environmental management, no doubt is an interdisciplinary subject, but mainly coordinates environmental planning by acting as catalyst in motivating other related branches and endeavouring to synthesize the outcomes of various environmental studies towards finding operational solutions to environmental problems.*

The underlying philosophy of management exemplifies an element of 'conscious choice'. Making a definite and determined preference among alternative proposals towards achieving desired objectives can be the hallmark of management. Environmental management does not stop with optimal allocation of natural resources alone but goes beyond by preparing strategies to overcome all 'intolerable constraints' imposed by the environment. This is a field of study to discerning man-environment interface where scientific principles are applied towards finding solutions to problems.

Environmental management is a fairly new and fast evolving discipline, but yet to gain universally accepted definition, notwithstanding the very broad scope and the involvement of diverse disciplines. However, a few definitions of environmental management are available in the literature, which may be presented as under:

S. Macgill puts it as, "An interface between scientific endeavour and policy development and implementation". According to Sharatt, 1995, "Management of the environmental performance of organizations, bodies and companies". Royston, 1978 states that "Environmental Management cannot hope to master all of the issues and environmental components it has to deal with. Rather, the environmental manger's jobs is to study and try to control by and each particular objectives". According Clarke to (1999) environmental management is "an approach which goes beyond natural resource management to encompass the political and social as well as the natural environments". Further Dorney (1989) puts it "environmental management – a generic description of a process undertaken by system-oriented professionals with a natural science, social science or less commonly, an engineering, law or design background, tackling problems of human-altered environment on an interdisciplinary basis from a quantitative and or futuristic viewpoint". There is one more definition, which is worth mentioning; Jolly (1978) states that it is "the process of allocating natural and artificial resources so as to make optimum use of the environment in satisfying basic human needs at the minimum and more, if possible, on a sustainable basis".

Existing literature on environmental management suggests that this field enquiry is quite wide by encompassing varied aspects relating to environment. Essentially this follows an interdisciplinary approach calling for integration of ecology, policy-making, planning and ultimately sustainable development. Generally environmental management comprises environmental planning, conservation of resources, environmental status evaluation and environmental legislation and administration.

This discipline looks at use and misuse of environmental resources and one hand, reduction of generation of pollution thereby improving lifestyle and well-being of human beings on the other. Further environmental studies focus on different facets and in this process, each discipline in the name of specialization, concentrates only on one facet to do an in-depth study. As a result, scientific information gets generated on a piece meal level on various dimensions of the problem. Given the fact that inputs from all different angles are warranted to solve environmental problems, a discipline is required to synthesize the outcomes of host of other disciplines to finding a holistic solution to environmental problems. Environmental management, in this milieu, assumes greater significance.

Irreversible nature of environmental problems warrant every individual, every academic discipline, every policy-maker, every administrator, every businessman, every social activist, and every institution in sharing responsibilities to devise means to protect the environment.

Each party in someway or the other exerts influence on the environment by drawing different forms of resource inputs and using the environment as waste receptor. None gets exempted. However, the manner and the extent of use and abuse do vary among different stakeholders.

Relevant here to mention the classification of major environmental categories of people viz., biosphere people, eco-system people, and ecological refugees. Biosphere people may constitute a larger proportion compared to other two sections. Eco-system people live in harmony with nature and cause less damage to environment, while the ecological refugees are the least damagers but the worst sufferers of environmental problems. Necessary to understand that the magnitude of pressure exerted on the environment by people do differ. As a result, in most cases, the impact shall be on those who are unconnected to those who have caused it. Precisely, this is called externality.

Managing the environment stems from the fact that environmental problems are becoming complex on the one hand and advances in environmental planning, monitoring impact and modelling assessment are occurring as discipline shall co-ordinate towards achieving sustainable development.

1.1 Economic Principles Governing Environmental Management

Understanding of economic principles becomes necessary for environmental management in firms besides dealing with a host of environmental issues. The first and foremost is "The creation and capture of value" by firms. In the process of converting inputs into output with the help of technology, the firm *ipso facto*, business concern creates value over and above the total cost of the resources required to produce them. In reality, owing to market imperfections and government intervention capturing of economic value by its producers become difficult (Reinharft, 2000).

More often than not technology opted by firms; in the production process involves spillover effects. In economic parlance it is called externalities. The costs that pollution and environmental degradation inflict on society, in the form of damage to human health, plant and animal life are the classic examples of externalities.

Theoretically this can be explained that private optimum may not coincide with social optimum owing to the presence of external cost. External cost is nothing but damages imposed on the society. Negative externality is a social menace needs to be controlled or abated.

The formidable challenge for environmental management is to make private optimum solution coincide with socially optimum level through appropriate methodology to reduce external cost. One of the methods is bring in environmentally benign technology. Whose responsibility is this? Undoubtedly environmental engineers are responsible for redesigning the technology towards achieving sustainable development.

Economic incentives/disincentives like subsidy, tax and depreciation allowance can only supplement the engineering solution, *ipso facto*, command and control method. Economic measures can never supplant engineering mechanism.

Regulation *vis-à-vis* market incentive is one of the unresolved controversies in environmental economics. Much of current literature supports economic/market approach towards pollution control. Even the World Bank's perception of "New environmentalism" emphasizes that whenever and wherever possible, market based initiatives should be used instead of command and control regulation to induce industry to pollute less. The developed countries have already built into their fiscal structure some market based incentives for highly polluting units.

The fact remains that India seldom employed incentive approaches but followed regulation/physical control/command and control method until 1992. This approach has been duly backed by legislations such as India's Water (Prevention and Control of Pollution) Act of 1981 and Environment Protection Act of 1986, towards combating pollution. The *modus operandi* of these regulations is to specify pollution standards and penalties for non-compliance, even to the extent of closing down erring units.

There is no gainsaying the fact that market instruments alone would be sufficient to achieve effective pollution control, nor will regulatory process by itself be adequate to win the purpose. The critical question is whether or not to give more weightage to market instruments. Is it necessary to combine market with regulatory procedure? To answer these questions, it is necessary to discuss the various types of instruments such as fiscal, market and regulatory procedures in detail. Necessary here is to address the dichotomy between market and state in the light of relative merits of different instruments.

1.2 Regulation

Regulatory method envisages fixing up of standards, which are also called maximum permissible level or tolerance limit to which the erring industrial units shall comply with. There are no across the board standards but does vary for different medium of disposal. Generally the prescribed standards range from 80 to 90 per cent of pollution to be abated. Though pollution standards are set in India at a level comparable with the standards in the advanced countries, particularly UK, the pollution control policy appears to be easily borne by the industry, nor even if passed on to consumer in the form of an increase in price, such a price rise is only marginal.

The Central Board for the prevention and control of water pollution prepared in the year 1984, an industry-wise Comprehensive industry Documents to help in evolving industry-specific minimal National standards based on the cost of various levels of effluent treatment. Normally, the 3 per cent level of annual turnover of the specific industry is accepted as the appropriate level of treatment to be installed by each industry.

According to the comprehensive industry document, the annual burden of treatment at prevailing standards as percentage of annual turnover remained within 12 per cent in many industries such as sugar, oil refinery, synthetic fibres, breweries, pesticides, etc.

1.3 Fiscal Incentives and Disincentives

This approach envisages economic disincentives such as charges or taxes and fiscal incentives such as depreciation allowance, exemption of capital gains, reduction in import tariff and reduction in union excise duty towards pollution control (Purohit and Rao, 1994).

An important fiscal incentive is to provide accelerated depreciation allowance for the use of pollution control equipments. In the Union Budget of 1993-94, the rate of depreciation on plant and machinery meant for environmental protection and control was raised from 40 to 100 per cent. Another fiscal incentive built into the tax system is the exemption of capital gains arising from transfer of immovable property as well as machinery for establishing business in a less congested place (normally outside a city).

Both these concessions are a part of the Income Tax Act, 1961. In regard to commodity taxes, there is a reduction in import tariff to 40 per cent. This concession is given for specified list of approximately about thirty-nine equipments. On domestically produced goods, the Union Excise Duty is levied on about twenty-three items at a lower rate of 5 per cent.

Another significant prescription for the problem of externality of pollution is charges/taxes. The justification for a pollution charge is fundamental in theory. The charge is a price extracted from polluters for using the environment and is intended to discourage them from doing so. To accomplish this goal, the tax cannot be nominal like India's water cess, but a true tax. The general economic solution to ensure sustainable use of the environment is to price the use of environmental resources high enough to reflect the cost imposed on other proximate, distant and future users.

Pollution abatement costs are lower for the society as a whole under a tax than with regulation. In the real world, effluent charges have been rated successful only in the field of water pollution control policy; they do not play an important role in air pollution control.

1.4 Market Approach

This approach introduces certain market incentives for firms to make mutual adjustments among themselves in such a way as to achieve desired goal at the least cost. Also the market approach does allow firms to decide on their own in selecting the type of technology, etc., to overcome the drawbacks of regulatory method. The point to note here is that market incentives would not supplant the regulatory process but would only allow certain financial incentives to supplement control mechanism.

The incentive schemes consist of 'bubble', 'offsets' and 'emission banks' (Crone, Theodore *et al.*, 1985). The bubble concept is designed to take account of the different incremental costs of controlling pollution both across the process within a particular plant and across plants and firms. A figurative bubble is placed around an entire plant, or area, treating it as a single source of emission rather than as a series of independent sources.

The bubble programme considers for instance, an industrial plant, which constitutes multiple sources of emission as single unit and treats all its sources. The aim of the method essentially is to control overall emission level. The incentive in this programme is that the factory owner is encouraged to concentrate only on those sources where the additional costs of pollution control are low and reduce pollution control where additional costs are high thereby keeping down the total pollution control cost.

The 'offset' programme is developed mainly to encourage new plants to open and old ones to expand without deteriorating air quality. The offset programme allows such concentration and expansions if the new emissions that result are more than offset by reductions in emissions from existing sources. In this process, the new entrant negotiates with existing firms by offering to buy emissions reduction for them. The main difference between 'bubble' and 'offset' programmes is that while the former may not necessarily reduce the amount of air pollution in the area, the latter does. Besides, while the 'bubble' applies only to existing sources, the 'offset' covers new sources as well.

The 'emission bank' programme is to supplement 'offset' programme in terms of timing the trade of emission reductions. This envisages that if a firm reduces its daily emissions below mandated levels, it can bank those reductions that is, hold them in reserve at a clearing house, for trade at some future date. It means that reduction of emission over and above the permissible level will be kept as reserve for sale for those big polluters whose abatement cost of pollution is very high. This programme simply means the offset scheme is more efficient by help, making potential polluters to straightway contact the clearing house inventory for trade, and they need not incur any expenditure in trying to locate offset partners.

Above-mentioned programmes like 'bubble', 'offset' and 'emission bank' would call for sophisticated electronic equipments for monitoring emission levels. Their adoption in developing countries like India could encourage the growth of electronic industries to create a strong base to make this adoption viable.

Another alternative approach uses marketable emission permits (tradable permits) to reduce environmentally damaging activities. Under this system, which has been used in the United States more than anywhere else, firms apply for emission permits, which are issued at a level so that aggregate emissions comply with regional pollution standards. These permits can be traded among users, from those firms with low costs of pollution abatement to those with high costs. All the above-mentioned market instruments are no rhetoric but formed the language of environmental economists in the recently concluded conference on climate change, held in Kyoto, Japan during December 1997.

Most of these market options were taken up for discussion by the participating countries. There was a conflict between US and the European Union over the proposal of 'Bubbling' reduction targets. The proposal was that the 15 members from the European Union as a whole would meet a target regardless of whether Germany and UK were required to reduce emissions or Portugal and Luxembourg being allowed to increase them by as much as 40 per cent over 1990 levels.

Reference was also made about 'Basket approach'. Under this the U.S. proposed all six main greenhouse gases to come under review as against the Japanese and European Union proposals that excluded the three secondary gases such as hydrofluoro carbons, perfluorocarbons and sulphur hexafluoride. Each one has a global warming potential between 4,000 to 24,000 times that of carbon dioxide. Basically the basket approach envisages across the board gas cuts, rather than a gas by gas approach. The three main gases are CO_2, methane and nitrous oxide.

1.5 Carbon Credit (CC)

This concept is an offshoot of an international agreement popularly known as the Kyoto Protocol*. Carbon credits envisage issuance of certificates to countries to bring down their emission of Green House Gas (GHG) which causes global warming. Estimates suggest that more than 60 per cent of GHG is from industries like cement, steel, textiles and fertilizers. Besides, gases like hydrofluoro carbons, methane and nitrous oxide impinge upon ozone layer leading to global warming.

The carbon credit is an incentive based programme, includes countries to cut down their GHG emissions as those countries,

---

* Kyoto Protocol is a voluntary treaty signed by 141 countries in agreement of reducing Green House Gas (GHG) emission by 5.2 per cent below 1990 level by 2012. The USA is yet to be a signatory of this treaty. The first phase of Kyoto Protocol will start from 2007 while the second phase starts from 2008. Any non-compliance of the first phase shall attract a penalty of 40 euro per tonne of CO_2 equivalent and in the second phase will be increased to 100 euro per tonne of CO_2.

which meet their targets, stand to benefit. Surplus credits gained by overshooting the emission reduction targets can be sold in the global market. Each credit is equivalent to one tonne of CO_2 emissions reduced. A country like India, whose GHG emission is much lower than the target fixed by Kyoto Protocol and, hence, she is entitled to sell surplus credit to northern industrialized countries. In this milieu trading process starts at two trading places are in the reckoning; the Chicago Climate Exchange and the European Climate Exchange, besides the open market.

1.6 Synergy of Regulation and Market

Notwithstanding the fact there are arguments coming up not in favour of regulation that this is purely an environmental engineering method. This does propose many incentives for adoption of pollution control. On many counts pollution tax scores over command and control method.

It is the pollution tax, more than a regulatory approach, which is consistent with a unified analytical framework for arriving at a solution to the environmental problem. Environmental regulations can have an educational effect that market-based approaches might miss. Anti-pollution publicity campaigns can accompany legal restrictions so that over time the idea that pollution is wrong is instilled in people. If the incentive were entirely economic, people might reduce pollution in response to price signals but they would not be made to feel that pollution is wrong (Kerr *et al.*, 1997).

A proper fiscal intervention for the developing countries such as India is the need of the hour. It is important to combine all the instruments such as regulation market incentive and if possible public expenditure on Research and Development.

In February 1992, the Government adopted a policy statement for abatement of pollution. It indicates the government's commitment to prevent further deterioration of the environment and asserts that it would make use of a mix of instruments including legislation and regulation, fiscal incentives, voluntary agreements, educational programmes and information campaigns. Further, the constitution amendments of 1992 assign the environmental protection and conservation function to local bodies. It is hoped that such initiatives result in a better environment in the days to come.

1.7 Environmental Policy

Essential to indicate the line of argument based on incentives, as the fundamental problem in managing environmental resources is the problem of incentives. Jan Bojo and Karl-Goran Maler argued that "environmental resources are often such that it is not in the best of interest of the individual to act in a way that is best for society at large. The basic objective of environmental policy is therefore to create an economic environment in which the incentives are correct, that is, to create a system in which the best interests of individuals, households, companies, local communities, organizations, state agencies, etc. coincides with the collective of public interest. Obviously, the design of mechanism to improve the incentive structure will depend not only on the characteristics of the resources, but also on the general economic and legal backgrounds."

1.8 Environmental Laws in India

1. The Air (Prevention and Control of Pollution) Act, 1981, amended in 1987.
2. The Water (Prevention and Control of Pollution) Act, 1974, amended in 1988.
3. The Water (Prevention and Control of Pollution Cess) Act, 1977.
4. The Environment (Protection) Act, 1986.
5. The Factories Act, 1948, amended in 1987.
6. The Motor Vehicles Act, 1972, amended in 1988.
7. The Wildlife (Protection) Act, 1972, amended in 1991.
8. The Forest (Conservation) Act, 1980, amended in 1991.
9. The Public Liability Insurance Act, 1992.

1.9 The Draft National Environmental Policy (NEP, 2004)

The NEP 2004, reaffirms India's commitment to a clean environment duly mandated in the constitution in Articles 48A and 51A(g), backed by judicial interpretation of Article 21. Necessary to mention that the NEP 2004 is in the initial stage with a draft copy online to receiving suggestions and comments by the Ministry of Environment and Forests of India.

The NEP 2004 sets out several objectives by keeping in view the formidable environmental challenges. They include the following:

(i) Conservation of critical environmental resources
(ii) Intra-generational equity: livelihood security for the poor
(iii) Inter-general equity
(iv) Integration of environmental concerns in economic and social development
(v) Efficiency in environmental resources use
(vi) Environmental Governance
(vii) Enhancement of resources for environmental conservation.

Realization of the stated objectives depends largely on the principles of mechanism to be adopted. The draft policy spells out a host of principles, which warrant "strategic interventions by different public authorities at Central, State and Local Governments levels". Besides it calls for partnership between public agencies and local communities. Importantly the whole exercise needs to be backed by legislation and the legal machinery.

Mainly, the principles enunciated exemplified the fact that human beings are at the centre of concern by upholding the right to development. Stress is laid on to integrate environmental protection as part of the development process. Exercising caution that inadequate scientific data should in no way be used to put off cost-effective measures to prevent ecological degradation.

The principles envisage attaching economic values to services of environmental resources that efficiency in use of the same shall be obtained. The other principles include cost minimization, equity, legal liability, public trust doctrine, decentralization, integration, environmental standard setting, preventive action and environmental offsetting.

1.10 Environmental Sustainability Index (ESI 2005) of Nations

The Yale Centre for Environmental Law and Policy and the Centre for International Earth Science Information Network at Columbia University in association with the World Economic Forum brought out the report on ESI 2005. As per this, India ranked 101 among 146 countries.

The methodology followed in the report has been by grouping participating countries on the basis of their Gross Domestic Product. Then each country is assigned an individual ESI score inferred from a data set of 76 variables, which are classified against 21 indicators and arrived as five broad components in the end stage. The major components include environmental systems, reducing stresses, reducing human vulnerability, social and institutional capacity, and global stewardship. Actual score of ESI of each country is discernible on a scale of 0 to 100. Incidentally, India, which has an estimated per capita GDP of $ 2530, obtained a ESI score of 452. Relatively, Finland and Norway topped the rankings by outsmarting certain industrially developed nations.

Many a force is at work behind the dismal ESI score of India. Both air and water qualities, which fell below the reference value remained a major cause. The exposition of ESI report is an eye opener that the ongoing preparation of the National Environmental Policy in India to incorporate correctives in the environmental planning and monitoring towards better management of environment (*The Hindu*, Feb. 9, 2005).

1.11 Environmental Management Systems (EMS)

Basically this is a mechanism to enhancing environmental performance of organizations. By following scientific way to approach environmental affairs; addressing both short and long term impacts on the environment. EMS executes order for efficient allocation of resources and eventually evaluate the whole exercise from the initial procedures and till the end process on a continues basis.

The key elements of an EMS include *inter alia*, policy statement containing the stated commitment to the environment, identification of potential environmental impacts of the activities and services, environmental goals of the organization, implementation of plans, training employees to be aware of their environmental responsibilities and to be ready for environment review.

An EMS is voluntary and not mandatory. It is also not regulatory but an arrangement made by organizations to respond to regulatory stipulations. Hence, an EMS can construed as an integral part of any organization with definite purpose of identification of potential impact and means of abating the same (Richard Welford, 1999).

An EMS is defined by the British Standards Institute as "*the organizational structure, responsibilities, practices, procedure, processes and resources for determining and implementing environmental policy.*"

An EMS is organization specific, across the prescription is not possible as the management structures, products and services to vary among organizations. There is no one-size-first-all EMS. However, certain commonalities in EMS organizations may be discerned such that planning, measurement and review or incorporated in all EMS.

1.12 International Standards Organization (ISO)

ISO primarily, is a non-governmental organization, came into existence from 1947 and found its location in Geneva, Switzerland. The function central to ISO is to formulate technical standards *vis-à-vis* environmental issues. Initially, ISO 14000 was introduced with a purpose of developing voluntary standards to facilitating firms dealing with environmental quality. Later in September 1996, the ISO brought out the first edition of ISO 14001, which exemplified the Environmental Management Systems (EMS) standard. ISO 14001 is a comprehensive package, includes EMS auditing, eco-labelling, performance evaluation and life-cycle assessment. ISO 14001 is essentially technical standards specified against which concerned organization shall receive certification. An updated version of second edition of ISO 14001 was released in 2004.

The methodology behind the preparation of the ISO standards is worth mentioning here. As stated earlier, it follows a voluntary consensus based approach, where the member countries across the world participate in the process. Negotiation will go on between countries on the proposed positions on the standards and the final version would emerge depending upon the official note on the drafts casts by the member countries. Different organizations like industry, government and NGOs do take part in this exercise.

1.13 Environmental Auditing

This forms an integral part of the Environmental Management System. The concept gained prominence during the early 1990s, with the publication of the British Standard BS 7750 in 1992 and 1994. Environmental audit acts as a tool to assess environmental performance of firms on a continuous basis. It is voluntary responsibility industries to undertake this exercise.

Undoubtedly companies stand to benefit from environmental auditing by means of gaining competitive edge over rivals. In addition, gaining opportunity to check environmental measures are satisfactory, and auditing promotes all round sustainable development.

As of now, this exercise has been voluntarily undertaken in various developed countries like U.S.A., U.K. and Canada. India is yet catch up with it. There is a need to sensitive this and it may be relevant to reiterate the standard definitions:

The International Chamber of Commerce (ICC 1989) defines it as:

> *"A management tool comprising a systematic, documented, periodic, and objective evolution of how well environmental organization, management and equipment are performing with the aim of helping to safeguard the environment by: (i) facilitating management and control of environmental practices; and (ii) assessing compliance with company policies, which include meeting regulatory requirements."*

According to the confederation of British Industry,

> *"The systematic examination of interactions between any business operation and its surrounding. This includes all emissions to air, land and water; legal constrains, the effects on the neighbouring community, landscape and ecology; and the public perception of the operating company in the local area ... Environmental auditing does not stop at compliance with legislation. Nor is it a 'green-washing' public relations exercise. Rather, it is a total strategic approach to the organization's activities".*

Another definition given by the eco-management and audit scheme, is:

> *"A management tool comprising a systematic, documented, periodic and objective evolution of the performance of the organization, management system and processes designed to protect the environment with the aim of: (i) facilitating management control of practices which may have impact on the environment; (ii) assessing compliance with company environmental policies."*

The objectives central to environmental audit are:

(a) Verifying compliance
(b) Identifying problems
(c) Formulating environmental policy
(d) Measuring environmental impact
(e) Measuring performance
(f) Confirming environmental management system effectiveness
(g) Providing a database for corrective action and future plans
(h) Developing the company's environmental strategy
(i) Communication.

The above stated objectives clearly explain that auditing is comprehensive, going beyond regulatory compliance, by taking firms towards greener pasture (Richard Welford, 1999).

Environmental auditing, of course, is not free from drawbacks. Already, companies do put up resistance to introduce pollution control measures and on top of it auditing will add on to cost of compliance, which ultimately becoming cost prohibitive. Understanding between an auditing team and industry personnel may not be smooth due to difference in level of knowledge of an industry. Understandably, the small-scale units might be reluctant to undertake auditing.

Also there exists incentive factors to induce companies to go in for environmental auditing. For instance, insurance companies would be ready to cover any unforeseen accident, should the companies undergo regular environmental audits. In the era information revolution, more and more of consumers have been revealing preference for environmentally friendly products. The competitive forces drive companies to demonstrate their products, the production of which inflicted less harm to environment. Regular environmental audits will help companies rate their relative merits on the environmental front.

1.14 Ecolabelling

An arrangement of marking of final products to distinguish whether or not a product is environmentally friendly. Germany was a pioneer in introducing ecolabelling way back in 1978. Now, many countries including Canada, the USA, and Sweden have started to adopt this practice. An independent agency does this job of judging the product *vis-à-vis* similar products. Ecolabelling is an eye opener where most developing countries have become environmentally conscious to influence the behaviour of consumers in choosing environmentally benign products on the one hand and the induces the manufacturers to bring down the environmental impacts of their products on the other (C.J. Barrow, 1999).

1.15 Natural Resource Accounting (NRA)

Conventional economic accounting seldom measured the use of natural resources in the process of economic activities. Consequently, the costs of environmental degradation and resource depletion remained outside the ambit of profit calculation by firms. Over a period of last three decades, there has been an increased realization that neglect of accounting of use of natural resource would not reflect the real value of goods and services and profit/loss as well.

Hence, natural resource accounting can alter the choice towards desirable development, *ipso facto*, development that takes cognizance natural resource use and its depletion (Kirit S. Parikh *et al.*, 1993).

While it may be easy to account for depreciation, value of capital used in a year, of artifacts like machines, but it is difficult to calculate depreciation value of not-man-made goods, viz., natural resources.

1.16 Environmental Impact Assessment

It is a tool of appraisal and the objective central to it is critical evaluation of potential impact of any proposed developmental project on the environment. This is a scientifically structured exercise with clear-cut procedures, well defined problem areas with adequate legal backing (Canter, L. M., 1996).

The major objectives are forecasting the spin-off of the developmental projects, discerning methods to combat negative effects, modifying projects to fit into local environment and ultimately to document the forecasting and options to facilitate decision-making.

By looking at the evolution, it is the National Environmental Policy Act of 1969, USA, which pronounced this concept for the first time. In India, the Ministry of Environments and Forests made it mandatory from 1994 onwards.

EIA is procedural, exemplified with following steps: (a) Screening, (b) Scoping and consideration of alternatives, (c) Base line data collection, (d) Impact prediction, (e) Public hearing, (f) Decision-making and (g) Monitoring the clearance condition.

EIA differs from a routine evaluation exercise; the assessment will be made *ex ante*. Because it deals with effects, which have not occurred previously, events sometimes may not occur. Hence, two elements, viz., future and uncertainty, are evident. This exactly warrants the expertise from the discipline economics. The benefit-cost analysis can be an appropriate method to assess the proposed plan objectively.

Development is a continuous process and its imminent spillover effects would also be increasing simultaneously. Benefit-cost analysis is one of the tools used to weigh the benefits owing to proposed project against the cost *ipso facto* damages. This is a formidable task where the positive and negative effects are felt in the long run. Discount rate need to be used appropriately to find out whether or not the project is viable. Willingness to pay and willingness to accept are other means which environmental economists use to measuring benefits over costs. Perceptions on environment by individuals vary largely and therefore the values placed on environmental resources too differ thereby hampering the benefit-cost analysis.

1.17 Institutional Approach to Environmental Management

Institutions comprise the rules of the game, based upon which all economic activities are performed. Douglass North puts it precisely as the "humanly devised constraints that shape human interaction". By and large, the constraints central to institutions revolve around property rights and the limits of government activity.

The best interest of individuals towards material resources seldom coincides with the best interest that serves the society at large. This is more so of environmental resources. From any given act, owner of resource enjoys the benefit at the margin, while externalizing the cost to be shared by the public (G. Hardin, 1968). Environmental policies come in general offer incentive/ disincentives to enable individuals to act in a way, which is beneficial for the whole society. Many a approach went into this direction, starting from classical, neoclassical and to modern economics. Neoclassical economists in particular, assumed away certain aspects like zero transaction cost and information symmetry and so on. New institutional economics takes cognizance of these and offers means to "reduce uncertainty in human exchange" (North, 1990).

Neoclassical economics, while dealing with environmental problems emphasized more on setting the prices right, with scant attention to institutional aspects (Erick G. Frubton and Rudolf Richter, 1999). New institutional economics becomes increasingly relevant in the context of recent economic problems. No doubt, institutional economics is an improvement over the neoclassical approach. Necessary to mention Ronal Coase, as he was the first economist to bring in the concept of transaction cost (Coase, 1937). This came as a revelation in resolving the problem of negative externalities, with a positive transaction cost. Momentum picked up slowly in identifying the existence of institutions (D.C. North, 1990).

New institutional economics takes four stand points to elucidate the improvements over new classical economics; the positive transaction cost, the concept of interdependence, moral attitudes and limited cognitive capacity and finally, self-interest motivation (Jouni Paavola and W. Neil Adger, 2002). Interdependence is appropriate usage as against externality as per their arguments. It looks justifiable to discern an agent's act will inevitably have an effect on another agent as long as the act of former is unintentional. Action or inaction will certainly bound to cause some change in the utility function of the other. Instead setting the price right as was done in the case of externality, property rights can be defined in the line's of Coase's argument and achieve efficient allocation of scarce environmental resources through negotiation. Interdependence exemplified the conflicts between both the agents over environmental resources, which can be resolved within the market realm or through the court, i.e. outside the market.

Transactions costs do play a critical role in environmental governance. Transactions cost *per se*, has been defined by Ronald Coase (1937) as "the cost of using the market system in explaining the existence of firm". However, the followers of Coase explained the concept of transactions costs as costs of information, cost of negotiation, monitoring and enforcement of compliance. Notwithstanding the fact that environmental governance posits non-market transactions, still transactions cost assumes importance in terms of cost of collection of information and decision-making. Arrow defines it as "cost of running the economy". The moot question is where were these costs earlier? Were they assumed to be insignificant or constant? It is evident from the literature, it is clear it is the cost of establishing contract, concluding contract, measuring, monitoring, negotiating and enforcement of compliance. Information cost of crucial part of transactions cost (Erick G. Frubton and Rudolf Richter, 1997).

'Limited cognitive capacity' is an important facet, which assumes relevance in this context (Jouni Paavola and W. Neil Adger, 2002). The limited cognitive capacity forbids agents revealing the true goal and preferences. Neoclassical literature underscores the fact that human behaviour based upon individual's motivations is self-centred subject to imperfect knowledge. New institutional economics replaces this with cognitive capacity of economic agents. The psychological concept of 'Cognitive Dissonance' introduced by Leon Festinger (1957) is appropriate here. According to him "cognitive dissonance is a state that an individual reaches ones she/he has an imbalance between cognition". Basically cognition implies an attitude, emotion, belief or value or even an mixture of these cognitions. The concept of cognitive dissonance is much deeper and uncovers profound insights. Even environmental psychologists tend to subscribe to this view through research studies that decisions made by agents were not in conformity with that of societal decisions. To quote their words "it manifests itself largely as a result of our insistence that we are right. It could actually be seen as the other side of the tenacity, but taken to an unhealthy extreme. This phenomenon causes people, even in the face of great natural destruction, for example, to perpetuate in keeping with their old habit, ways or habitations and to stubbornly insist that they could be wrong, have made an error or even be in danger, for so much of their previous action was right" (Cornelia Meseke, 1998).

The Macmillan Family Encyclopaedia cites that "cognitive dissonance is a theoretical construct of social psychology. First advanced by Lean Festinger, that attempts to explain certain aspects of decision-making and as individuals behaviour before and after the decision-making process. Festinger assumed that people strive towards an internal consistency between their belief and their actions or between one belief and another. He termed the lack of such consistency dissonance and asserted that when such dissonance occurs, individuals unconsciously seek to reduce it by changes in behaviour, changes in belief, and selective exposure to new information and opinions congruent with their actions. An important hypothesis of the theory is that the greater the difficulty a person has in making a decision the greater the tendency to rationalize or justify that decision."

Cognitive dissonance envisages disharmony between attitude and action, in other words, an incompatibility between belief and behaviour. Cognition is to do with mental frame of mind manifesting as attitudes, emotion, belief or value. It is argued that a single person may hold more than one value or attitude as result contradictions between cognition arise.

'Free rider' is yet another aspect of institutional approach. Free rider is one, who enjoys benefits more than their his/her fair share, but seldom contribute or shoulder or share the cost involved in making the service or product. Many a instance can be cited; for instance, an individual 'A' trying to enjoy the services of public good, without contributing anything from one's end.

Public goods are, basically, meant for everyone, and no one can exclude from using it nor one's use does not preclude the other from accessing the same.

How do we say a person can free ride with a public good? An individual 'A' may use public good but many evade paying tax. However, revenue accrued through taxes being utilized for providing public good. Most others pay but individual 'A' does not pay, the problem may look trivial, but if individual 'A' syndrome spreads by manifesting into many free riders than the real problem emerges. Consequent to increase in free riders, the taxes on commodities would raise and the corollary effects of increased tax increased prices of goods would bring down the level of demand and eventually end up with low production or provision of public goods.

Another facet is that neoclassical economics stuck with self-interest motivating ultimate preference, institutional economics brings forth pluralism in motivations. Motivation beyond self-interest is quite a reality as economic agents look for welfare of large section of society. Multiple motivations most often facilitate identifying goals and motivations of individuals over environmental issues (Jouni Paavola and W. Neil Adger, 2002).

The impact of globalization on environment is another very crucial dimension crying for attention. A proper knowledge of Environmental Management is necessary to address these issues. Although environmental studies have been undertaken in Developing countries at a piece meal level, a concerted effort to initiate Environmental Management Education at tertiary level is lagging behind. A systematic programme of Environmental Management would facilitate facing many challenges, to converting opportunities and to take measures to safeguard against certain untreatable facets of globalizing process.

Under the globalization phase, the corporate sector faces a predicament in terms of facing regulatory stipulations on the one hand and necessity to demonstrate competitive strength on the other. In particular, small scale sector units have been facing this formidable challenge. A systematic environmental management can help the corporate sector to perform better by ensuring the desired level of environmental quality without compromising the ability of organizations to produce goods and services and to stand upto global competition. Needless to say that big companies would seize opportunities in such a way that their rivals cannot match through proper environmental planning and environmental management systems.

1.18 Millennium Development Goals (MDGs)

The MDGs envisage, a long-term, comprehensive vision of human development. This calls for the collective efforts by the international community, *ipso facto*, 'global partnership' to accomplish certain very vital socio-economic goals. On tracing the origin, this forms an offshoot of the Millennium Submit in New York held in September 2000 (Anil B. Deolalikar, 2005).

Millennium Development Goals (United Nations 2005)

1. Eradicate extreme poverty and hunger
2. Achieve universal primary education
3. Promote gender equality and empower women
4. Reduce child mortality
5. Improve maternal health
6. Combat HIV/AIDS malaria and other diseases
7. Ensure environmental sustainability
8. Develop a global partnership for development.

It is relevant to reiterate the goal of ensuring environmental sustainability. Under this, emphasis being laid an halving the proportion of people without access to safe water, one of the targets to be achieved by 2015, from their level in 1990. In this milieu, this book assumes significance. A systematic empirical research work on potable water in rural parts of India and Tamil Nadu will be presented in the following chapters:

1.19 Study Background

In developing countries the fundamental issues of social sector are gaining prominence. The basic needs of the public, particularly the rural poor continue to attract the attention of planners and policy-makers. The basic needs include *inter alia* primary education, health care, safe drinking water, sanitation, housing and roads. These basic provisions are intrinsic to community development and in turn economic development of the rural poor. Development unmindful of these primary requirements will be incomplete and lopsided. Provision of potable water to rural mass is a case at issue. This is important due to the fact that access to safe water has a direct bearing on the health of the poor, particularly the rural poor.

The fact remains that the total water on earth is limited; continuous pressure from agricultural, industrial and domestic sectors leads to qualitative and quantitative problems to this finite and fragile natural system. Of the total water resources present on earth, 97 per cent is confined to oceans, 2 per cent got locked as ice and just one per cent is available for direct human use as freshwater. A major chunk of our nation's water, as high as 84 per cent goes for agricultural activities; 12 per cent is utilized for industrial and energy sectors and the remaining 4 per cent for domestic purposes (Jyothi and Kirit, 1999).

Provision of potable water on a sustainable basis is a basic necessity. Concerted efforts have been made both at the centre and state levels right from the First Five Year plan period. But yet nearly 15 per cent of the total population is left with little access to safe water. A management of water resource towards provision of water with adequate quantity and acceptable quality for drinking purpose is a stupendous task. Indeed the issues pertaining to water supply system are so profound starting from socio-economic problem, environmental, institutional, financial and human resource management.

The percentage of population with little access to safe water constitutes one of the three major variables based on which deprivation index is arrived at. Deprivation index forms one of the three main indices of human poverty index. In the deprivation index, besides access to safe water, the percentage of the population with little access to health services and the percentage of the under weight children under the five year age group were also taken into account. The average of the three variables is considered in the preparation of deprivation index (Thirlwall, 1999). The fact that lack of access to safe water to the poor is a crucial variable in deprivation index emphasizes the involvement of human factors along with technological problems in water supply and sanitation programmes.

While all the water supply schemes generate assets such as bore well, piped water supply through overhead tank and hand pumps etc., the question of their operation and maintenance merits research investigation. Another issue pertaining to water collection is the role of women. It has been the legacy; particularly in rural area women continue to be subjected to the hardship of traversing long distances to collect water. In this context one of the major challenges is to initiate gender sensitive strategies, thereby reducing the burden of water collection and to involve them to participate in water management.

Ultimately the problem of rural water supply (RWS) revolves around provision of water on a sustainable basis, which is a many-folded issue. Provision of water to the target groups on a continuous basis is central to it. Corollary to this is depletion of ground water; a finite natural resource constrained to be over-exploited to meet the requirements of increasing population. And the deterioration of water quality, both due to natural conditions and human interventions, is a matter of serious concern. Achieving sustainability here envisages provision of water without gaps, without depleting the natural resource and without causing water borne health hazards to users.

An organized role of local communities is appropriate from the perspective of environmental economics (Harou *et al.*, 1998).

Community participation in water supply assumes significance because after all the users may have to accept their responsibilities. It is to be remembered that community participation does not simply mean adopting the decisions ratified by the local people. In a strict sense, it means participation in decision-making and management processes; such an involvement to become really involved need be built over time.

Water quality and human health are directly related issues. Improved water quality and increased quantities and adequate sanitation* facilities would bring forth health benefits. Improved water supplies mitigate the incidence of many water-borne diseases. It is worth quoting Halfdan Mahler, former Director General of the World Health Organisation (WHO), who said,

> "*The number of water taps per 1000 persons is a better indicator of health than the number of hospital beds*" (Sachchidananda, 1999: p.14).

Safe water eliminates the infective agents associated with water-borne diseases. Availability of greater quantity of water can improve health by allowing improved personal hygiene and sanitation.

Economic aspects of providing drinking water to the public unfold a number of issues. At present, modern programme *ipso facto* mission approach is central to water supply and sanitation. This necessarily involves capital investment by the Centre or the State towards creation of sources. It is the operation and maintenance costs that can keep the systems function on a regular basis. In this regard the following questions arise:

- Whether "*demand responsiveness*" or supply oriented factors which one is crucial for expansion of provision of this basic service?

---

* The term sanitation does not confine to latrines alone, it encompasses personal hygiene, proper garbage disposal, drainage system and community well-being.

- What is the extent of subsidy involved in providing water to rural poor? Are there cross-subsidies between urban and rural and the rich and poor?
- If cost sharing is agreeable in principle what is the rationale behind calculating tariff for rural water supply?

However uniform tariff rates may affect the poor more than the rich. Hence, there is a need to strike a balance between economic value of water to users, the cost of providing services to users and the prices charged for these services.

Improvements in water provision can be a crucial factor in controlling water-borne diseases and improving living conditions, especially in a country like India where a sizable portion of the population is constrained to live with inadequate supply of water. The prime aim of the International "Drinking Water Supply and Sanitation Decade (1981-1990)" is to make potable water accessible to as many households as possible. On the one hand domestic water supply serves as a basic component of welfare in its role as a direct consumer commodity and on the other hand it acts as an element of socio-economic infrastructure. Provision of an adequate amount of domestic water supply may result in community stability that may stimulate success of other components of development (Biswas, 1987). Notwithstanding the fact that success in economic activities depends on host of other factors, inadequate water supply can be a significant constraint.

1.19.1 Statement of the Problem

Despite the efforts made at the central, state and local bodies level, nearly 16 per cent of the population in our country has not been covered with safe water, more so with sanitation. Even where provided, there are numerous inroads in the distribution and maintenance of the sources. Provision made by the state and the problems thereof are just tip of the ice burg. The socio-economic, technological and environmental issues involved are profound, as many of them still remain unresolved. Whether water is treated as an economic good or social good or both. Whether the provision need be demand responsive or supply based. What is the extent of subsidy the state can provide for rural water supply? If cost sharing is agreeable in principle, whether to start with sharing capital cost or sharing operation and maintenance cost. Who should decide on the technology and its cost if costs are to be shared? The role of women and the community participation in managing water supply unfolds issues like time spent, distance travelled and the involvement of local people in organizing the facility.

As stated earlier provision of potable water to the rural population is a multifaceted problem. The need of the hour is to develop a framework for improved water provision on a sustainable basis. The traditional approach was characterized by central decision-making, external determination of requirements rather than "economic demand" for service, absence of cost-sharing arrangements, greater involvement of government machinery rather than local participation in deciding location, installation, operation and maintenance of water supply. The launching of a National Drinking Water Mission in 1986 later came to be known as the Rajiv Gandhi National Drinking Water Mission, witnessed a paradigm shift from 'supply oriented' approach to 'demand responsive' method. This implies a switch over to modern method from traditional approach, which assumes socio and economic significance.

A crucial question is the quantum of water required for domestic purpose, (the fixed norm of 40 litres per capita per day) and the rationale behind the norm. Then comes the question of convenient distance within which the sources need to be located. Whether the number of hand pump/stand post for every 1000 persons is distributed equitably across the study district. Choice between three different major sources such as (a) traditional sources like springs, wells, lakes, river and tanks; (b) mechanical "contravention" brought from outside the villages like hand pumps and (c) very advanced systems like piped water supply and water treatment plant like desalination plant. The whole question is whether to treat all the systems together as one and adopt holistic method to manage them towards better provision of water. Modern approach is a package consisting of five different stages, viz., identification of suitable sources, adopting systematic methods of drilling deep bore wells, putting up the hand pumps to bring the water above the surface, create hygienic atmosphere around the source by providing platform, drainage facility, soaking facility and finally, proper operation and maintenance of the above items. If problem occurs in any one of the stages the systems go defunct. More important is the question of sustainability of maintaining the level of consumption and quality of water. Is the quality compatible to the standards fixed by the WHO? What are the health problems of polluted water consumption? Sustainability is achievable if and only if the people at large participate in resource mobilization and in cost sharing towards water supply. On top of everything, the awareness of people about the linkage between health and safe drinking water. What is the rural water supply pattern in India that emerged from NSSO 54th round?

Water use plays a crucial role in ensuring socio-economic development particularly when it fulfils domestic purposes. The present study title, albeit, reads drinking water supply, does not envisage water for drinking purpose alone. The context is much wider in terms of water use in domestic sector. At household level water is required for various different purposes like cooking, bathing and washing etc.

1.19.2 Objectives of the Study

The present study in the chosen study area sets out the following objectives to:

- discern the rural water supply (RWS) with the help of secondary sources of information to understand the pattern of water use at the study district and all India level.
- analyze the cost aspects, factors influencing water use, distance travelled, time spent and the participation of rural households in organizing and availing the services in the select villages.
- understand the environmental dimensions of drinking water at the village level with respect to depletion of natural resource, degradation of water quality, and the vulnerability of women and children to degradation of environment.
- outline an alternative method of calculating tariff for rural water supply.

1.19.3 Hypotheses

I. The respondents used the modern schemes as a principal source and traditional source as a supplementary source for collecting water for different consumption purposes (NSSO 54th round).

II. All the regions received potable water for drinking and cooking purposes in equal proportion.

III. The family size, land holding, per capita income, female head education, occupation, house value, area (wet, mixed, dry and hill) cooking trip per day, distance and time are the key determinants of consumption of water.

IV. There is relationship between environmental degradation in terms of depletion of natural resource, viz., the ground water level and the burden of women in general and children particular.

1.19.4 Methodology

In order to realize the set objectives, Tiruchirappalli district in the state of Tamil Nadu is chosen. This is one of the thirty districts in the state, comprising 8 taluks, 14 blocks, 408 village Panchayats and 2376 habitations. Of which 311 sample village households were selected across 4 taluks, 4 blocks, 5 village Panchayats and 46 habitations.

1.19.4.1 Method of Sample Selection

The present study has used multistage sampling methods, viz., systematic proportionate stratified random sampling method to select the sample villages. The criteria adopted to stratify the five select villages to choose 311 households includes the following ecological zones area irrigated, area, less irrigated, area, which is partially irrigated and partially less irrigated, and Hilly area with special characteristics such as village where scheduled caste/tribes are concentrated. Totally five villages were selected and grouped under four categories, viz., Wet, Mixed (partially wet and partially dry), Dry (arid) and Hilly region. In the three select villages, of the total households of each village 10 per cent of the sample households are chosen. In the case of the remaining two villages, where the characteristics are mixed, only 5 per cent of the sample households are chosen from the total (see Fig.1.1).

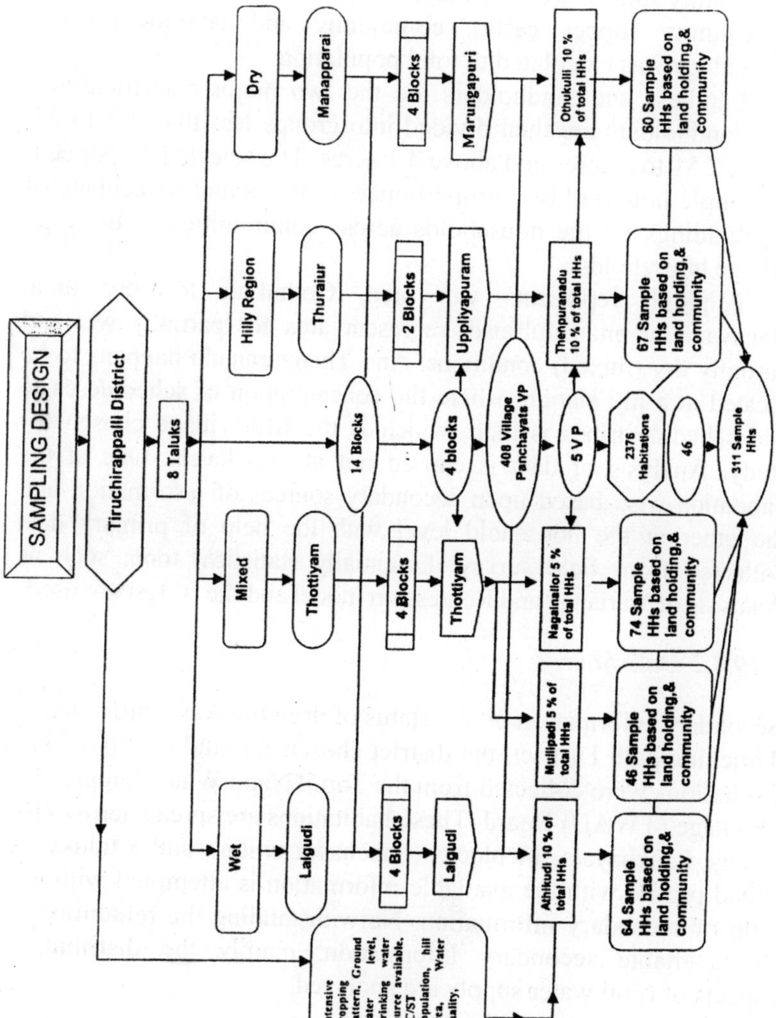

Fig. 1.1 : Sampling Design of Tiruchirappalli District.

Household list and caste particulars are collected from the village Panchayat office. From this list landholders and landless particulars are obtained from the Village Administrative Officer (VAO). Total population (households) is classified on the basis of community like Scheduled Castes/Tribes (lower caste) and Other Community (upper caste), community and landholding-wise percentage was calculated to total population.

Landless and landholders are the two major classifications. The landholders are then divided into groups less than 1.1 to 2.5 acres, 2.51 to 4 acres and above 4.1 acres. The selected 10 per cent of sample households is proportionate to the actual percentage of landholdings by the households across communities to the total village households.

Athikudi represents wet area, Oothukuli for dry area; Nagayanallur and Mullipadi represent area for partially wet and partially dry (mixed) conditions. And Thenpuranadu happens to be located at a hill station, where the concentration of schedule caste and schedule tribes is high, which is the fifth village chosen for study. Analysis of data is carried out at two levels. One at the habitation-wise based upon secondary sources of information and the other at the household level with the help of primary data collected from field survey. Essentially statistical tools such as Analysis of Variance and Regression model and the 't' test are used.

1.19.4.2 Data Source

Secondary information on the status of drinking water provision at Tiruchirappalli District, the district chosen for study, across 2376 habitations were collected from the Tamil Nadu Water Supply and Drainage (TWAD) Board. These habitations are spread across 408 village Panchayats, 14 blocks (Panchayat union), and 8 taluks. A broad profile with the available information is attempted with the help of secondary information. Notwithstanding the reliability of the available secondary information, mainly the distributive aspects of rural water supply are analyzed.

1.19.4.3 Primary Household Survey Period

The primary household survey was conducted with the help of a detailed interview schedule (Annexure II) during first May 2000 to end of October 2000. The survey period covered summer and rainy seasons as well. In addition, the National Sample Survey Organisation (NSSO) 54th Round 1999 data on rural water supply in India used for analysis.

1.19.4.4 Tools of Analysis

Simple statistical tools* such as 't' test, regression model and ANOVA for testing of hypotheses, mean, standard deviation and co-efficient of variation are used along with bar and pie diagrammes. Regression model is used to analyze both secondary and primary sources of information. The Ordinary Least Squares (OLS) method is followed with linear formations for estimating the values. In terms of explanatory power the linear formulations are more suitable. For the preliminary analysis, a large number of variables are included, however only five to six variables were used for the actual analysis. The correlation matrices are used to drop less important variables and thereby avoid multi-colleniarity problems. For the final regression analysis number of different combinations are tried to arrive at a final list of variables with a good fit in terms of explanatory power. Block rate pricing method is used to estimate the tariff rates for pipe service connections with the help of the actual village level data.

In sum, the actual data analysis of both secondary and primary information has been carried out at different levels, presented in third, fourth and fifth chapters of the present study. First, the NSSO data were analysed with a hypothesis testing using paired 't' test. Secondly, the TWAD Board re-survey data were analysed with a regression model. Thirdly, primary household survey information was analysed through regression equation and Duncan test to test the stated hypothesis. And, finally, Block rate pricing method was applied to estimate the rural water tariff for house service connections.

---

* The software, Statistical Package for Social Sciences (SPSS) is used to carry out the calculations.

2

CONCEPTUAL FRAMEWORK AND REVIEW OF LITERATURE

2. 1 Conceptual Framework

In a broader sense, water resource management as a concept may outline a framework for numerous water related decisions. Given the fact that socio-economic development processes are related to the water resource, owing to interaction with water and human activities. It is imperative to conceptualize the problem in hand with respect to economic, environmental, and institutional aspects.

2.1.1 Economic Aspects

The debate on whether or not to treat water as an economic good began since the International Conference on Water and the Environment, 1992. Albeit, many agreed to treat it as an economic good, the issues pertaining to role of water remained unresolved. This is because depending upon situations water is treated as a basic good, with social, economic, and environmental implications. It is justifiable to treat it as an economic good because even the definition of economics by great economist Robbins confirms as

> "*the science, which studies human behaviour as a relationship between ends and scarce means which have alternative uses*".

Potable water is scarce and water can be put into alternative uses such as drinking, cooking, bathing and recreation.

The next question is what kind of economic good? It is generally believed that it is both a public and a private good. Addressing this rhetoric issue involves discussion on values and facts (Perry *et al.*, 1995) on treating water as private good, production and allocation of water would be through responding to market sources. Consumer sovereignty, in terms of amount that users are willing and their ability to pay for water, may also be a determining factor. However, this treatment does not consider the distribution of income in society. When compared to rich, the poor might not be in a position to pay as much as the rich for water, while the marginal value of water is higher for the poor. On the other hand, as public good, water is treated as a basic need that must be made available at required levels to all. Certain others believed that water bestows important environmental benefits in most cases, and should not be allocated to other users simply on grounds of willingness to pay. These groups emphasize that at least up to some minimum level of availability to certain groups and for certain purposes as well below market prices charging for water will pave the way for the greater benefit to the society as a whole. Once a basic level of service (drinking water) is attained, additional supplies could properly be allocated by market forces. To sum up, water serves many different objectives and can be treated both as a private and public good. The appropriate blend of values and facts in proper policy formulation for water requires a deeper analysis than by the simple-minded dogmatism of proponents, either as a basic need or a free market good.

Water use plays a crucial role in socio-economic development particularly since it is one of the basic needs for all domestic purposes. The prime aim of the International Drinking Water Supply and Sanitation Decade, 1981-1990 period is to make potable water accessible to as many households as possible (Biswas, 1987). Importantly, domestic water supply forms the basic component of life sustenance. Further it acts an element in establishing socio-economic infrastructure. Ultimately, the adequate provision of domestic water supply promotes community stability which in turn may become a catalyst in improving other components of development. Needless to argue that success in economic activities depends on the other crucial factors. However, inadequate water supply can be a potential constraint.

Merit good argument is another facet of clean drinking water. Musgrave and Musgrave (1973) takes the credit of having introduced this concept. Merit goods include *inter alia*, minimal shelter, primary education, basic sanitation, access to basic health care and clean drinking water. The functional definition is

> *"Those kinds of commodity which society appears to consider intrinsically good or bad, and so adopts measures to stimulate or discourage their consumption. For example, it may be decided that education is desirable, not simply because it increases the productivity of labour but because it is inherently a good thing. Resources may then be devoted to making it more widely available e.g. through the state-school system, then would be the case if left to the market forces. Similarly consumption of hard drugs is considered intrinsically undesirable and therefore made illegal. It should be noted that there is an element of paternalism in policies towards merit goods. Society decides that the preferences of individuals cannot be left to determine the levels of consumption of such commodities"* (Pande and Mithani, 1990: p. 161).

Musgrave admits the fact that merit goods are subjected to several interpretations. However, one can infer the idea that in the process of resource allocation, if everything is left to individual's preferences of commodities, than the end result may not be efficient. Resource allocation entails the state interference in directing certain goods *ipso facto* merit goods in ensuring minimal supply. It is in this context, the clean drinking water assumes significance as a merit good.

Santhakumar (1998) and Pushpangadan and Murugan (1995) in their empirical studies on drinking water have referred to merit goods. Merit goods are those which yield benefits to users and the benefits received are far greater than their actual expectations. Preferences of individuals in this regard take a back seat while the "paternalistic preference' of the state assures mere importance in so far as drinking water is concerned.

Merit good argument can be acceptable only to the extent where the state interferes to make good the deficiencies and to ensure minimum supply of this basic necessity. Leaving entirely this process to the State's control may not prove to be worthwhile. A blend of state, individual's commitment to accept user pay principle and collective community participation would retain the status of clean drinking water as merit good.

Production of a commodity entails a sacrifice of an alternative product that could have been produced had resources been diverted towards it. The value of foregone product is the opportunity cost. The marginal cost principle ultimately rests with equality of marginal benefit with marginal opportunity cost. The principle of drinking water pricing can be explained under the neo-classical framework in the following manner. Consider a situation where certain quantum of water is drawn from ground water source for consumption. The micro economic principle suggests that every successive unit of consumption of water brings down the marginal benefit. In other words, the marginal benefit of consuming water falls as the quantum of water consumption increases.

The diagrammatic form given in a workbook (Harou *et al.*, 1998) may be reproduced as under:

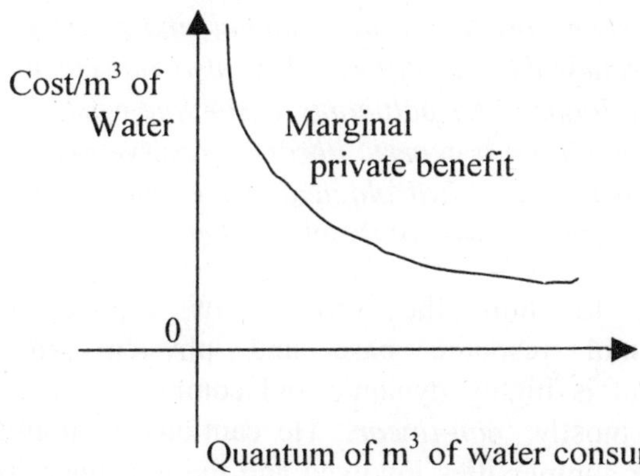

The above diagram provides a partial explanation, about the demand side only. An extraction of one litre of water from a source for consumption represents one litre of less water that could have been consumed by another household. Hence extraction and consumption of water involve imposition of cost on the society. The upward sloping curve represents the marginal social cost associated with consumption of water.

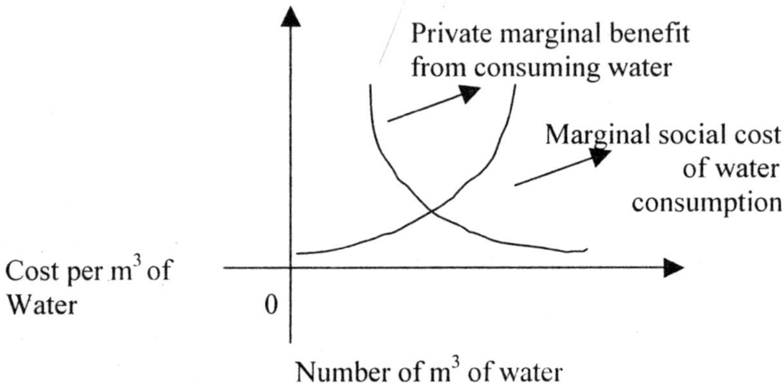

2.1.2 *Environmental Aspects*

Economic analysis of use of environmental resource base and their analysis must be based on a sound understanding of the environmental functions and life supporting services provided by the ecosystem. In the words of Maler (1997: p. 252),

> "*Ecosystems provide water, animal and plant food and other renewable resources. They also recycle nutrients, control floods, filter pollutants, assimilate waste, pollinate crops, maintain a generic library, preserve and generate soil, operate the hydrological cycle and maintain the gaseous consumption of the atmosphere*".

According to him the process of interaction between environmental resource base and physical and chemical environment is highly dynamic and complex. These interactive forms are mostly '*non-linear*'. He cautions economists to take note of the complexities involved and the non-linear relationship between economic and ecosystems while constructing models of '*natural world*'.

It is relevant to note

> *"The environmental resource base is dynamic and complex consisting of biological communities that interact with the physical and chemical environment in time and space. Thus the resource base can display threshold effects – meaning that the flow of services can be interrupted."*

Demand for environmental resources can be two fold: as an amenity and as an input – the former has a direct bearing on the well-being of consumers while the later goes for production.

Conceptually, population growth has a bearing on environmental degradation. The resource management system at the household level largely depends upon family size. Dasgupta and Maler showed empirical evidence to the fact that children were not merely for the old-age support but also to promote the workforce. Bakane-Thoane (1997) also supported the view through her study in rural Lesotho, that the economic value of children to rural households proved to be a major determinant of fertility. The implication is that there is a positive correlation between fertility and the need for workers particularly in rural areas. Nerlov's* (1991) argues,

> *"For example, as forest recede up the mountains sides, parents may perceive a greater need of having an additional child to gather firewood, more realistically; similarly in a poor agricultural setting lower environmental quality may be associated with a greater livestock component in total production. Arguably, children have a comparative advantage over adults in tending livestock in contrast to the heavier labour of planting, tilling and harvesting crops. Thus environmental deterioration may well enhance the marginal productivity of children at least relative family productivity."*

This apparent 'nexus' between environmental degradation and population growth may form the basis for further research

---

* Filmer and Pritchett (1996: 4).

investigation. For instance, whether family size in rural areas has a bearing in water scarce areas and distance to travel, to fetch potable water and so on.

In order to check excess use of water, the state fixes price, perhaps per cubic metre of water consumed. Consequent to fixing of price, there may be a reduction in water consumption. But the point is the price that the consumers' pay might not reflect the '*true social cost*' related to water consumption. This means that the price fixed by the state is well below the price that should motivate households to consume the '*socially optimal amount of water*'.

2.1.3 Institutional Aspects

The institutional arrangement to provide water is a matter of concern in this realm. Whether water is provided free of cost to all households, can water be treated a free good any longer, are some of the questions which merit attention. Given the fact that access to safe water is a basic human right, concerted efforts have been made at the Central, State and Local body levels right from the First Five Year Plan period. But the problems relating to recovery of Operational and Maintenance (O&M) cost are yet to be resolved, needless to say about the recovery of capital cost. Many a change can be brought in the existing institutional mechanism to overcome the problem. One possible way is through correcting and getting the prices right. A tariff, which ensures sustainable water supply, needs to be evolved.

Water pricing theories guide resource allocation, particularly a scarce resource such as drinking water (Jacob, 1997). There are a number of theories, which explain the pricing of urban/rural water supplies. Marginal cost pricing, average cost pricing, long-run marginal cost pricing, block rate and fixed rate and so on. All the theories basically try to equate price with marginal cost or average cost in order to ensure efficiency.

Water pricing policies are of three major kinds, viz.

(1) Flat rate
(2) Constant rate
(3) Block rate

Flat rate pricing: A specific, fixed rate is levied on the consumer irrespective of the amount of water used. For each tap connection the user has to pay a fixed rate and use any amount of water he needs. This system can be followed only in regions where there is excess water source. The consumer will not have any tendency to economize water since there is no increase in the charge for increase in consumption of water.

Constant rate pricing: A constant, fixed charge for each unit is levied on the consumer. A meter is needed to monitor the number of units drawn by the consumer and according to the meter reading charges are calculated. In this rate water is charged at a uniform rate, there is no increase in rate on consumption above a reasonable limit.

Block rate pricing: In this system unit price varies according to the quantity of consumption. Tariffs are fixed up to certain levels and charges are calculated taking this into consideration. Block rate pricing is of two types:

(i) Declining Block rate
(ii) Increasing Block rate

In declining block rate, the unit price falls gradually as the water consumption increases. A minimum charge is fixed up to a certain limit and after that for each discrete quantity of water different rates are fixed which is declining in their value. In increasing block rate, the unit price increases gradually as the water consumption increases. After the minimum charge, block rate for each discrete quantity of water increases. So a person consuming more water has to pay a higher rate.

Conventionally water resource management had followed supply based approach with scant attention to water demand. Then at a later stage realisation came in the form of better manner through balancing both demand and supply aspects. Given the fact that there is cost escalation of creating new sources, the limited financial resources need to be utilized to achieve economic efficiency. The provisions of Agenda 21 of United Nations Conference on Environment and Development give impetus to water resource management. The recommendations of UNCED emphasize the need for pricing mechanism, levying of water tariffs and certain economic instruments towards achieving demand management.

Water pricing can be an effective tool in achieving sustainable development in urban and rural water provision. Besides,

> "*Efficient pricing systems would increase the revenue to meet operation and maintenance costs, recover capital investments and generate funds for the improvement and expansion of water supply services. It would also contribute to the protection of the environment by reducing the quantity of wastewater*" (United Nations, 1997a: p. 2).

Water pricing assumes a crucial role in the sustainable development of rural water supply due to two reasons. Efficient pricing shall enhance the revenue to meet operation and maintenance costs on the one hand and help achieving reduction in wastage of potable water. Even the provisions of Agenda 21 of the United Nations Conference on Environment and Development emphasized this view that there is a need for appropriate pricing policies, as a strategy to achieve effective demand management, in promoting efficiency of water use and discouraging waste.

In the context of rural water supply, users-pay principle can best be construed as an economic tool. This principle envisages the responsibility to be borne by the users by paying charges for the use of water resource. Every user of resource is to be charged with the full-cost of the usage. Which includes not only the cost of the provision but also the cost inflicted upon the system by damages caused due to usage and the opportunity cost.

Rationale of pricing of water considers provision of drinking water as an economic activity, which entails cost at various stages. The processes include lifting the water from the source, treatment of water where possible and finally, transmitting to the distributing tank. All the three stages involve costs of various inputs. Pricing of water becomes imminent if the costs are to be recovered from users. In this context, the available theories and approaches merit discussion.

As against the accounting approach, which does not guide resource allocation, pricing based on marginal cost is theoretically agreeable for efficiency in resource allocation. Generally prices are based upon how a consumer values a product against its costs. Both consumer's valuation and costs would vary, and resources get diverted to most valued users. The policy prescription equates price with marginal cost to achieve ideal output and consumption as well. The basis of pricing rests on consumer's valuation of a commodity in relation to costs. Price has direct relationship with changing value and costs. The change in value and costs act as checks and balance the production and consumption pattern. Price sends two signals, one in discouraging consumers from an excess consumption and secondly, restricting the production to a required level.

The foregoing description, albeit brief, helps conceptualizing the problem in proper perspective. Allocation of water resources across the competing sectors is a complex phenomenon. Provision of water to domestic sector is crucial. The socio-economic aspects need to be discussed in the environmental background of water resource in order to achieve sustainability. Institutional approach to water resource management calls for pricing the water supply to achieve optimal allocation and check wastage of resources.

2.2 Review of Literature

The fact remains that there is dearth of research studies on drinking water supply in India, a few empirical investigations carried out in different parts of country by various authors can be summarized as under.

Pushpangadan and Murugan (1996) made use of the information provided by Rajiv Gandhi Drinking Water Mission reports and estimated the replacement cost, operation and maintenance costs across all states. They supported the view that user financing towards capital, operation and maintenance costs can be the means of raising sources for sustainable rural water supply in developing countries. Such a change in policy would help achieve efficiency, equity and sustainability.

They estimated capital cost by using annual expenditure data. About 90 per cent of the Accelerated Rural Water Supply Programmes of the Centre (ARWSP) and 60 per cent of the

Minimum Needs Programmes (MNP) were allotted for capital formation. Further,

> "*Using these proportions, the total capital cost is estimated for each year. Since the life of the system is assumed to be 15 years, we need only to consider the capital expenditure starting from 1980-81. Capital cost thus obtained in a year is then distributed uniformly over the next fifteen years, the average life of the system. The sum of such distributed costs is taken as the replacement costs in current prices. The costs in current prices are then arrived at by deflating price indices.*" (p.12)

Similarly, for the operation and maintenance cost, owing to non-availability of data, 6 per cent of the cumulated capital expenditure was taken, which is in line with the Mission's suggestions. The actual estimates suggested that 64 per cent of the total expenditure on ARWSP and MNP was needed to keep the total stock of capital constant, and that 34 per cent of the total money being spent for operation and maintenance in rural water supply sector. Finally, they concluded that the rural water is unsustainable and hence suggested user finance.

Another study by Pushpangadan *et al.* (1996) on travel time, user rate and cost of supply of drinking water in rural Kerala is worth mentioning. They used the data, which was collected after the launching of National Drinking Water Mission of 1986. In ascertaining the performance of the Mission approach, an all India Census Survey was conducted during 1991-93 across all states and on aspects of rural water supply. Data from water census and validation survey were used. They expressed that

> "*Coverage by habitation is not a real measure of availability of drinking water in the State*" (p.18)

Their estimates revealed that only 0.8 per cent of the population were fully covered, while 67 per cent remained uncovered. Of the partially covered population of 32 per cent, most of them received less than half a bucket a day. By applying Becker's model on allocation of time in rural households, they brought empirical evidence to identify that travel distance and uncertainty in supply as significant factors affecting the demand for public sources. The study concluded with a note that there is need to broaden the definition of coverage incorporating consumption, quality and settlement pattern of the villages.

Reddy (1999a) made a study on rural water supply in Rajasthan state during 1994. Four villages across command and non-command areas with 89 sample households were taken up for the purpose. He found that households did not incur direct cost on drinking water, but incurred indirect costs such as time spent and distance travelled to collect water. In regard to factors influencing water use, the regression results brought certain aspects to light. Negative relationship between per capita use and family size, positive relationship between high income and per capita use, positively related even with per capita time spent. However, distance travelled to fetch water did not turn out to be a significant variable in relation to per capita consumption.

His study relied up on Contingent Valuation Method (CVM) to elicit information on willingness to pay for water supply. He found that variables such as distance, time, total annual expenditure, and annual income, percentage of household expenditure spent on health care were positively related with willingness to pay for improved water supply.

The policy implication of the study included that provision of hand pumps in the endowed regions be continued. Increased coverage is possible if the quantum of water consumption can be measured, as it was actually lower than 40 lpcd in the study area under review. More importantly, the study rejected the notion that the willingness to pay for improved water supply was 5 per cent, but it was less than 2 per cent of the total expenditure regardless of the economic background of the region. The need for pricing of improved water supplies was emphasized by means of discriminatory pricing thereby the low income households are less burdened.

The World Bank Water Demand Research team comprising eleven principal members made a study on determinants of rural water demand in select regions of Latin America, Africa, and South Asia during 1987-90. The team brought to light the major findings and discussed the policy implications. '*Supply driven*' strategies of governments failed to bring in desired results and hence suggested a need for paradigm shift towards '*demand based*' methods. The crucial aspects relevant for household demand for improved water service included education of family members, occupation, size and composition of family; and measures of income, expenditure and assets. Besides this, the relative merits of traditional source of water *vis-à-vis* the improved water supply with respect to cost, the quality, and reliability of the supply, and finally, the attitudes of households towards public policy in the water supply.

Their empirical results showed that income of households did not prove to be the principal determinant as the proportion of income allotted for improved water supplied varied widely. Education as factor influenced better as educated households were willing to pay more for improved water provision. The gender of the respondent turned out to be significant, as women were willing to pay for better water service, notwithstanding the fact that they had little control over cash resources. Another relevant factor under consideration was occupation. The willingness to pay was higher among the respondents employed in formal sector. Finally, the family size and composition showed little effect on households' willingness to pay for improved service.

The characteristics of existing alternatives as against the improved water supplics were assessed with respect to costs, quality and reliability of supply and level of service. In regard to policy questions, the team addressed two important issues. What kind of improved water services best suited for a given village? Secondly, how to decide on modalities to induce the users pay for the improved services. However, the study did not address institutional questions such as the respective roles of public agencies, the private enterprise, non-governmental organizations and the users themselves. The team also cautioned against the uniform and across the board policy for all villages. They suggested that appropriate policies would differ depending up on the prevailing situations at the community level. In communities where the households were willing to bear the full costs of private water connections, the strategy should be to encourage private connections to enhance resources to the State. In communities where the cost of provision is high but people are willing to pay a significant percentage of income towards better service, the strategy suggested include the provision of public taps on the one hand and encourage households to have a metered connection. Lastly, in villages where the people are reluctant for paying any money, subsidies would be given towards provision of water supply.

Sachchidananda (1999) had analyzed the sociological dimensions of rural water supply in India, specially referring to Bihar. The study covered 1300 respondents across 130 villages in the state. Relevant social variables such as education, caste, religion, sex, exposure to media, cultural constraints and more importantly the role of women and Non-Governmental Organizations (NGOs) were taken into account in this study. Major findings of his study included the following: more than 40 per cent of respondents lacked adequate access to drinking water facility. More than 85 per cent of sample households were deprived of sanitation facility. Majority of people used open air, riverbanks, forest and roadside drains. Women's organizations for water supply never existed in rural Bihar. Not surprisingly, many parts of the State experienced acute shortage of water during summer, consequently the village inhabitants had to depend on traditional sources such as ponds, *chauan, dari* and from pits dug in riverbed. The failure is on the part of Panchayats and the state to repair and maintain the source.

Hoek *et al.* (2001) made a case study of irrigation water as a source of drinking water in Pakistan. They argued most regions in South Asia, the Middle East and East Africa found ground water unsuitable for drinking purpose owing to high concentration levels of arsenic, fluoride, iron and salt. Hence, they considered it necessary to look for an option of using irrigation water for domestic use. They pointed the incompatibility between suppliers of drinking water and irrigation planners as an impediment in enjoying the 'health benefits' of irrigation water. On health and hygienic practices, their survey results of 200 families found quantity of water mattered more than the quality of water particularly with the incidence of diarrhoea cases.

Santhakumar (1998) made an attempt to identify the inefficiency in the existing system of rural water provision. Unilateral decision, made by the Government in source creation and quantity supplied, was one of the major lacunae. This 'autonomous decision' devoids the actual users in exercising their choice of location of public service. Secondly, the inappropriate choice of institutional mechanism in executing the provision of the merit good, was yet another major source of inefficiency.

Two separate surveys were conducted in Kerala in seeking evidence to the above stated allegations. Santhakumar confirmed the public provision did not serve the intended purpose due to not easily accessible location of physical facilities like street taps. Distance travelled to access remained a discouraging factor. According to him, the institutional mechanism for state intervention is necessary where 'specific requirements of the locations' are the basis of water provision. A uniform and across the board strategy may not be fruitful. Emphasis was made on replacing state intervention by organisation like Grama Panchayats that funds be routed through Panchayat rather than through Central agency.

Suggestions were made to recover the cost of the schemes partially, which may induce the users to seek 'cost effective schemes'. Finally, he concludes by 'stating in societies', where people are functionally capable to exercise choices on consumption, paternalistic characterisation of any good may lead to gross inefficiency, if such characterisation of any is widely different from the choice of the people. This shows that 'even in the case of merit goods, its characterisation should be the one that states care of preferences of the citizens'.

Niyathi (1996) highlighted the problems facing Rural Water Supply (RWS) at the macro level. They included financial crunch, improper estimation of project cost, inadequacy of low cost technology, inefficient maintenance of RWS and non-existence of rural water pricing policy. The policy suggestion pleaded against the standardized design to be applied in all areas.

Satyan (1996) conducted a survey of 84 Panchayats under the Thiruvananthapuram district Panchayat to find out the status of water scarcity on the one hand the people's participation to overcome the problem on the other. The study confirmed about 58 per cent of the households suffered from water scarcity during summer, owing to drying of deferent sources. The study did not stop with the survey alone but went further in conducting seminar to sensitise the problem thereby invoked the participation of the actual stakeholders under phases. In phase I, local labourers were mobilized in renovating the traditional sources like ponds and public wells. And in phase II envisaged full coverage of Grama Panchayat with small schemes.

Chakravarthy and Biswas (1997) discussed that about 23 per cent of the total rural populations do not have any safe drinking water source and they have provided with less than 40 litres per capita per day. Rajiv Gandhi National Drinking Water Mission aims at providing the unserved population with 10 to 40 lpcd. The authors recommended that to achieve this goal, the totally uncovered or very poorly covered habitations should be taken up on priority and the Central and State Governments should provide adequate funds to cover all of them. The efforts to tackle quality problems such as fluoride, arsenic, brackishness and iron need be made. And a combination of cost effective technological options may be utilized to make safe water available in these affected habitations. Further they added, to tackle the problem of depletion of groundwater, location specific recharge structures should be constructed and dried source should be reactivated. Emphasis is made on the co-ordination between irrigation schemes and drinking water with lower cost. In scarcity areas, especially where wells operated by handpump have dried up, a scheme should be evolved to rejuvenate, to improve traditional structures such as dug-wells, tanks, etc. with appropriate innovations to improve the supply of quality water. Preparation of the people to take over the responsibility should be given the highest priority by imparting well structured, need-based training to the beneficiaries, local artisans, field level departmental functionaries and local Panchayat functionaries.

Yadav (1999) reported that more than 65,000 villages in the country do not have the access to a safe public source of drinking water. Availability of safe drinking water people living in villages have to depend on traditional water sources such as dug-wells, ponds, rivers, etc., which do not ensure quality and quantity. About 80 per cent of all the diseases are due to unhygienic conditions and unsafe drinking water in developing countries (WHO). Every year 1.5 million children under five years die of water related diseases in India. The country loses over 200 million man-days each year due to water borne diseases and lack of sanitary conditions. The rural Indian women spend many hours daily in collecting, transporting and managing water. The time and energy thus spend could be utilized productively and leisure if she is provided with safe drinking water.

They stated further, the social structure in many a village further accentuates the inadequacy of safe drinking water. The division of village community between 'high' and 'low' castes over access of water sources is often marked in most of the rural India. It was reported in some villages in Rajasthan that to deprive Harijans, access to safe drinking water, the high caste people damage the handpumps and standposts located in Harijan colonies. In some villages they went to the extent of dumping dead animals into Harijan dugwells so as to make it unsuitable for drinking. The problem of safe drinking water in India is enormous and has many facets. To solve it, strong political will and sufficient resources will be required.

The author also suggests that there is an urgent need of a national drinking water policy. The policy should set norms for safe drinking water. There is a need for an involvement of the people. Even in installation of a handpump the concerned village people are not consulted about their location and or maintenance, though crores of rupees are being spent in various rural water supply schemes.

Khanna (1997) the chose a village named Nanimorsal in Sayla taluk of Surendranagar district in Gujarat. Scarcity of drinking water prevailed throughout the year. The problem is accentuated in summer. Groundwater has depleted due to the extraction of water for irrigations. She finds that everyday people especially women, spent six to seven hours in collecting drinking water. A majority of the families are dependent on the small pits dug in the riverbed called *'virda'*. It takes nearly two hours to collect 5-6 liters of water from a *virda*. They have to wait for nearly 5-6 hours for their turn to collect water and women have to wait for nearly six hours to fill two pots for their daily requirement of water. The women thus spend 10–12 hours a day in collecting drinking water. But they can hardly afford to waste so much time as they also have to cook, take care of animals and clean the house. Lack of even adequate water for bathing poses a serious health hazard. Most people are in a position to bathe only once every 8-10 days.

In many places dams have been built near the villages but the water is provided for irrigation and not for drinking. In addition water from these dams is supplied to for off towns rather than villages nearly. This study concludes that the construction of rainwater harvesting structures is one of the options for the conservation of water.

Chaddha (1999) found that India's groundwater is not in a very good state. The annual recharge of water is for less than what is consumed. The situation is more alarming in urban areas due to population pressure and industrial growth. The total groundwater sources, which are annually recharged, provide around 43 million cubic metres (mcm) of water out of which only 7 mcm is reserved for irrigation. The total need is assessed at 64 mcm at the end of the Eighth Five-Year Plan.

One viable solution would be to go for recharging through rainwater harvesting. The excess water is not harvested even when there is a flood. We should make a deep well through a channel and push the water deep inside. It will act as a storage tank. It will also help in reducing the concentration of fluorides and nitrates. But artificial recharging can ease the ground water crisis because it helps in protecting water resources and assures a constant supply of clean water. The author concludes that we have enough water. We only need to manage the available water resources properly. Instead of developing big water systems, we should go for smaller ones. In other words, we should decentralise the water system. Different areas should have there own water system so that it can be managed properly.

Agarwal (1997) explained the argument made in the parliament debate by quoting the Prime Minister's words, 'water can also catch fire' the problem of water is going to become even more complicated. The problem of water is not limited only to India. In the recent period, water becomes increasingly an agenda in political (election) manifesto. All political parties make a promise to provide safe water to all. The extent of success in this direction has proved to be discouraging. Underlying point here is that political parties are aware of the actual needs of the mandates and this is a testimony of the seriousness of the problem of potable water in rural areas. Even there are wide-ranging discussions on cleaning up of mother Ganga, Yamuna and Cauvery. Linking of rivers and rainwater harvesting has become the subject matter for politicians to articulate. But the author lamented that performance in realizing the proposed promises were dismal.

Agarwal (1999a) argued that to provide safe drinking water to all rural areas during the Ninth Plan, the Ministry of Rural Development has revised the guidelines for implementing the Rural Water Supply Programme (RWSP). This would involve exercising control on over extraction of ground water, more funds for repair and rehabitation of infrastructure, increasing people participation, reserving 20 per cent funds for the states and establishing stronger links with watershed development programmes. The main objective of the guideline and to ensure safe drinking water to all rural areas and to preserve the quality of water. The norms stipulated that 40 litres per capita per day (lpcd) for humans might be provided for drinking, cooking, bathing, washing utensils and ablutions.

Pathak (1999) discussed that by means of artificial recharge and adopting both conventional and unconventional measures, the ground water potential can be improved through additional storage and safeguarding of sources, for example, roof top rainwater harvesting structure which is the direct method of rainwater harvesting. But it cannot be successfully implemented without involving the community. He also suggests that it can be possible when a planned information, motivation and educational effort take place. This will encourage people to participate and reap full benefits. It is essential to involve the community or get ourselves in educating them about the facts and figures of technical inputs.

The development of ground water resources also shows a divergent trend. It is being overexploited in regions wherever available in quantity, resulting in regional imbalance. The regions with available storage space suffer due to recharging conditions and overexploitation in the adjoining areas. As such rain water if properly harvested through roof harvesting methods and other ground water recharge measures would help in creating additional storage, when the water resource are concerned the need are galloping but supply became scarce. Community development doesn't only educate the people but it seeks their involvement in maintaining and managing the water supply system.

The author concludes to strengthen the water resources, by both conventional and non-conventional means, community participation is must in the overall development of the water sector, especially the ground water resources in the Rural Water Supply Programme, by way of systematic planning for motivation and proper education of the community. NGOs can play a major role in this respect to help the government efforts. Efforts should be made to educate the community about the various activities by way of displaying posters, booklets for working and maintenance of hand pumps, manual on water conservation etc. However, there is a need to intensify these activities through regular government budgetary support as part of execution costs of water supply schemes and in their maintenance costs also.

Critical Remarks

The foregoing review, though not exhaustive, highlights the important issues pertaining to rural drinking water supply in the Indian context. This exercise facilitates identifying the appropriate theoretical variables to be considered for the present study besides finding the research gaps. Notwithstanding the fact there is dearth of studies in water supply at the domestic level and with a focus on drinking water, the present study discerns to probe the provision of water at the habitation and at the household level.

Besides, the references to certain empirical studies are quoted in the subsequent chapters of the thesis.

There have been studies made in India on rural water supply from time to time. Most of the empirical studies relating to water use are management centred on water use in agriculture *ipso facto* irrigation purposes. Research investigations on industrial water use and domestic water provision are relatively scanty, more so with empirical investigation on rural drinking water supply. However, concerted efforts towards probing issues relating domestic water supply were made by a few scholars in India. For instance, Reddy (1993, 1996, 1999a, 1999b), Pushpangadan and Murugan (1994, 1995, 1996, 1997, 1998), Santhakumar (1998), Sachidananda (1999), World Bank Water Demand Research Team

(1993), Satyan (1996) and Niyathi (1996) were the empirical works carried out in India. It is to be admitted that the review made in this chapter cannot be claimed to be exhaustive. But earnest efforts have been made to access the available studies in this country, the review of which is included in the foregoing pages of this chapter.

From the preceding review, the present study could identify different theoretical and policy aspects and variables, in the realm of rural drinking water supply. They include, starting from demand for water, various schemes for water provisions, distance travelled to collect, time spent, scarcity, family size, coverage of habitations, liters per capita consumption per head (lpcd), equity, gender, sustainability, cost of provision, ground water table, water quality, pricing of water, environmental conflicts, community participation and willingness to pay for improved water supply.

The methodology adopted in various studies was aimed at probing issues more at piece meal level. Hardly any attempt is made so far in India to look at this problem in a holistic manner by integrating both economic and environmental aspects towards finding a solution to the problem. This is not to discount the merits of the earlier studies conducted but to justify the necessity of the present study.

In the light of the literature review made in this chapter, the present study proposed to estimate the demand for domestic water in general and cooking and drinking in particular. This is, in fact, the need of the hour as there are a large number of criticisms on the existing state norms of 40-50 lpcd in vogue. Secondly, the quality of different water sources and the health impacts thereof formed a part of the present study. And more importantly the pricing of rural water is proposed with the help of actual field level data. The earlier studies provided adequate guidelines to estimate the water tariff in rural areas.

3

NATIONAL AND STATE SCENARIOS OF RURAL WATER SUPPLY

International scientific communities warned India that she might face water famine in another two decades. Drinking water scarcity is an offshoot of drought conditions besides fodder scarcity and inflicts a host of other hardships on the poor. Solving this problem temporarily and let alone a permanent solution will be a formidable task for any Government. Provision of safe drinking water on a sustainable basis entails co-ordination of state and the people at large. In most cases the state would provide a source of water but end up with a failure for want of proper operation and maintenance of the same. In certain other cases, state may be ready to render service but there will be a dearth of water source. There are instances where people collectively organize themselves in creating a community source. Therefore, water management in India is so complex that hydrologists, social scientists, geologists and environmentalists have a role to play in understanding and streamlining the system. In this context it is relevant to discuss the socio-economic and environment related issues of drinking water provision at the village level across the country. This chapter intends to trace plan allocation, financial implications and environmental aspects, institutional measures and the people's participation in the provision of drinking water supply in rural areas of India.

3.1 Water Institutions

The literature on Institutional Economics (Saleth, 1994) suggests that Water Institutions comprise water law, water policy and water administration. Given the fact, water is a state subject, under the constitutional provision a number of policies and programmes have been initiated both by Central and State Governments from time to time towards provision of total rural water supply. They include: The International Decade for Drinking Water Supply and Sanitation (1981-90), The Rajiv Gandhi National Drinking Water Mission (1986), and the Government of India (1987). These arrangements can be considered as supply side institutions.

3.1.1 National Initiatives: Plan Allocation

Even before Independence, organised effort got initiated with the formation of Bhore Committee to look into this service on a nation wide scale. During the First Five Year Plan (1951-56), water supply and sanitation schemes were funded under community development works. Only in September 1954 the National Water Supply and Sanitation Programme became a part of the health schemes, followed by setting up of Public Health Engineering Department. No notable changes had taken place during the Second Five Year Plan period (1956-61) excepting the expansion of the Public Health Engineering Departments in order to cope up with the increasing workload. A preliminary survey of the problems of water supply was made during the Third Five Year Plan (1961-66). The three Annual Plans (1966-67), (1967-68) and (1968-69) had witnessed no marked changes in programmes.

The Accelerated Rural Water Supply Programme (ARWSP) was introduced during the Fourth Five Year Plan (1969-74). This central scheme had ensured cent-per-cent assistance to the States and Union territories towards the water supply to villages. The major thrust of the Minimum Needs Programme (MNP) during the Fifth Five Year Plan (1974-79) was to provide safe drinking water that forms an integral part of the basic needs of the rural poor.

Launching of Sixth Five Year Plan (1980-85) witnessed an increasing awareness both nationally and internationally on the urgency of the protected water supply to sustain the process of economic and human resource development. The global concern gathered momentum leading to the United Nations Water Conference in Argentina in 1977. As a follow up measure, decadal campaign started among member countries eventually declaring 1981-90 as *the International Drinking Water Supply and Sanitation Decade*. Needless to mention, India as a signatory to the Resolution had extended its support to the action plan. During the Seventh Five Year Plan (1985-90), the RWS continued to be a part of the MNP. Additional progress was in the form of re-defining the per capita norm and the problem villages in regard to RWS. No new improvements had taken place during the two Annual Plans (1990-91 and 1991-92) in this realm. Another milestone in the history of RWS was launching of *Rajiv Gandhi National Drinking Water Mission (RGNDWM)* during this period. Defining water as safe if it is free from biological and chemical contamination the RGNDWM had proposed certain interesting norms which included provision of 40 litres per capita per day (lpcd) for human beings, an additional 30 lpcd for cattle in desert districts, one hand pump or stand post for every 250 persons, access to water sources within 1.6 K.M. in the plains and within 100 metres elevation differences in hilly areas (Ghosh *et al.*, 1995).

Even the National Water Policy (1987) declared water to be an economic good and a renewable natural resource to be conserved on a sustainable basis. In view of the fact that economic growth and employment opportunities by themselves may not suffice to improve the living conditions of the poor the Ninth Five Year Plan (1997-2002), has proposed certain basic minimum services which include, provision of safe drinking water in rural areas.

Allocation for water supply and sanitation was 2.47 per cent in the First Five Year Plan of which only 0.71 per cent was earmarked for rural water supply. The allocation rose to 3.85 per cent in the Eighth Plan of which 2.52 per cent was allotted to rural water supply. However, in terms of per capita cost of plan outlay towards rural water sector it was abysmally low during the early plan period. It increased five fold between Fifth and Sixth Plan period. This increased priority began after the advent of Rajiv Gandhi Drinking Water Mission and the pace kept up till the end of the Eighth Plan period (Table 3.1) and (Fig. 3.1). It may be inferred that allocation for rural water supply had been relatively less when compared to urban water supply. Secondly, the increase in allocation was marginal over the span of last five decades.

Table 3.1 : Development plans outlays/Expenditure and allocation to the sector

(Rs. in crores)

Development Plan	*Total Plan Original*	*Water supply and sanitation sector*				
		Total	*% of the plan outlay*	*Rural*	*% of the outlay*	*Per capita cost (in Rupees)*
First Plan 1951 – 56	1960.00	48.49	2.47	14.00	0.71	1.4
Second Plan 1956 – 61	4600.00	91.00	1.98	28.00	0.60	
Third Plan 1961 – 66	8576.00	105.70	1.23	67.00	0.78	2.41
Annual Plans 1966 – 69	6625.40	102.70	1.55	19.67	0.29	
Fourth Plan 1969 – 74	15782.50	458.90	2.91	158.33	1.0	20.11
Fifth Plan 1974 – 79	39426.20	1091.60	2.77	489.78	1.24	
Annual Plan 1979 – 80	12176.50	429.52	3.52	234.16	1.92	
Sixth Plan 1980 – 85	97500.00	3907.80	4.00	2154.24	2.21	108.83
Seventh Plan 1985 – 90	180000.00	6522.47	3.62	3556.72	1.97	
Annual Plan 1990 – 92	137033.55	4427.29	3.23	2705.92	1.97	213.69
Eighth Plan 1992 – 97	525273.50	16373.03	3.85	10728.75	2.52	

Source : As quoted in Ghosh et. al. (1995).

Thirdly, it can be construed from the plan allocation that the rural population is provided with adequate water supply. Perhaps it is difficult to confirm whether all the villages across the country are provided with safe drinking water supply. An in-depth study at the micro level is called for to clarify such issues.

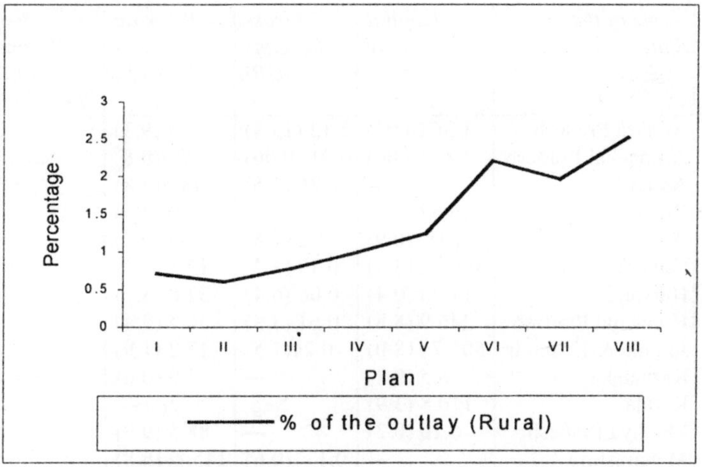

Fig. 3.1 : Percentage of the plan outlay (Rural).

As a result of planning efforts, definitely there is an increase in terms of coverage of population, but the vulnerable sections of society, particularly schedule caste and schedule tribes are yet to be adequately served. Hence, the thrust should not only be on merely increasing the total coverage but extending the service to underprivileged population so as to ensure equity (Bijlani, 1998).

3.1.2 Financing of Rural Water Supply

Financing of this sector assumes significance from the point of view of economics. A number of schemes have so far been launched both at the central and state level to create a water sources. Cost of providing this public utility is a matter of great concern for economists. It is only through careful planning of cost aspects of RWS, efficiency, equity and sustainability are achievable. Basically, financing comprises two components, viz., capital, operation and maintenance costs. As the budgetary transfers always remained inadequate to the sector, financing becomes more crucial to meet the inadequacies.

Table 3.2 : State-wise Financial Results of Rural Water Supply Schemes (RWSS) Quinquennial average for the period 1989-90 to 1993-94.

(Rs. crores)

Sl. No.	*Name of the State / UT*	*Capital outlay*	*Gross Receipts (GR)*	*Working Expenses (WE)*	*%age Recovery of WE Through GR*
1.	Andhra Pradesh	1.56 (0.05)	2.12 (13.8)	82.9 (9.3)	2.6
2.	Arunachal Pradesh	1.85 (0.06)	0.01 (0.06)	7.5(0.8)	0.02
3.	Assam	—	0.26 (1.6)	34.5(3.8)	0.21
4.	Bihar	426.6 (15.3)	—	39.0 (4.3)	0.00
5.	Goa	25.18 (0.9)	1.2 (7.8)	1.95 (0.2)	58.2
6.	Gujarat	369.8 (13.3)	0.19 (1.2)	17.5 (1.9)	2.06
7.	Haryana	11.23 (0.4)	0.06 (0.4)	32.8 (3.7)	0.9
8.	Himachal Pradesh	246.9 (8.8)	0.61 (3.9)	30.5 (3.4)	1.9
9.	Jammu & Kashmir	501.7 (18.0)	0.24(1.5)	17.2 (1.9)	1.4
10.	Karnataka	6.5 (0.2)	—	5.9 (0.6)	0.00
11.	Kerala	110.8 (3.9)	Neg.	—	—
12.	Madhya Pradesh	6.10 (0.2)	—	88.5 (9.9)	0.00
13.	Maharashtra	—	0.1 (0.6)	145.8(16.8)	0.16
14.	Manipur	100.2 (3.6)	0.01(0.06)	1.4(0.1)	2.6
15.	Meghalaya	111.4 (4.0)	—	—	—
16.	Mizoram	15.9 (0.5)	0.2(1.3)	3.2(0.3)	2.5
17.	Nagaland	43.2 (1.5)	0.03(0.19)	9.5(1.0)	0.05
18.	Orissa	13.5 (0.5)	0.02(0.13)	28.8(3.2)	0.10
19.	Punjab	2.6 (0.09)	1.9(12.4)	32.6(3.6)	8.5
20.	Rajasthan	840.8(30.2)	7.9(51.6)	54.5(6.1)	15.2
21.	Sikkim	30.3 (0.4)	—	0.9(0.10)	—
22.	Tamil Nadu	4.19 (0.15)	—	81.3(9.1)	0.00
23.	Tripura	55.8 (2.0)	—	3.7(0.4)	0.00
24.	Uttar Pradesh	0.24 (0.008)	Neg.	112.1(12.6)	—
25.	West Bengal	—	Neg.	19.7(2.2)	—
26.	Pondicherry	—	0.4 (2.6)	2.4(0.27)	26.7
27.	Union Government	27.5 (0.9)	0.03(0.19)	48.8(5.5)	0.05
	All India	**2779.3**	**15.4**	**889.0**	**1.72**

Source : Water and Related Statistics, Central Water Commission, July 1998. Figures in brackets indicate percentage to the total.

Generally, it is the State Government's responsibility to provide tap connections, hand pumps, stand post, and construct Over Head Tanks (OHT) and so on. The State then hand over the responsibility of maintenance to the local bodies.

Financial constraints have continued to hamper progress over the decades. Secondary source of information on the financial results of RWS during 1974-75 to 1993-94 for India revealed certain important features. The quinquennial averages clearly showed that the working expenses towards RWS increased at a higher pace than the gross receipts. As a result, the percentage recovery of working expenses through gross receipts was fairly low. Lack of accountability can be one of the reasons for the unprecedented rise in working expenses. Further the State-wise financial results also brought to light the dismal recovery of working expenses through gross receipts. In states like Tamil Nadu, Karnataka, Madhya Pradesh and Tripura the recovery has been zero. On the contrary, Rajasthan revealed a different picture with the highest percentage of the capital outlay, and recovery with minimum working expenses (Table 3.2). This only reflected the financial constraints and the inability of State Governments to mobilize funds through user charges and so on. The quinquennial averages showed a picture where the working expenses increased from Rs. 56.8 crores to Rs. 905.8 crores between 1974-75 to 1978-79 and 1989-90 to 1993-94. But the percentage recovery of working expenses through gross recovery declined from 2.4 to 1.7 during the same period (Table 3.3).

Table 3.3 : Financial results Rural Water Supply Scheme (RWSS) during 1974-75 to 1993-94 All India Quinquennial Average.

(Rs. in crores)

Sl. No.	*Year*	*Capital Outlay*	*Gross Receipts (GR)*	*Working Expenses*	*Percentage Recovery of (WE) Through (GR)*
1.	1974-75 to 1978-79	109.34	1.3	56.8	2.4
2.	1979-80 to 1983-84	488.6	2.8	237.7	1.3
3.	1984-85 to 1988-89	1202.7	6.1	577.5	1.0
4.	1989-90 to 1993-94	3405.7	15.3	905.8	1.7

Source : Water and Related Statistics, Central Water Commission, July 1998.

A study on drinking water supply in Rajasthan demonstrated how the estimates of household's willingness to pay for drinking water formed an input in rural water pricing policy. Further it confirmed that assured safe water supply on a regular basis motivated the households to pay for water. The study

> *"rejects the thumb rule of 5 per cent of total expenditure the household would be willing to pay. For the willingness to pay for water is much less than 5 per cent (less than 2 per cent) irrespective of the economic condition of the region. However, the willingness to pay is substantially higher than the existing urban water rates on a per unit basis. The ability of the household to pay for social consumption items like health and education is about 5 per cent of the total expenditure. The share of the willingness to pay for water in the total expenditure may go up with the realization of health benefits from improved water supplies. This is possible because people are now aware of the link between the two"* (Reddy, 1999: p. 120).

The Indian scenario necessitates a case for pricing of rural water. Besides, recovery rate can be enhanced with more community participation rather than entrusting the entire responsibility with the state. Financial strategy should be intrinsic to water supply and sanitation projects. This in turn calls for efficient cost recovery procedures. Pricing of rural water supply will be a better choice to run the schemes on a sustainable basis. In rural areas, pricing will be feasible only for house connection. An intricate problem which poses challenge is the mindset of the rural users with respect to water rates/charges since the general pattern through out history has always been to treat water as free good.

3.1.3 Role of State in Rural Water Supply

The recent Supreme Court ruling states, "*clean drinking water is a fundamental right of all citizens*". This forms part of Article 21 of the Constitution, which guaranted right to life (Agarwal, 2000). Provision of drinking water to villages is a State subject as per Indian Constitution. The Constitutional Amendment Act of 1992 empowered the Panchayati Raj Institutions to be responsible for operation and maintenance of the sources created with a financial autonomy to decide appropriate means of raising funds to strengthen the base to keep system going. In India, right from the beginning of the First Five Year Plan funds were allowed in the respective budget of the State Governments. Although many a State and Central Programmes were started over a period of time, RGNDWM (1986) is a milestone in the history of rural water supply in India.

Under this mission approach, villages across the country were divided into habitations[1]. Each habitation is to be provided with at least one source of safe drinking water such as hand pump or stand post or tap connection. The 1991 census data showed that 55.5 per cent of rural households have had access to safe drinking water facility. Kerala and Mizoram stood low in this respect and this may be due to dependence on locally available sources of water. Punjab, West Bengal, Sikkim, and Haryana were some of the states with good coverage of drinking water supply. During 1991-94, a nation-wide survey was conducted to assess the performance of the mission approach and it was found that 82 per cent of the rural population got benefited through this programme (Table 3.4) and (Fig. 3.2). The operation and maintenance was reckoned to be major problems of this mission approach. Efficient provision of rural water supply does not stop with mere installation and commissioning of the sources alone but depends more on ensuring continued functioning, acceptance by the users and above all self-mobilizing capacity of operational and maintenance costs; in rural areas technical know-how and financial position are relatively weak. Government sponsored survey on Rajiv Gandhi Drinking Water Mission came out with the finding that in most places inadequacy of resources for operation and maintenance caused the schemes non-functional. The immediate blame lies albeit with the government machinery, (i.e.) the local body like, Panchayats, which are entrusted with the responsibility of operation and maintenance of the sources.

---

[1] An entity with a minimum population of one thousand and the distance between two habitations should be not less than one km.

Table 3.4 : Status of water supply in village habitations in India – 1999.

S. No.	*State & UT*	*Habitations*			
		Not covered	*Partially covered*	*Fully covered*	*Total*
1.	Andhra Pradesh	0	24683	45049	69732
2.	Arunachal Pradesh	548	1227	2403	4178
3.	Assam	3901	26202	40566	70669
4.	Bihar	1069	564	203803	205436
5.	Goa	34	27	344	405
6.	Gujarat	437	4639	25193	30269
7.	Haryana	32	0	7513	7545
8.	Himachal Pradesh	3750	13592	28025	45367
9.	J & K	2430	4047	9249	15726
10.	Karnataka	1522	10498	44662	56682
11.	Kerala	880	6719	2164	9763
12.	Madhaya Pradesh	3563	17709	138596	159868
13.	Maharashtra	1515	31811	43798	77124
14.	Manipur	77	510	2204	2791
15.	Meghalaya	869	1276	6494	8639
16.	Mizoram	2	624	285	911
17.	Nagaland	428	703	394	1525
18.	Orssa	1978	4709	107412	114099
19.	Punjab	5845	3123	4481	13449
20.	Rajasthan	4715	38163	61188	104066
21.	Sikkim	0	732	947	1679
22.	Tamil Nadu	0	16971	49660	66631
23.	Tripura	726	1604	5082	7412
24.	Uttar Pradesh	0	0	274641	274641
25.	West Bengal	0	22547	57830	80377
	Union Territory				
26.	Andaman and Nicobar Islands	11	6	487	504
27.	Dadra and Nagar Havali	128	190	198	516
28.	Daman and Diu	0	1	28	29
29.	Delhi	0	0	200	200
30.	Lakshadweep	0	10	0	10
31.	Pondicherry	0	0	276	276
32.	Chandigarh	0	0	24	24
	Total	**34460**	**232887**	**1163196**	**1430543**

Source : Annual Report 1999–2000, Ministry of Rural Development, Government of India, pp. 201.

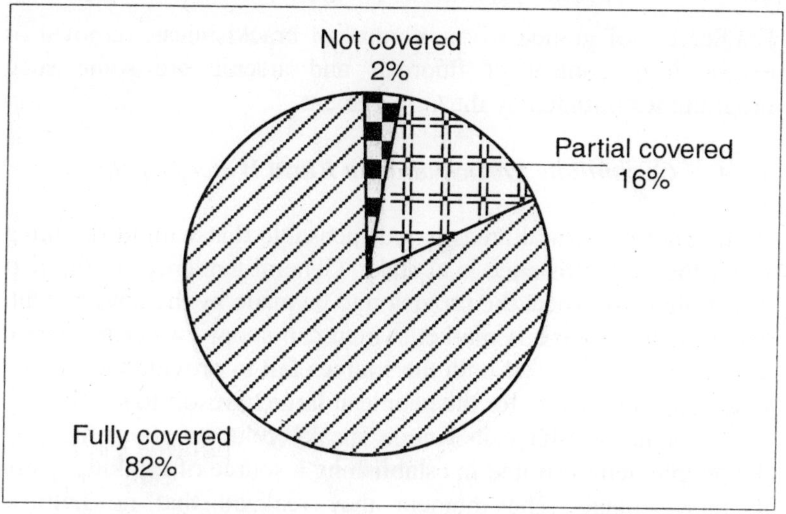

Fig. 3.2 : Status of water supply in village habitation in India – 1999.

State Governments have been endeavouring from time to time in modifying the norms towards achieving results. At present provision of one hand pump for every 150 persons from the existing norm of 250 persons and enhancing the per capita per day rate of 40 lpcd to 70 lpcd are recommended. The intended beneficiaries shall have to share 10 per cent of the capital cost and full operation and maintenance cost.

However, both the Central and State Governments have so far paid scant attention to the problem of operation and maintenance of the system. This is evident from the absence of definite policy towards tackling this problem. The problem is compounded by the rural water users' notion that water should be made available free of cost. Excepting a few, majority of the rural water users hold this view. The need of the hour is a permanent and viable solution to this problem before long.

Recent report (Govt. of India, 1999-2000) from the Ministry of Rural Development clearly signalled a paradigm shift from Government oriented approach to people oriented, from centralized to decentralized and from supply driven to demand driven and community based rural water supply programme. On the quality front, submissions were launched to provide safe drinking water to those habitations where water quality is poor.

Eradication of guinea worm, control of brackishness, removal of excess iron, control of fluorosis and arsenic are some such programmes initiated by the Government.

3.1.4 Community Participation in Rural Water Supply

Water supply in rural areas is indispensable that without drinking water the very existence is at stake. General tendency on the part of people is to expect the provision to be made by the government. The next alternative is market, which can supply water at a price with a profit motive. If both the sources fail to provide the facility it becomes inevitable for the people at large to resort to self-help.

Olvanna, a village in Kerela speaks volumes about the way the people demonstrated in establishing a source of drinking water in their village. The moment they realized that no help is forthcoming, the people of Olvanna village joined together to raise money through sale of jewels and properties. Surprisingly they were able to construct overhead tanks and lay pipelines by using their local expertise rather than depending on qualified engineer. Consequent to the use of traditional knowledge, the villagers brought down the cost from Rs. 50,000 to just Rs. 5,000. Other problem villages in Kerala are trying to emulate the same by effectively organizing themselves to create some sources of water without depending much on the Government (Nair, 1998).

It is worth recalling the experience of Karnataka in implementing 'Karnataka Integrated Rural Water Supply and Environmental Schemes' (KIRWS & ES). This scheme aimed at providing "*an alternative delivery system through participatory approach*". Under this scheme the village community is a part of a decision-making body apart from the Government, Non-Governmental Organizations (NGOs); the private sector is also included in planning and executing. However, the operation and maintenance of the system will be left to the care of village communities. Ultimately it is the village community that assumes a role in all the three stages. Functionally, the Village Water Supply Committee (VWSC) is formed consisting of Panchayat members and selected members from the community with the Panchayat President as the ex-officio Chairman of the Committee. About one-third of the total members are women. The main idea of the scheme is to inculcate the sense of sharing costs, as sustainability of the system rests with user financing and maintenance. The VWSC members take the responsibility of mobilizing community contributions by means of household connection fee and water tariff to meet the operation and maintenance costs. At times the village Panchayat come to rescue when the VESC faced certain difficulties like irregular power supply and mechanical failure of motor pumps (Veerashekharappa, 2000).

Community participation is thus an alternative approach through creating community-based problem solving capability. Here the changes are directed towards locally felt needs unlike the ones decided by outside agencies. These endeavours motivate the community as a whole to participate, thereby making them learn certain skills of problem identification and generating solutions for the same. Further a feeling that the community participants shall have a stake in the provision of facility is created through this. Now the question that arises as to whether the community participation *per se* is adequate for achieving the provision of safe water for all. The answer is obviously no. Because only in the event of total state failure, community participation becomes imminent, in places where state functions well the community participation can only supplement the existing sources.

3.1.5 Sustainability of Rural Water Supply

Sustainability is an often-quoted paradigm in environmental economics. In the absence of substitute for dinking water the question of sustainability becomes increasingly important. There are two basic arguments that have come forth in this context. Provision of water by means of creation of source through scientific identification, installation of hand pump/stand post and operating and maintaining the system continuously is one way of looking at the sustainability aspect. Lack of finance makes the system unsustainable. Therefore, to achieve sustainability, rationalized water tariffs ought to improve revenue position, which in turn meet the operation and maintenance expenses. The other argument highlights the traditional water supply systems[1]. Rainwater harvesting, watershed management and check dams are the traditional methods to ensure sustainability. The issue is to decide whether modern (mission)[2] approach *versus* traditional method or a blend of both, is ideal to understand the complex question of sustainability.

There is a growing concern and enthusiasm right from hydrologists to common man across the country over the rainwater harvesting. Thanks to the recent drought in Gujarat and Orissa. According to the Chairman of the Central Ground Water Board, about 210 billion cubic metres of rainwater can be retained as groundwater and more than 75 per cent of this can be utilized. After all rainwater carries zero price, quality-wise very little bacteria and other organic matters.

> According to the Citizens' report
>
> "*the principle of water harvesting is to conserve rainfall according to local needs and geophysical conditions. In the process, ground water is also recharged. Traditional water harvesting systems have met the domestic and irrigation needs of the people. The available historical and archaeological evidences suggest that effective systems of water management had been established and were operated by small communities in many regions of the country as early as the 4th Century BC*" (Agarwal and Narain, 1997: p.17).

Rainwater harvesting is basically a traditional method of recharging ground water source. It is rooftop rainwater harvesting

---

1 **Traditional sources**: (a) open well (shallow), (b) Oorani, (c) tank (irrigation), (d) Agricultural well (open), (e) pond, and (f) spring, temple tanks, spring channel.

2 **Mission sources**: (a) Hand pump (i) shallow bore well with Tara hand pump, (ii) shallow bore well with pumps other than Tara hand pump, (iii) deep tube well with India mark II hand pump, (iv) deep bore well with hand pump other than India mark II hand pump, and (v) sanitary dug-wells with hand pump, (b) Infiltration wells, (c) infiltration gallery, (d) piped water supply schemes through overhead tanks (OHT), (e) extended pipeline, (f) Ground Level Water Reservoir (GLWR).

which is frequently quoted and experimented. Under this, each and every drop of rainwater is streamlined to reach the watertable rather than just letting it flow on the ground. A rough estimate of cost of this recharge structure to practice rainwater harvesting worked out to be Rs. 5,000 to Rs. 10,000. Invariably all the buildings will have a storm water pipe from the terrace. The idea is to direct the rainwater to reach the filter bed that has a pipe at the bottom that is connected to a shallow well. This will replenish the level of water in the well and in the long run the quality of water would improve (*DPG News Review*, 1999). The whole idea becomes rhetoric in rural areas where concrete buildings are small in numbers, unlike in urban areas.

Rainwater harvesting is an environmentally benign method of recharging the groundwater. The concept of rainwater harvesting is gaining significance, as there are many success stories in our country in the recent period. The Centre for Science and Environment (CSE) had conducted a survey of different villages that suffered drought in Gujarat and Western Madhya Pradesh during last 1999, which brought forth the following facts. Those villages that had experimented rainwater harvesting and watershed development in the recent past enjoyed good drinking water source and even had some water for irrigation. Conversely, neighbouring villages that neglected their traditional systems were confronted with severe drinking water scarcity. Other famous success stories include the following. Anna Hazare in Ralegaon Siddhi and Manegaon villages in Maharashtra could convincingly eradicate water scarcity. Hundreds of villages in Alwar district of Rajasthan were rescued by the non-governmental organization called Tarun Bharat Sangh, that taught the residents to build several thousand small check dams to enable wells and underground aquifers to recharge. They reportedly gave life to the dying rivers. Rich business groups from Mumbai came forward voluntarily to fund the construction of water harvesting structures in Saurastra. A dynamic District Collector in Dewas town of Madhya Pradesh, has encouraged the local people to practice rooftop rainwater harvesting thereby reducing dependence on scarce municipal water. There are innumerable further cases exemplified by NGOs and sincere officials in rainwater harvesting across different states of India.

Sustainability of groundwater is equally relevant as evidently groundwater is the major source of drinking water across the villages in India. There is no gainsaying the fact that water resources are renewable one, since the recharging rate should be greater than the extraction rate. In India the scenario of groundwater level is so deplorable.

> *"In most parts of the country groundwater exploitation is as high as 80 per cent. Only in 5 per cent of our country, is water present at a depth of 0 to 5 meters, 97 per cent has water at 3-10 metres and 58 per cent areas have water below 40 metres"* (Iqbal, 2000: p.55).

Many methods have been adopted over several years to store rainwater in tanks and allow it to percolate down to ground thereby recharging it. The feasibility of percolation depends largely on the 'geological formation', which may vary from region to region.

> *"The distribution of underground water is not uniform and its availability is subject to wide spatio-temporal variations depending on the underlying rock formation, precipitation pattern and other hydrological conditions"* (*The Hindu*, 1999: p. 7).

There is a relationship between groundwater depletion and mechanical and technical problems involved in operating and maintaining the sources such as hand pumps and stand post. As water table goes down the extraction of water becomes more and more difficult, eventually rendering the machines unutilized and finally, end up with mechanical failure.

The foregoing discussion brings forth certain questions for further discussion. What are the relative merits of modern (mission) approach over the traditional system? Is it possible for the State (through mission approach) to achieve the set target of providing a source of drinking water across all habitations in the country? Is there a need to combine both traditional and modern methods towards the ultimate goal of provision of drinking water? Mission approach keeps the groundwater source as its base, while the traditional systems are more flexible depending upon the prevailing local hydrological conditions. The state considers that water provided through hand pumps, stand posts, and house service connection taps is protected. As much as 90 per cent of water supplied in rural areas depends largely on groundwater source. Other sources such as water in lake, tanks and ponds are unprotected and hence unsafe.

The paradoxical situation of '*scarcity amid plenty*' is applicable to rural water supply too. In most cases, it is not the lack of absolute quantity of water but the problem is of improper and inequitable distribution amongst consumers. Water after all has no substitute unlike other items such as oil and coal.

Many reasons can be cited for the negligence of traditional water systems. An important historical reason is

> *"Centralization of power in the pre-colonial and colonial periods saw rapid changes in traditional systems. The responsibility of managing small water bodies passed from the local community to centralized state agencies. The concept of water as a 'national asset' was used to justify this transfer as if the local community could not be entrusted with national property. Disinvested of their customary powers and responsibilities, communities became apathetic to the maintenance of reservoirs and water channels. The increasing political empowerment of village Panchayats did not help the matter"* (Kothari, 2000: p.III).

Discussion of traditional system of water harvesting is not necessarily meant to discourage mission approach, since this brings in research and development and ensures science and technology inputs into the water supply schemes. Also mission approach envisages water quality assurance, water conservation, operation and maintenance and other sustainability aspects.

There is no gainsaying the fact that our traditional system of rainwater harvesting was based on science and common sense. These practices ought to be revived, and linked to modern methods and knowledge. No doubt, provision of drinking water to the rural population of India is a formidable task. Keeping in view the fact that though both Central and State Governments have already invested Rs.15,000 crores in this respect, and estimates indicates an additional 15,000 crores more would be required for total solution of the problem.

Even after a lapse of fifty years of independence nearly 26 per cent of rural population have little access to safe drinking water. The conditions have been improving over the last decade owing to efforts taken by the Central and State Governments. But the whole question is whether the provision made so far is sustainable? One major impediment with the mission approach *ipso facto* state's effort is the problem of lack of finance for operation and maintenance of potable water sources. Inadequate financial position only reflects the inefficiency of the states to mobilize fund for this purpose besides the populist policies. The need of the hour is to rationalize the tariff structure of both house service connection and the property tax thereby raise the revenue to meet the operation and maintenance of the system on a sustainable basis.

Community participation is reckoned as a powerful instrument to meet the aspirations by people themselves. Though not all the states, certain states in southern part of India such as Kerala and Karnataka exemplified their collective strength towards this goal.

Water quality is as problematic as the quantity of water. There is no dearth of evidence to show the health hazards due to water quality deterioration. Rural water users are aware of the link between health and safe drinking water, but seldom they treat or purify their source of drinking water. Urban dwellers on the other hand are relatively better in terms of awareness and in treating the water either through on-line or off-line processes.

The upshot is the complexities involved in understanding and trying to find a permanent solution for rural water supply. There is no gainsaying that traditional systems need to be preserved and strengthened. Now there is a paradigm shift in the role of state from provider to facilitator and hence only a collective effort by the state, local people and the NGOs should further endeavour to identify scientific sources without compromising the traditional wisdom to improve the rural water supply.

3.2 Analysis of National Sample Survey Organisation data on Rural Water Supply

The National Sample Survey Organisation (NSSO) has had conducted several rounds of survey from time to time, the 44th, 49th and 54th rounds are noteworthy from the point of view of drinking water and sanitation. The 54th round of survey was conducted during January-June 1998 and got published in 1999. This round has covered a wide spectrum of details pertaining to drinking water and sanitation in this country. Sample design used in the NSSO 54th round is given in Annexure-III.

The analysis of NSSO data bringsforth several interesting results over the access, usage and quality of principal and supplementary[1] sources across modern and traditional[2] schemes of water supply. Over the last one decade, it is evident from Table 3.5 that the access to modern[3]/mission sources had increased to 69 per cent in 1998 from 54.3 per cent in 1988 (Fig. 3.3). Dependence on modern source by the households has been on the increase, while the access to traditional means as principal source recorded a fall during the same period.

For other domestic uses such as cooking, bathing and washing utensils, the proportion of households depended on modern means, as supplementary source was lower. More than 60 per cent of the households resorted to modern facilities as principal sources for domestic purposes. In the case of traditional means, more than 50 per cent of households resorted to this as supplementary source for cooking, bathing and washing utensils.

---

[1] *Principal and supplementary sources*: If a household, during the last 365 days, obtained drinking water from more than one source, then the one most commonly used was treated as the principal source and the next one (in terms of frequency of use) was treated as the supplementary source. Thus, if a household used source A for 5 months of the year, source B for 4 months, and C for 3 months, then A and B were treated as the principal and the supplementary source, respectively. (NSSO 1999)

[2] *Traditional sources*: Well, tank/pond resvoir for drinking, other tank/pond, river/canal/lake, spring.

[3] *Modern (Mission) sources*: tap, tubewell and hand pump, and tanker.

Table 3.5 : Access to Principal Sources of Drinking and domestic use of water-percentage distribution of households – 1988, 1993 and 1998.

Source	*Principal source of drinking water*			*Principal and supplementary – 1998*					
				Cooking		*Bathing*			*Wash-ing utensils*
	1988 (44th)	*1993 (49th)*	*1998 (54th)*	*PS*	*SS*	*PS*	*SS*	*PS*	*SS*
Modern	54.3	63.4	69.0	69.6	45.1	60.1	43.3	64.9	44.7
Traditional	45.1	36.5	30.7	30.0	53.3	39.2	55.5	34.7	53.9
Others	0.6	0.3	0.2	0.4	1.6	0.4	1.2	0.3	1.3
All India (rural)	**100**	**100**	**100**	**100**	**100**	**100**	**100**	**100**	**100**

PS : Principal Source, SS : Supplementary Source.
Source : Computed from 44th, 49th and 54th rounds of NSSO (1999) data.

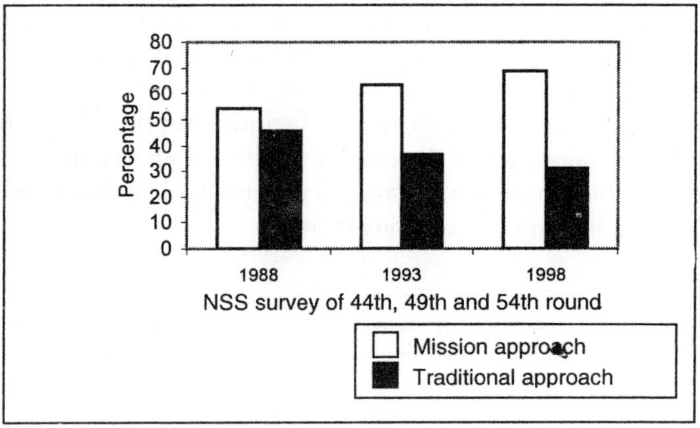

Fig. 3.3 : Percentage distribution of households by principal source of drinking water.

The trend that emerged from the 44th, 49th and 54th round of surveys is worth mentioning. Firstly, the modern facilities as principal source have kept up an increasing pace over the decade *vis-à-vis* the traditional source. Secondly, traditional means recorded a substantial fall during the same period as principal source. And, thirdly, other domestic uses depended largely on traditional facilities as supplementary sources. The implications of these trends are far reaching. By over-emphasizing mission/ modern schemes the State paid scant attention to the traditional facilities. Despite the concerted efforts of the Central and State programmes, one-fifth of the rural population is still deprived of access to potable water. This may be due to the negligence of traditional sources. Therefore, there is need for a holistic approach by way of paying enough attention to traditional means, which would be sustainable in the long-run.

Although the 54th round contains data both on rural and urban areas as well, the details regarding sources, consumption, quality and distance travelled towards fetching water with respect to rural areas across different states are considered in this study. For this purpose, zone-wise classification of states are prepared across which the above stated aspects are analysed. On the whole, modern sources remained a major contributor as principal source to the extent of 69 per cent, while the traditional sources contributed the rest as stated earlier. Exceptionally the state of Kerala stands different in terms of larger dependence on traditional scheme of water as principal source. This does not necessarily mean any under provision of public water supply in Kerala (Table 3.6). The public distribution of rural water supply is reported to be a failure due to

> *"The characterisation safe water as pipe water, and institutional framework of free distribution by the state agency, are the root causes of the ineffectiveness of public water supply in rural Kerala"* (Santhakumar, 1998: p. 22).

Given the fact that both modern and traditional schemes serve as principal and supplementary sources for domestic use, an element of uncertainty arises over the extent of dependence on both schemes as sources by the households. Further, the implications of over emphasis of any one, be it modern or traditional, will be known only through an empirical verification of dependence.

Table 3.6 : Principal sources of drinking water.

(In percentage)

Zone wise analysis	*State*	*Principal Source*			*Supplementary*		
		Modern	*Traditional*	*Others*	*Modern*	*Traditional*	*Others*
South Zone	Andhra Pradesh	73.0	26.2	0.8	46.7	50.8	2.5
	Karnataka	80.5	19.5	0.0	60.2	39.8	0
	Kerala	11.9	87.8	0.3	23.2	76.6	0.3
	Tamil Nadu	81.7	18.3	0.0	54.2	45.5	0.0
North Zone	Haryana	80.9	19.1	0.0	75.9	24.0	0.1
	Punjab	97.5	2.4	0.5	96.3	3.2	0.5
	Rajasthan	55.6	43.9	0.4	39.9	58.2	1.9
Central Zone	Madhya Pradesh	57.2	42.7	0.1	36.98	60.6	2.3
	Uttar Pradesh	72.3	27.6	0.2	44.8	52.4	2.7
West Zone	Gujarat	80.5	19.4	0.1	41.2	58.4	0.4
	Maharashtra	65.9	33.9	0.2	41.7	57.9	0.4
East Zone	Bihar	70.9	28.5	0.5	39.1	58.4	2.5
	Orissa	56.4	42.2	1.3	41.9	55.8	0.1
	West Bengal	79.8	19.7	0.5	64.5	30.3	5.2
North-Eastern Zone	Assam	56.8	42.3	0.9	20.7	79.0	0.3
	Arunachal Pradesh Manipur, Meghalaya, Mizoram, Nagaland, Sikkim, Tripura	69.1	28.1	2.8	30.4	65.6	4.0
North-Western Zone	Jammu & Kashmir, Himachal Pradesh, Chandigarh, Delhi	99.6	0.4	0.0	31.2	67.4	1.4
Southern Zone	Andaman & Nicobar Islands, Dadra & Nagar Haveli, Goa, Daman & Diu, Lakshadweep, Pondicherry	90.6	9.3	0.0	40.0	59.7	0.2
All India		**68.98**	**30.66**	**0.4**	**45.7**	**52.9**	**1.4**

Source : Computed from NSSO 54th round.

3.2.1 Hypothesis I

The respondents (NSSO 54th round of survey) used the modern schemes as a principal sources and traditional schemes as a supplementary source for collecting water for various domestic consumption purpose.

3.2.2 Null Hypothesis

There is no significant difference between the modern and traditional schemes as principal and supplementary sources for the NSSO respondents in the country as a whole.

3.2.3 Alternative Hypothesis

There is difference between the modern and traditional schemes as principal and supplementary sources for the respondents in the country as a whole.

A paired 't'-test is used to test the stated hypothesis. Here the pairs represent the modern scheme as principal use and modern schemes as supplementary source on the one hand, and on the other hand traditional schemes as principal use and traditional schemes as supplementary sources.

On the basis of the test results, the null hypothesis gets rejected, meaning that there is a significant difference between the modern and traditional schemes to act as principal and supplementary sources. It is necessary to look at the differences within the scheme as principal and supplementary sources and differences between the schemes as principal and supplementary sources.

In the case of modern scheme the difference is statistically significant as a principal and supplementary sources, with a mean difference of 25.07 at 5 per cent level. The traditional scheme too showed a statistically significant difference as principal and supplementary sources with a mean difference of 24.02 at 5 per cent level (Table 3.7).

The next question is the difference between the schemes as principal and supplementary sources. The difference between the modern and traditional schemes as principal source is significant with a mean difference of 42 at 5 per cent level. But the difference between the modern and traditional schemes as supplementary source did not turn out to be statistically significant.

Table 3.7 : 't' test results.

Variable	Number of Pairs	Corr	2-tail Sig	Mean	SD	SE of Mean
PM Modern source as principal						
	18	–.999	.000	71.1222	19.919	4.695
PT Traditional source as principal						
				28.4056	19.766	4.695

Paired Differences					
Mean	SD	SE of Mean	t-value	df	2-tail Sig
42.7167	39.679	9.352	4.57	17	.000
95% CI (22.980, 62.454)					

Variable	Number of Pairs	Corr	2-tail Sig	Mean	SD	SE of Mean
SM Modern source as supplementary						
	18	–.997	.000	46.0489	18.661	4.398
ST Traditional source as supplementary						
				52.4222	18.606	4.395

Paired Differences					
Mean	SD	SE of Mean	t-value	df	2-tail Sig
-6.3733	37.236	8.777	-.73	17	.478
95% CI (-24.895, 12.148)					

Variable	Number of Pairs	Corr	2-tail Sig	Mean	SD	SE of Mean
PM Modern source as principal						
	18	.548	.018	71.1222	19.919	4
SM Modern source as supplementary						
				46.0489	18.661	4

Paired Differences					
Mean	SD	SE of Mean	t-value	df	2-tail Sig
25.07333	18.367	4.329	5.79	17	.000
95% CI (15.937, 34.210)					

Variable	Number of Pairs	Corr	2-tail Sig	Mean	SD	SE of Mean
PT Traditional source as principal						
	18	.543	.020	28.4056	19.766	4.659
ST Traditional source as supplementary						
				52.4222	18.606	4.385

Paired Differences					
Mean	SD	SE of Mean	t-value	df	2-tail Sig
-24.0167	18.368	4.329	-5.55	17	.000
95% CI (-33.153, -14.880)					

The implications of the results of the hypothesis testing are profound. Merely by expanding modern schemes the effective coverage of rural water supply cannot be achieved. It is evident that traditional sources play an important role as principal source to some extent and supplementary source to a greater extent.

An observation worth reckoning here is the gradual increase in modern source and the moderate decline in traditional source as principal means of water. In regard to supplementary source of water, the states like Tamil Nadu, Karnataka, Haryana, Punjab and West Bengal depended again on modern sources as supplementary uses. All the remaining states in India largely resorted to traditional means as supplementary sources. An alarming scenario emerges that the traditional sources across the country are declining over the last decade between 1988 and 1998. This trend is a serious matter of concern as reduction in traditional sources will exert pressure of modern sources may ultimately cause a crisis in rural water supply.

By classification of sources, the tube-well, hand pump served the purpose over the others, as 501 out of 1000 households on average all over country depended on this wells and taps are the major sources as per the NSSO report. Tanks, ponds, canal and lakes constituted less than 20 per 1000 households. Tamil Nadu, North Western Zone, and southern Union territories registered well in terms of number of taps per 1000 households. Central zone, Eastern zone and Karnataka State recorded higher proportion of hand pumps per 1000 households. Kerala is the only state in the country, which showed 851 out of 1000 households of having served by well (Table 3.8).

The NSSO tried to capture the water quality problems too. The water supply through tube-well, hand pumps attracted more number of complaints followed by well and tap. Among the tap users, the states like Kerala, Bihar, West Bengal, Assam, North Eastern zone, North Western zone and southern union territories more than 10 per cent of households faced with quality problems. Hand pump users in states like Kerala, Punjab, Bihar, Orissa, West Bengal, Assam North Eastern zone, and southern union territory recorded more than the all India average with respect to quality problems. And well users in state like Kerala were found large in proposition but low in reporting quality problems. The NSSO data

Table 3.8 : Quality of drinking water – Sample Households' perception.

Zone wise analysis	*State*	*Tap*			*Tube-well and hand pump*			*Well*			*Tank and pond reserved for drinking*		
		HHs per 1000 (1)	*Per 1000 HHs*		*HHs per 1000 (1)*	*Per 1000 HHs*		*HHs per 1000 (1)*	*Per 1000 HHs*		*HHs per 1000 (1)*	*Per 1000 HHs*	
			Quality problems (2)	*Satis-factory (3)*		*Quality problems (2)*	*Satis-factory (3)*		*Quality problems (2)*	*Satis-factory (3)*		*Quality problems (2)*	*Satis-factory (3)*
(1)	(2)	(3)	(4)	(5)	(6)	(7)	(8)	(9)	(10)	(11)	(12)	(13)	(14)
South Zone	Andhra Pradesh	262	41	959	469	85	911	206	75	923	26	306	694
	Karnataka	266	5	985	539	28	973	156	48	952	19	0	1000
	Kerala	106	146	854	14	258	742	851	40	958	15	95	905
	Tamil Nadu	500	42	957	311	96	900	142	148	849	24	449	552
North Zone	Haryana	311	11	988	499	37	959	191	62	935	0	0	0
	Punjab	148	92	908	827	151	849	23	368	630	0	0	0
	Rajasthan	192	27	971	362	60	941	329	29	967	61	144	849
Central Zone	Madhya Pradesh	50	9	991	522	37	961	394	54	947	0	914	86
	Uttar Pradesh	88	19	541	635	63	887	221	76	633	4	0	426
West Zone	Gujarat	466	96	904	317	22	976	161	126	874	25	105	895
	Maharashtra	411	35	947	244	85	916	298	33	967	1	644	356
East Zone	Bihar	7	127	857	703	226	765	279	202	788	0	1000	0
	Orissa	29	34	967	532	140	856	337	169	830	14	679	321
	West Bengal	41	171	649	756	280	688	182	98	449	9	65	43
North-Eastern Zone	Assam	73	273	727	495	325	653	278	321	675	21	137	793
	Arunachal Pradesh Manipur, Meghalaya, Mizoram, Nagaland, Sikkim, Tripura	283	191	726	185	481	499	194	347	639	47	145	749
North-Western Zone	Jammu & Kashmir, Himachal Pradesh, Chandigarh, Delhi	578	101	895	139	121	876	88	57	940	5	646	354
Southern Zone	Andaman & Nicobar Islands, Dadra & Nagar Haveli, Goa, Daman & Diu, Lakshadweep, Pondicherry	626	115	886	63	159	841	254	105	895	1	0	1000
All India		**187**	**56**	**903**	**501**	**130**	**853**	**258**	**98**	**832**	**13**	**219**	**686**

1. No. of HHs per 1000 served by the source, 2. DW affected by any one of the known and unknown causes, 3. Satisfactory quality.
Source: Computed from NSSO 54th round.

Table 3.8 : *(Contd. ...)*

Zone-wise analysis	State	Other tank, pond			River, canal, lake			Spring		
		HHs per 1000 (1)	Per 1000 HHs		HHs per 1000 (1)	Per 1000 HHs		HHs per 1000 (1)	Per 1000 HHs	
			Quality problems (2)	Satisfactory (3)		Quality problems (2)	Satisfactory (3)		Quality problems (2)	Satisfactory (3)
		(15)	(16)	(17)	(18)	(19)	(20)	(21)	(22)	(23)
South Zone	Andhra Pradesh	3	0	1000	23	234	735	4	0	1000
	Karnataka	2	0	1000	17	88	912	1	333	667
	Kerala	7	0	1000	1	0	1000	3	0	1000
	Tamil Nadu	5	346	654	1	1	999	2	567	433
North Zone	Haryana	0	0	0	0	0	0	0	0	0
	Punjab	0	0	0	1	1000	0	0	0	0
	Rajasthan	23	181	820	27	206	857	0	0	0
Central Zone	Madhya Pradesh	1	0	1000	19	387	613	13	179	821
	Uttar Pradesh	1	0	0	1	280	546	47	0	1000
West Zone	Gujarat	0	439	531	7	628	372	0	0	0
	Maharashtra	0	1000	107	26	335	666	14	30	970
East Zone	Bihar	1	647	353	3	141	860	3	897	104
	Orissa	21	468	490	27	223	724	23	318	683
	West Bengal	2	196	107	2	237	595	2	0	1000
North-Eastern Zone	Assam	69	645	356	43	440	301	11	935	65
	Arunachal Pradesh									
	Manipur, Meghalaya, Mizoram, Nagaland, Sikkim, Tripura	19	540	460	33	430	538	203	111	867
North-Western Zone	Jammu & Kashmir, Himachal Pradesh, Chandigarh, Delhi	13	209	791	42	539	461	127	31	968
Southern Zone	Andaman & Nicobar Islands, Dadra & Nagar Haveli, Goa, Daman & Diu, Lakshadweep, Pondicherry	0	0	1000	13	859	142	22	187	813
All India		**6**	**392**	**554**	**13**	**319**	**673**	**17**	**92**	**906**

1. No. of HHs per 1000 served by the source, 2. DW affected by any one of the known and unknown causes, 3. Satisfactory quality.

Source: Computed from NSSO 54th round.

confirms that tap, tube-well and hand pumps the so-called safe water as claimed by State Governments, turned out to be more problematic at least quality-wise (Table 3.8).

Table 3.9 : Distance Factor.

Zone-wise analysis	*State*	*Within the premises (Per 1000 Households)*				
		Tap	*Tube-well and hand pump*	*Well*	*Tank and canal*	*Other tank*
South Zone	Andhra Pradesh	310	142	141	39	0
	Karnataka	284	107	348	83	255
	Kerala	598	83	162	86	0
	Tamil Nadu	169	189	139	56	0
North Zone	Haryana	250	399	86	0	0
	Punjab	480	898	192	0	0
	Rajasthan	497	106	62	64	427
Central Zone	Madhya Pradesh	598	83	162	86	0
	Uttar Pradesh	763	588	153	67	0
West Zone	Gujarat	653	212	201	0	0
	Maharashtra	487	136	195	356	0
East Zone	Bihar	777	460	184	0	0
	Orissa	208	69	205	0	0
	West Bengal	278	268	195	43	107
North-Eastern Zone	Assam	189	576	464	619	719
	Arunachal Pradesh Manipur, Meghalaya, Mizoram, Nagaland, Sikkim, Tripura	390	510	376	156	381
North-Western Zone	Jammu & Kashmir, Himachal Pradesh, Chandigarh, Delhi	504	670	88	67	0
Southern Zone	Andaman & Nicobar Islands, Dadra & Nagar Haveli, Goa, Daman & Diu, Lakshadweep, Pondicherry	509	375	360	152	0
All India		**411**	**342**	**227**	**96**	**349**

Source : Computed from NSSO 54th round.

Distance travelled to fetch water is a crucial policy variable. The provision of modern sources by the state follows distance as one of the norms. The NSSO data threw lights on this aspect also. The principal sources such as tap, tube-well and hand pump, well, tank/pond reserved for drinking, other tank/ pond, river/canal/lake, spring, and tanker were established with a distance less than 0.2 km. from the habitat for all the states in the country. The proportion of traditional means as principal source per 1000 households within the premises is less when compared to modern sources (Table 3.9).

Punjab, Uttar Pradesh, Bihar, North-western zone are those states which registered a higher proportion per 1000 households depending on modern sources (tap, tube-well and hand pump) with in the premises. Besides, Kerala, Assam, Madhya Pradesh, Gujarat, Maharashtra, Southern zone and North-eastern zone are the states, which performed well in any one of modern sources with in the premises.

With respect to traditional sources as principal means, by and large there is low provision within the premises in all the states. Assam is the only state, which registered a relatively better score in terms access to traditional source within the premises as principal source.

3.2.4 *Insufficiency of Principal Source of Water*

It is not unusual to find households facing problem of insufficiency of water during summer months i.e. from April to June. The NSSO 54th round brought out certain interesting facets of scarcity of potable water.

The problem of insufficiency was evident in all the major principal sources viz., tap, tube-well (hand pump) and well. More than 50 per cent of the sample respondents per 1000 households reported the problem with taps (Public Fountain), followed by well and tube-well (hand pump). Relatively, hand pumps were reportedly less problematic, due to lesser extraction of ground water than the taps (power pumps).

Compared to other zones in the country, the southern, the western and the north-eastern zones started to face the insufficiency of water from January onwards.

Information is available on the measures taken towards solving scarcity by the local body. Only one-fourth of the total respondents expressed that there were no measures taken in this context. About 4.7 per cent expressed the measures taken by the local bodies. Just 1.7 per cent of the respondents purchased water at the all India level, water purchased is the highest in the state of Rajasthan, and about 24 per cent obtained water from the neighbouring households. Less than one per cent agreed the role played by the voluntary organisation (Table 3.10).

3.2.5 Type of Container used

Water container for drinking purpose is a matter of concern. At the all India level, nearly 6.9 per cent did not store water for consumption, while 37.1 per cent used earthen (mud pot), 16 per cent used iron galvanized and the same proportion of stainless steel were used as containers and other types such as brass, copper, and plastics constituted less than one per cent (Table 3.11).

More than 90 per cent of the respondents in Haryana, Rajasthan and Gujarat reported to be using earthen containers. The Tamil Nadu state ranks first in the usage of plastic containers followed by Kerala and Assam. The southern zone as a whole showed a higher proportion of use of stainless steel. A higher proportion of use of iron-galvanised containers was reported in Uttar Pradesh.

Treatment of water to quality is a crucial aspect of drinking water. At the all India level, more than 75 per cent had not taken any step to treat the water before consumption. Among the rest of the proportion, only 15 per cent used plain cloth for filtering water for consumption. Only 4 per cent resorted to boiling of water and one per cent adopted chemical treatment (Table 3.12). This is an important fact of rural water supply as this has a bearing on the health of human beings.

3.2.6 Discussion of NSS data

Indeed the NSSO 54th round had made a substantial contribution to rural water supply scenario' in India. The 54th round is comprehensive by giving an aggregate picture on this vital issue of basic necessity. It is holistic because the survey covered both

Table 3.10 : Per 1000 number of HHs with specific principal source of drinking water reporting insufficient from principal source in specific months of the year and measures taken.

Zone-wise analysis	State	Tap				Tube-well and hand pump				Well			
		J-M	*A-J*	*J-S*	*O-D*	*J-M*	*A-J*	*J-S*	*O-D*	*J-M*	*A-J*	*J-S*	*O-D*
(1)	(2)	(3)	(4)	(5)	(6)	(7)	(8)	(9)	(10)	(11)	(12)	(13)	(14)
South Zone	Andhra Pradesh	122	658	66	7	111	436	40	6	78	689	75	12
	Karnataka	150	560	82	30	129	317	14	21	51	666	0	0
	Kerala	451	593	106	102	159	345	0	0	219	640	26	9
	Tamil Nadu	55	456	109	15	24	343	89	16	33	403	276	57
North Zone	Haryana	99	576	415	95	178	434	309	172	138	230	193	138
	Punjab	11	282	98	16	0	32	19	0	0	198	34	0
	Rajasthan	6	183	49	13	34	152	49	33	7	119	20	6
Central Zone	Madhya Pradesh	26	535	68	6	29	257	12	3	7	365	19	1
	Uttar Pradesh	54	356	37	19	7	61	13	4	9	145	33	7
West Zone	Gujarat	120	332	101	69	11	198	41	1	27	389	125	34
	Maharashtra	239	868	93	42	105	435	24	0	99	532	36	1
East Zone	Bihar	0	0	0	0	4	50	9	3	2	342	50	0
	Orissa	81	285	0	0	23	174	20	16	50	727	28	4
	West Bengal	144	295	19	0	28	88	9	3	76	241	19	2
North-Eastern Zone	Assam	139	130	0	13	91	13	4	22	253	38	0	52
	Arunachal Pradesh Manipur, Meghalaya, Mizoram, Nagaland, Sikkim, Tripura	183	94	8	133	95	28	15	55	139	118	9	29
North-Western Zone	Jammu & Kashmir, Himachal Pradesh, Chandigarh, Delhi	67	631	186	71	22	118	48	24	4	192	34	0
Southern Zone	Andaman & Nicobar Islands, Dadra & Nagar Haveli, Goa, Daman & Diu, Lakshadweep, Pondicherry	93	394	19	6	0	167	0	0	39	217	4	0
All India		**121**	**528**	**95**	**35**	**38**	**168**	**25**	**10**	**64**	**397**	**45**	**10**

J-M: January, February, March, A-J: April, May, June, J-S: July, August, September, O-D: October, November and December.

Table 3.10 : Per 1000 number of HHs with specific principal source of drinking water reporting insufficient from principal source in specific months of the year and measures taken.

Zone wise analysis	*State*	*No. of HHs per 1000 among those reporting insufficiency of DW from Principal Sources (PS) for some part of year who report*				
		No measures taken	*Water supplied by local authority*	*Water supplied by charitable body*	*Water obtained from neighbours*	*Water purchased*
		(15)	(16)	(17)	(18)	(19)
South Zone	Andhra Pradesh	363	27	8	125	20
	Karnataka	274	2	0	99	25
	Kerala	60	41	1	686	10
	Tamil Nadu	321	24	6	188	29
North Zone	Haryana	27	4	20	565	45
	Punjab	91	0	0	308	0
	Rajasthan	137	7	4	53	147
Central Zone	Madhya Pradesh	142	6	2	210	5
	Uttar Pradesh	239	7	10	443	7
West Zone	Gujarat	107	102	7	276	3
	Maharashtra	168	166	13	151	8
East Zone	Bihar	189	0	0	486	0
	Orissa	396	11	2	20	10
	West Bengal	356	77	9	272	4
North-Eastern Zone	Assam	436	0	4	318	0
	Arunachal Pradesh	405	16	10	50	6
	Manipur, Meghalaya, Mizoram, Nagaland, Sikkim, Tripura					
North-Western Zone	Jammu & Kashmir, Himachal Pradesh, Chandigarh, Delhi	322	46	7	81	1
Southern Zone	Andaman & Nicobar Islands, Dadra & Nagar Haveli, Goa, Daman & Diu, Lakshadweep, Pondicherry	195	151	0	151	0
All India		**238**	**47**	**7**	**241**	**17**

J-M: January, February, March, A-J: April, May, June, J-S: July, August, September, O-D: October, November and December.

Table 3.11 : Material of container in which drinking water is stored per 1000 distribution of HHs.

Zone-wise analysis	*State*	*No. of HHs per 1000 with*								*Other metal*
		No storage	*Storage in container of material*							
			Earthen	*Plastic*	*Other non-metal*	*Iron (galvanised)*	*Copper*	*Stainless steel*	*Brass*	
South Zone	Andhra Pradesh	3	324	21	8	5	7	387	195	48
	Karnataka	1	255	55	26	11	189	368	63	32
	Kerala	85	54	131	46	6	7	203	7	462
	Tamil Nadu	0	22	209	6	5	20	604	115	20
North Zone	Haryana	24	903	16	4	35	3	8	4	3
	Punjab	487	356	64	19	28	-	29	2	16
	Rajasthan	3	944	2	13	2	1	21	11	2
Central Zone	Madhya Pradesh	0	451	3	6	36	1	143	311	49
	Uttar Pradesh	180	135	13	16	571	24	25	18	18
West Zone	Gujarat	12	934	-	8	2	-	44	1	0
	Maharashtra	-	493	14	2	8	19	356	101	8
East Zone	Bihar	142	316	15	26	371	2	19	4	105
	Orissa	1	526	7	15	43	3	40	115	250
	West Bengal	72	438	30	31	111	18	27	151	122
North-Eastern Zone	Assam	27	444	133	40	188	2	49	31	85
	Arunachal Pradesh Manipur, Meghalaya, Mizoram, Nagaland, Sikkim, Tripura	45	324	173	78	39	45	31	34	
North-Western Zone	Jammu & Kashmir, Himachal Pradesh, Chandigarh, Delhi,	51	553	164	28	56	49	17	52	230
Southern Zone	Andaman & Nicobar Islands, Dadra & Nagar Haveli, Goa, Daman & Diu, Lakshadweep, Pondicherry	9	135	132	10	32	33	603	11	35
All India		**69**	**371**	**42**	**17**	**162**	**21**	**161**	**86**	**70**

Source : Computed from NSSO 54th round.

Table 3.12 : Number of HHs per 1000 filtering /Chemically treating /boiling their drinking water in different states.

Zone-wise analysis	*State*	*Per 1000 no.of HHs*				
		Filtering		*Chemical treating*	*Boiling*	
		With plain cloth	*By other process*			
South Zone	Andhra Pradesh	218	36	7	26	713
	Karnataka	90	13	14	28	855
	Kerala	84	33	50	493	340
	Tamil Nadu	76	16	15	81	812
North Zone	Haryana	26	8	1	4	961
	Punjab	1	11	4	3	981
	Rajasthan	397	18	4	2	579
Central Zone	Madhya Pradesh	243	31	13	4	709
	Uttar Pradesh	3	11	7	2	977
West Zone	Gujarat	745	64	5	4	182
	Maharashtra	415	26	19	12	528
East Zone	Bihar	32	18	5	7	938
	Orissa	85	16	7	18	874
	West Bengal	46	17	8	13	916
North-Eastern Zone	Assam	117	193	67	216	407
	Arunachal Pradesh Manipur, Meghalaya, Mizoram, Nagaland, Sikkim, Tripura	81	200	28	340	351
North-Western Zone	Jammu & Kashmir, Himachal Pradesh, Chandigarh, Delhi	43	24	14	86	833
Southern Zone	Andaman & Nicobar Islands, Dadra & Nagar Haveli, Goa, Daman & Diu, Lakshadweep, Pondicherry	173	77	9	366	375
All India		**152**	**29**	**12**	**43**	**764**

Source : Computed from NSSO 54th round.

modern and traditional schemes of rural water supply. This massive exercise is quite useful in fringing to light certain items, which were hitherto ignored. For instance, quality of drinking water has been taken note of in this survey. The quality of potable of water is closely associated with the health of the users. Types of water container as a variable are considered in this survey. More importantly, insufficiency of potable water during certain month is considered as a crucial variable in the survey. On the whole, the NSSO survey focused more on 'supply side' of the rural water supply in India.

However, there are certain lacunae, which merit discussion. The whole exercise lacks focus on demand side of water supply. The current paradigm is 'demand responsive' in effective water management. In fact, information relating to quantum of water required for various domestic uses should be useful in estimating, (at least in making approximate estimation) the demand for domestic uses. Any demand estimation would ultimately help in cutting down the cost of wasteful investment in this realm. The fixed target of rural water supply can be made cost effective.

Despite the inclusion of the variable hygiene in the survey, hardly any attempt is made to capture the impact of unsafe water on the health of the respondents. Contrary to the claims made by the state agencies that modern schemes are safe and provide potable water with adequate treatment of water to large section of population, the reality is different. It is evident from the NSSO data that the respondents complained about the quality problems even from the modern schemes such as hand pumps and stand posts. Hence, there is scope for incorporating health impact as a variable in the survey.

Time factor has been neglected. Time spent to travel in fetching water varies from region to region in rural areas. This aspect can be included in the future surveys of rural water supply as it may prove to be beneficial in estimating the foregone benefits of time spent in water collection.

Gender is yet another neglected item of the 54th round of NSSO. Water collectors are by and large women in rural areas of India. This survey did not collect any information on the role played by women in general and children in particular. The 54th round had not taken note of the community participation by the people *ipso facto*, the user groups. In particular, the choices of location of water source by the local people, scope for training local manpower to operate and maintain the public sources are missing in the survey. By adding the qualitative information a great deal of success can be achieved.

The survey omitted a very crucial aspect, viz., equity. Whether or not distribution of public schemes served all sections of population across all communities in all regions, this question has not been addressed in this survey.

3.3 Rural Water Supply in Tamil Nadu

Geographically the state of Tamil Nadu has spread across 13 million hectares of area, which is 4 per cent of the total area of India and is ranked eleventh in size among the Indian states. The average annual rainfall is 925 mm with a minimum 400 mm to a maximum of 4300 mm. The state has three distinct rainy seasons, viz., South-West Monsoon, North-East Monsoon; of the two, the state receives its maximum rainfall during the North-East Monsoon. The coastal line of the state stretches for about 920 kms. from Pulicate Lake in the North to Kanyakumari in the South. There are 34 river basins in the State, which are grouped into 17 river basins. The Cauvery basin is the largest and its coverage is more than one-third of the State area. More than one-third of the irrigated area of the state depends on the release of water from Karnataka, an upstream state, where the river Cauvery originates. The three major basins include *inter alia* Palar, Ponnaiyar, Vaigai and Tamiraparani (Government of Tamil Nadu, 1999).

Provision of drinking water to all villages is the responsibility of the State Governments. The Government of Tamil Nadu had formed the Tamil Nadu Water And Drainage (TWAD) Board during 1971 and entrusted the responsibility of providing drinking water and drainage facilities to the entire state except for Chennai metropolitan area. The introduction of a state sponsored Minimum Needs Programme (MNP), in 1974-75 gave impetus to rural water supply schemes.

3.3.1 The Tamil Nadu Water and Drainage (TWAD) Board

TWAD Board is a State Government undertaking. Chairman, a Managing Director and about ten outside Directors constitute the Board. The Directors are responsible for formulating the board's policies. The programmes are implemented by the Engineering Executives. The rules and regulations followed by the state Public Works Department (PWD) are applicable for this Board.

3.3.2 Norms of TWAD Board

Apart from adopting the norms of Government of India and Government of Tamil Nadu, the TWAD as an implementing agency, have its own norms and guidelines for preparing outline proposals for rural water supply system. The salient features of norms of TWAD Board are indicated below.

Population size	*Components*
< 150	One Hand Pump (HP)
150 – 500	Power scheme with OHT of 1000 litres and distribution system for 1000 metres
501 – 1250	Power scheme with OHT of 30000 litres and distribution system for 1500 metres
1251 – 3000	Power scheme with OHT of 60000 litres and distribution system for 2000 metres
3001 – 6000	Power scheme with OHT of 1 lakh litres and distribution system for 2500 metres
> 6000	Power scheme with capacity of OHT as per the requirement and less than 1.5 lakhs litres

In case of power pump schemes one public fountain (stand post) has to propose for every present population of 150. Hours of pumping should be a minimum of 8 hours in case of individual power pump scheme and 12 hours in case of comprehensive water supply schemes (CWSS). 50 per cent of the requirement is being fixed as the capacity of OHTs. Ceiling on per capita cost is rupees 2500 and cost per thousand liters of water should not be greater than rupees 17.0

40 litres per capita per day for humans to meet the following requirement:

Purpose	*Quantity (LPCD)*
Drinking	3
Cooking	5
Bathing	15
Washing utensils and innovation	7
Ablution	10

The Board executes programmes with financial assistance from Government of Tamil Nadu, Government of India and by taking loans from external agencies like LIC, World Bank, DANIDA and HUDCO. The Board is responsible for both rural and urban sectors. The annual budget of the Board is around Rs. 400 crores and of which, 60 per cent is allocated every year for rural water supply. Through conducting periodical survey the Board assesses the status of rural habitations and in the process a database is maintained.

The total number of habitations in the state is 66631 according to 1999-2000 re-survey by the TWAD Board; of which 83.9 per cent of the habitations are fully covered* and 16.1 per cent of the habitation are partially covered with respect to rural water supply. The state comprises 385 Panchayat unions (blocks) and 12619 village Panchayats (Table 3.13) and (Fig. 3.4).

3.3.3 Schemes and Sources of Water Supply

Since 1974 the State has initiated various schemes to improve water supply. As on 1999-2000 the State has 34090 power pumps; 136421 hand pumps and 376477 house service connections.

* If all the population of a habitation is able to get daily, not less than 40 litres of protected and potable water, within a distance of 1.6 km. from the habitation, on all the days of a normal year, then it is classified as 'Fully covered' habitation.

Availability of stand posts is one per 1000 population and access to hand pumps is 3.7 per 1000 population. The performance with regard to creation of stand posts is far from satisfactory. In rural Tamil Nadu, the house service connection facility is a recent phenomenon. So far the state has provided 376477 house service connections with 44 house service connections per 1000 households in rural areas.

The State Government is also bent upon removing illegal house service connections. It is a general practice to remove excess stand posts in the event of provision of house service connection (Table 3.14).

Table 3.13 : Status of coverage of rural habitation during – 2000.

District & State	*Fully covered habitation*	*Partially covered habitation*	*Not covered habitation*	*Total*
India	1212243 (85.2)	187139 (13.2)	23282 (1.6)	1422664
Tami Nadu	55929 (83.9)	10702 (16.1)	-	66631
Tiruchirappalli	1354 (56.9)	1022 (43.01)	-	2376

Source : TWAD Board (2000), Chennai 5. Figures in parentheses indicate percentage to total.

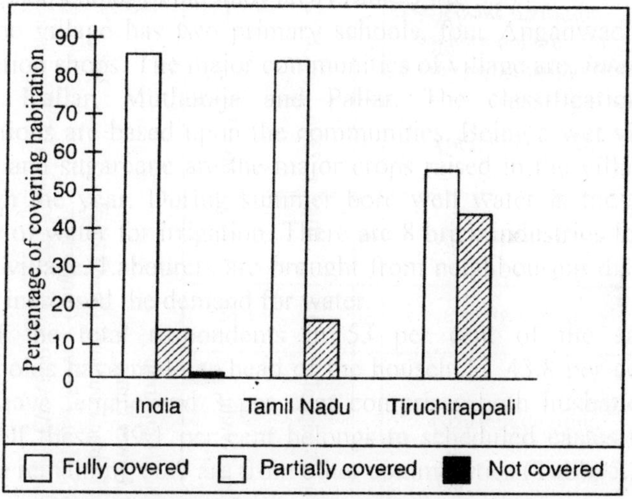

Fig. 3.4 : Coverage of habitation - drinking water supply.

Table 3.14 : Details of rural water supply – Tiruchirappalli and Tamil Nadu – 1999.

District and State	*No. of Union*	*No. of Panchayat*	*Total no. of habi.*	*Total No. of Habitation Where hand pump Scheme available*	*Total No. of Habi.. Where P.P Scheme available*	*No. of HSC available as on 10/99*	*No. of PF available as on 10/99*	*No. of excess HSC to be removed from the existing HSC*	*No. of excess PF to be removed from the existing PF available*	*Total No. of HSC permissible*	*Total No. of PF permissible*
1	2	3	4	5	6	7	8	9	10	11	12
Tiruchirappalli	14	408	2376	2252	906	26333	12964	411	1710	71635	12114
Tamil Nadu	385	11823	66631	—	34090	376477	382467	39756	42058	934934	361241

Habi.: Habitation.
PP: Power Pump
PF: Public Fountain (Stand Post)
HSC: House Service Connection
Source : TWAD Board (2000), Chennai 5. Figures in parentheses indicate percentage to total.

Budgetary allocation for rural water supply is worth mentioning since over a period the allocation has been increasing for this purpose. Of the total, the percentage outlay in 1992-93 for rural supply was 41, which increased to 71 per cent in 1997-98. At the national level, about 3 per cent of the total budget is allocated for rural water supply and Sanitation. Interestingly there is budget provision for operation and maintenance for the ongoing water supply schemes. However the issue of lack of operation and maintenance cost becomes a major hurdle in deciding the performance of various schemes. More discussion on this will follow in the subsequent chapters (Table 3.15) and (Fig. 3.5).

Table 3.15 : State Expenditure on rural water supply.

(Rs. in lakhs)

Particulars	*1992-93*	*1993-94*	*1994-95*	*1995-96*	*1996-97*	*1997-98*
Urban	3139.01	2811.02	3846.73	15193.62	5578.09	8770.15
Rural	10077.03	10549.17	10181.03	19552.32	24173.78	32123.20
Maintenance	800.00	1000.00	1200.003	2000.00	3483.00	3831.00
Others	10500.00	10594.69	8090.02	947.97	449.45	299.25
Total	**24516.04**	**23287.99**	**23317.78**	**37693.91**	**33684.32**	**45023.60**
Percentage outlay for rural	41	45	44	52	72	71

Source : TWAD Board (2000), Chennai 5. Figures in parentheses indicate percentage to total.

It is relevant to look into the contributions made by state, centre and other agencies towards rural water supply. For instance the decadal (1990-91 to 1999-2000) average contribution made by the state for this purpose was 35.8 per cent. Similarly the contribution made by LIC is 31.6 per cent and the Central Government's contribution was 32.5 per cent. Here the contributions made by the state are the highest besides the LIC's loan amount, which shall also be repaid by the state. The contributions made by international agencies such as World Bank, UNICEF and DANIDA were reportedly less than 5 per cent of the total outlay (Table 3.16) and (Fig. 3.6).

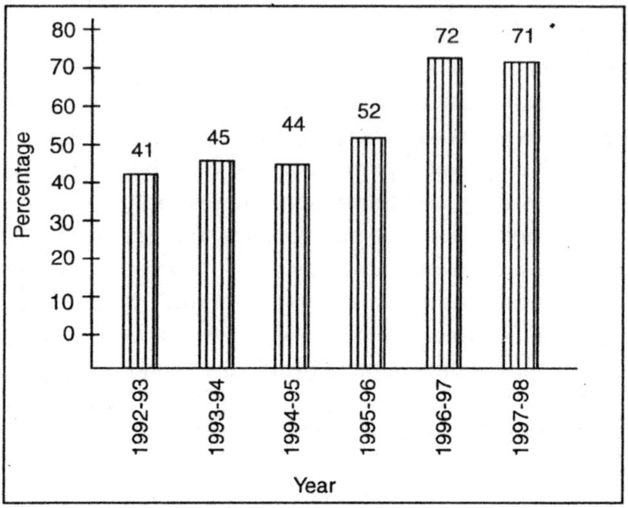

Fig. 3.5 : Percentage out lay to rural water supply.

Table 3.16 : Year-wise fund release by Agencies.

(Rs. in lakhs)

Year	*MNP*			*ARWSP*	*Grand Total*
	State Government	*L.I.C.*	*HUDCO*		
1990-91	1500 (27.0)	2049.95 (36.9)	—	2004 (36.1)	5553.95
1991-92	2097.08 (34.3)	1978.91 (32.3)	—	2039 (33.4)	6114.99
1992-93	3936.73 (45.1)	2566.87 (29.4)	—	2215 (25.4)	8718.60
1993-94	3320.00 (35.6)	2729.14 (29.3)	—	3278 (35.1)	9327.14
1994-95	3320.00 (32.1)	3152.27 (30.4)	—	3884 (37.5)	10356.27
1995-96	5120.00 (38.2)	3492.18 (26.1)	—	4789 (35.7)	13401.18
1996-97	8000.00 (47.4)	3531.15 (20.9)	—	5343 (31.7)	16874.15
1997-98	6000.00 (33.4)	6201.36 (34.4)	—	5834 (32.3)	18035.36
1998-99	11000.00 (37.3)	8000.00 (27.1)	—	10527.51 (35.6)	29527.51
1999-2000	11000.00 (27.7)	19623.00 (49.4)	160.00 (0.4)	8968.00 (22.6)	39751.00
Decadal Percentage	35.8	31.6	0.04	32.5	

Source : TWAD Board (2000), Chennai-5.

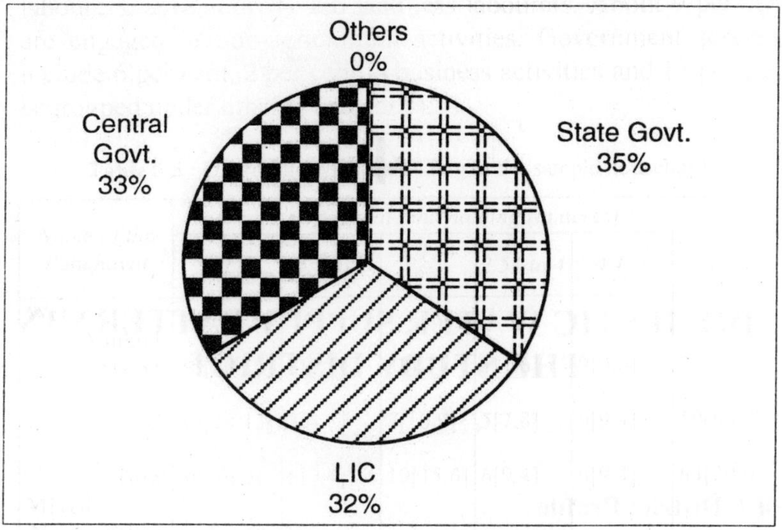

Fig. 3.6 : Decadal average of fund release.

4

DOMESTIC WATER SUPPLY PATTERN IN THE STUDY DISTRICT

4.1 District Profile

The Tamil Nadu State comprises 30 districts as per the recent information from the Assistant Director of Statistics. Tiruchirappalli district chosen for this study is bounded by Namakkal, Perambalur, Ariyalur, Thanjavur and Pudukkottai districts. The total area of Tiruchirappalli district is 4403.83 sq. km. in area, situated between 10 and 11.30 of the Northern Latitude and with an altitude of 78 m. above the sea level. The district is a typical semi-arid area with the temperature ranged from maximum of 39.4 centigrade and minimum of 19.7 centigrade. The district is endowed with two major rivers, viz., Cauvery and its major tributary Coleroon, serving as irrigation sources to the district; other small rivers include Naniyar, Ponnaniar. And the canals in the district are Pullambadi canal, Pudukkottai canal, Kattalai vaikkal, Uyyakondan, Iyyanvaikkal and Peruvalai Vaikkal.

As per 2001 census the birth rate is 20 per 1000 population while the death rate is 6.1 per 1000 population. The infant mortality per 1000 live births is 42.7. The life expectancy at birth is 60 for male and female. These are combined rates for both rural and urban areas. The literacy rate is 79.16 per cent to the total population. The district consists of 8 taluks, 14 panchayat union blocks and 408 villages, panchayats and 2376 rural habitations.

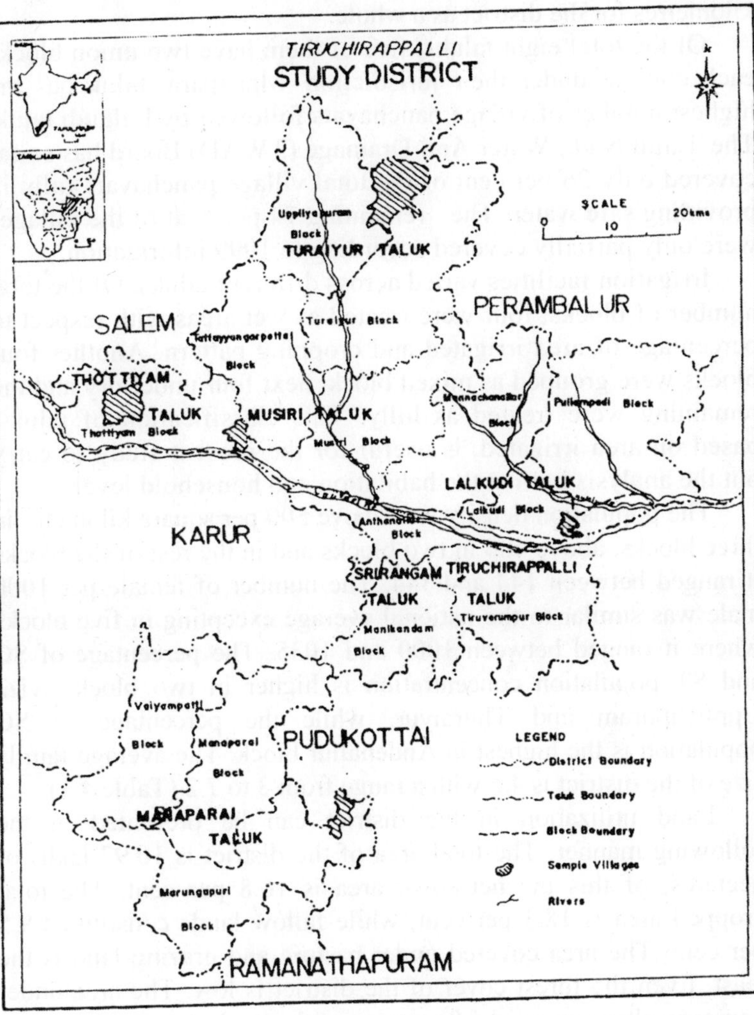

Map of Ramananthapuram

The total population of the district according to 2001 census was 23,88,831, and of the total, the rural population constituted 60 per cent. The density of population was recorded as 542 per square kilometres for the district as a whole.

Of the total eight taluks, five of them have two union blocks each coming under their jurisdiction. Manaparai taluk has the highest number of village panchayats followed by Lalgudi taluk. The Tamil Nadu Water And Drainage (TWAD) Board has so far covered only 26 per cent of the total village panchayats fully in providing safe water. The remaining 74 per cent of the villages were only partially covered according to 1999 information.

Irrigation facilities varied across different taluks. Of the total number of blocks, four were treated as wet areas with respect to percentage of area irrigated and cropping pattern. Another four blocks were grouped as mixed block, next four under dry and the remaining were treated as hilly. This classification of taluks, based on area irrigated, is useful for the present study to carry out the analysis both at the habitation and household level.

The population density was above 500 per square kilometre in three blocks, above 400 in two blocks and in the rest of the blocks it ranged between 144 and 344. The number of female per 1000 male was similar to the national average excepting in five blocks where it ranged between 1000 and 1035. The percentage of SC and ST population concentration is higher in two blocks, viz., Uppliyapuram and Thuraiyur, while the percentage of SC population is the highest in Andenallur block. The average family size of the district is 4.5 with a range from 3 to 7.2 (Table 4.1).

Land utilization in the district can be presented in the following manner. The total area of the district is 10.97 lakhs of hectares; of this the net sown area is 16.8 per cent. The total cropped area is 18.3 per cent, while fallow lands constituted 9.5 per cent. The area covered under pasture and grazing land is the least. Even the forest cover of the district is low. The area under non-agriculture covered 6.8 per cent of the total.

The principal crops raised in the district are paddy, millets, pulses, sugarcane, groundnuts, gingili and cotton. Of these the dominant crops include paddy, sugarcane and cotton.

Table 4.1 : Block-wise Basic Information of the study district.

Name of block	*Population density*	*Female per 1000 male*	*Percentage of SC population*	*Percentage of ST population*	*Average family size*	*Percentage of agri. Workers to T.W.*	*Percentage of agri. Labourer to*	*Percentage of Irrigated area*	*Bovine population per Sq. KM.*	*Percentage of village electrification*	*Percentage of rural Literacy*
Andanallur	593	975	24.75	0.01	4.47	47.25	35	77.97	130	100	86.95
Manikandam	511	999	16.20	0.17	4.62	24.74	36.24	89.02	128	100	78.92
Lalgudi	643	1003	21.85	0.09	4.28	29.28	17.72	96	-	100	92.10
Pullambadi	240	1011	14.49	1	4	66.28	45.02	33.95	85	100	74.72
Thiruverambor	291	973	20.68	0.29	4.46	20.49	69.20	93.20	-	100	100
Uppliyapuram	278	988	24	5	4	89	58	75	214	100	100
Thuraiyur	200	1035	22.1	6.7	4	85.3	52.3	62.1	62	100	72.55
Musiri	344	997	21.43	0.18	5	50.2	58.04	40.42	486	100	75.62
Thottiyam	430	989	21	-	4.41	81	71	58	3432	100	-
Thathayangar pettai	238	996	18	-	4	30	47.03	51.97	193	100	75.64
Manachanallur	145	997	19.4	0.7	7.23	41.14	29.16	62.9	-	100	76.44
Manapparai	420	971	3.1	0.7	7	14.7	51.1	52.6	-	100	63.31
Vaiyampatti	295	1000	16	0.28	5	37.33	79.12	47.24	-	100	40.81
Marungapuri	234	1002	19.5	-	5	51.7	69.5	46.0	4091	100	100

Source : Statistical abstract of Tiruchirappalli district during 1998-99.

As per the rural District handbook census 1999, electrification is cent per cent. The number of electrified agricultural pump sets is 46,963. Of the total power consumed, 71 per cent goes for agriculture, 4.2 per cent for industry and 18.6 per cent goes for domestic use and the rest goes as miscellaneous.

There are 328 post offices, 1276 telegraph offices, 1553 schools and 23,318 Anganwadis (noon-meal scheme centres) functioning in the rural district.

With regard to operational landholdings, the large holders comprised 15.1 per cent of the total, 14.9 per cent are medium holders, 12.8 per cent are small holders and the rest 57.3 per cent of the landholders are marginal farmers. The average size of landholdings is 1.04 hectares. (Table 4.2).

Table 4.2 : Number and Area of Operational Landholdings.

(Year 1995-96)

Land class of holdings (In hectare)	*Number*				*Area (in hectares)*			
	SC	*ST*	*Others*	*Total*	*SC*	*ST*	*Others*	*Total*
Marginal (upto 1 hectare)	2803	329	200462	228824 (57.3)	5507.7	169.4	79182.6	89467.7
Small (1.1-2)	4562	509	45924	50995 (12.8)	5607.6	766.5	65577.8	72574.5
Medium (2.1-10)	1413	785	57282	29267 (14.9)	1028.6	3377.5	94110.8	247394
Large (more than 10)	1415	856	57891	29949 (15.1)	10374.3	8537	105013.5	260198
				399461				

Note : Figures in parentheses indicate percentage to total.

Irrigation potential depends mostly on groundwater resources in this district. Nearly 61 per cent of the total land gets irrigated by ground water source. Tanks serve to the extent of 6.2 per cent, while canals serve to the extent of 31.98 per cent of the total (Table 4.3) and (Fig. 4.1).

The livestock population in the district is crucial as provision of rural water has to cater to the requirement of livestock too. Total livestock population according to 1994 livestock census was

2276292. Of this 33.6 per cent consists of cattle population, 26.8 per cent of sheep, 30.5 per cent of goats, 4 per cent of pigs and 5 per cent of other animals such as horse, donkeys, and dogs.

Table 4.3 : Area irrigated by source.

(Area in hectare)

Water source	*Numbers*	*Net irrigated*	*Gross area*	*Percentage to total*
Canals	135	43942	51138	31.98
Tanks				
a. Large	115	3970	9912	6.2
b. Small	1652	4697		
Ground water				
a. Public	-			
b. Private tube-wells	3605	4294	4891	3.1
c. Dug-wells	63177	45013	51668	32.3
d. (i) With pump sets	58056	42294	42294	26.5
(ii) Without pump sets	5121			
Total			**159903**	

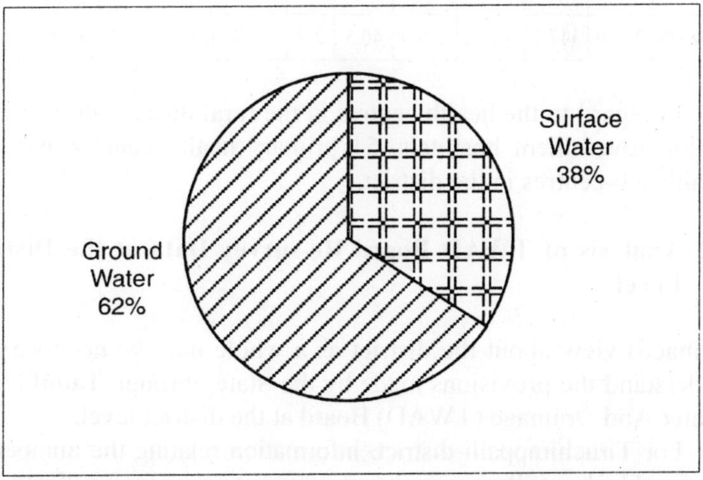

Fig. 4.1 : Area irrigated in rural Tiruchirappalli district (Percentage).

The workforce in the district is similar to the state figures. The workforce is maximum in agricultural labour category, followed by cultivators; the remaining are other workers, which include government employees and company workers.

Rainfall (annual) data for two years (i.e.) 1997-98 and 1998-99, showed a deficit of 82.7 per cent from the normal for the year 1997-98. While the level for 1998-99 it was more than normal. North-east monsoon brings more rain than the South-west monsoon. Excess rainfall is disastrous as it results in flood. Tiruchirappalli district experienced such flood during 1977-78, 1992 and 1999. The average normal rainfall in the district is 831.7 mm. (Table 4.4).

Table 4.4 : Time series data of rainfall by seasons.

(In mm)

Year	*South-West Monsoon*		*North-East Monsoon*		*Winter Season*		*Hot Weather Season*		*Total*		*% (+ or – or =) from normal*
	Normal	*Actual*	*Normal*	*Actual*	*Normal*	*Actual*	*Normal*	*Actual*	*Normal*	*Actual*	
1997-98	273.3	137.4	394.8	563.9	40.5	1.0	134.0	57.6	842.6	759.9	-82.7
1998-99	272.0	347.2	385.2	559.9	40.5	2.0	134.8	135.1	831.7	1044.2	-

In regard to the health centres in the rural district, there are 10 major government hospitals, 51 primary health centres and 306 health sub-centres in the district.

4.2 Analysis of TWAD Board Re-survey Data at the District Level

A macro view about the district as a whole may be necessary to understand the provisions made by the State, through Tamil Nadu Water And Drainage (TWAD) Board at the district level.

For Tiruchirappalli district, information relating the number of taluks, blocks, village panchayats, executing agencies, financing agencies, habitations, population, houses, soil conditions, distance between two habitations, water quality, number of water sources, cost of installation, liter per minute, the number of house service connections, and sanitation were obtained from the TWAD Board re-survey. However, socio-economic variables received only scant attention by the board. The purpose here is to assess the status of the state induced water sources across the rural areas of the district. Creation of sources such as hand pumps, and power pumps are the major sources provided by the state. The Centrally sponsored schemes like Accelerated Rural Water Supply Programme (ARWSP) and the state sponsored Minimum Needs Programme (MNP) have been creating assets in rural areas in the form of hand pumps and stand posts. Whether the sources created commensurate with the norms prescribed, the liter per capita consumption by the people, cost of provision of sources, the extent of house service connections given, sanitation facilities and the overall performance of the state created sources merit an in-depth study.

As indicated in the methodology for the purpose of secondary data analysis, the entire rural district is divided into four categories viz., wet, mixed, dry based on the percentage of area irrigated and another area where schedule caste and schedule tribes population were high in concentration. The categorised blocks are: (a) wet: Andenallur, Manikandam, Lalgudi, Thiruverambor; (b) Mixed: Manachanallur, Thottiyam, Manapparai, Thathayangarpettai; (c) Dry: Marungapuri, Musiri, Vaiyampatti, Pullampadi; and (d) Hilly: Thuraiyur, Uppliyapuram.

4.2.1 Demographic details of the District

According to 1991 census the total rural population of the district was 1,44,6003. As per the TWAD board re-survey (1999) it was 19,72,551. The decadal growth rate worked out to be 36.4 per cent. Among the four categories of blocks, the percentage of decadal growth rate of the total population was higher in region where SC&ST population being high. In the same region by taking SC&ST alone, the growth rate was 63.65 per cent. The other three categories ranged between 30.34 and 38.25.

The average population of a habitation in the district was 915, which ranged between 50 and 2,500. The mean value of population was higher in areas where SC and ST concentration is high, followed by wet villages, dry, and mixed villages (Table 4.5).

Table 4.5 : Population growth rate in rural Tiruchirappalli district during 1991 census and TWAD re-survey 1999.

Area	*Total population 1991*	*Total population 1999*	*SC/ST 91*	*SC/ST 99*	*Decadal growth rate*		*Ultimate population (Projection)*	
					T. Population	*SC/ST*	*2005*	*2015*
Wet								
Sum	487706	674391	118251	167730	38.28	41.8	1157255	836904
Mean	757.31	1047.19	183.62	260.45				
%	33.73	34.19	33.88	33.14				
N	644							
Mixed region								
Sum	407421	531038	80620	108717	30.34	34.85	911261	699134
Mean	466.69	608.29	92.35	124.53				
%	28.18	26.9	23.1	21.5				
N	873							
Dry								
Sum	362089	494215	78402	112207	36.49	43.1	848073	621345
Mean	568.43	775.85	123.08	176.15				
%	25.04	25.1	22.5	22.2				
N	637							
Hill region								
Sum	188787	272907	71740	117403	44.55	63.65	468308	323959
Mean	850.39	1229.31	323.15	528.84				
%	13.06	13.8	20.6	23.2				
N	222							
Total	**1446003**	**1972551**	**349013**	**506057**	**36.4**	**44.99**	**3384898**	**2481341**

Source : TWAD re-survey 1999.

4.2.2 Types of Schemes

The performance of the agency, viz., the TWAD board can be assessed by means of the number and types of schemes created across the district. The different categories include hand pumps and power pumps (OHTs), Combined Water Supply Scheme (CWSS), Gravity scheme and pipeline extension. Under the above said schemes the following sources were created; they include, deep bore well, shallow bore well, open well, infiltration well, infiltration gallery and treated surface water. By and large the schemes and the sources depended on ground water sources.

It is necessary to look into the actual schemes implemented and the sources thereof in the study district. Regarding hand pumps, the total number of hand pumps installed was the highest in wet villages, followed by mixed, dry and hill region. The reason for this is individual's creation of own sources, as it is less costlier to install hand pumps.

The Non-Governmental Organization (NGO) also played a vital role in creating a large number of hand pumps in wet villages than in other regions. On an average each habitation has 4 hand pumps in wet, 2 in mixed, 2 in dry and 3 in hilly region. Compared with the Government norms, for every 156 population there was one hand pump in wet villages and mixed, while in dry villages for every 186 population there was one hand pump and in hilly region it was for every 238 population. The data suggests that Government norm is fulfilled only in wet and mixed villages but not in other categories of villages. Nearly 5.2 per cent of the total habitations hand pump facilities were not provided.

4.2.3 Service Reservoirs (SR)

This is supposed to be a predominant source provided by the State Government. There are two types of service reservoirs; Over Head Tanks (OHT) and Ground Level Water Service Reservoir (GLWSR). Under OHT category, there exists two types; one is circular OHT and Rectangular or square OHT.

As high as 96.6 per cent of the OHTs were located inside the habitations other than SC and ST colonies. Just only 2.4 per cent of the OHTs were located in areas where SC and ST population were concentrated. This scenario is a matter of concern with respect to equitable distribution of water by the State (Table 4.6).

Table 4.6 : Location of schemes.

Area	*Service reservoir location*			*Type of SR*	
	In side the SC/ST colonies	*In side the habitation*	*Out side the habitation*	*RCC*	*Masonry*
Wet	18	420	5	288	137
Mixed	9	498	6	301	127
Dry	—	169	2	210	67
Hill region	4	167	—	117	51
Total	**31 [2.4]**	**1254 [96.6]**	**13 [.096]**	**916 [70.57]**	**382 [29.43]**

In regard to Over Head Tanks (OHT), the total number was 1,298 in the district, according to TWAD Board data 1999. About 32.36 per cent of the total OHTs were in wet villages, 30.28 per cent in mixed villages, 24.3 per cent in dry villages and 13.02 per cent in hilly region.

The capacity of OHT, ranged from 5,000 liters to 2,50,000 litres. Construction of OHT with a capacity of 2,50,000 litres requires special permission from the Government. As against the government norm of 30,000 litre of OHT per habitation, the facilities created by and large at the (rural) district as a whole have not fulfilled the norm. However, in a few habitations OHT capacity exceeded the government norm (Table 4.7).

By taking the district as a whole, 54 per cent of the total habitations did not have OHT provision. This does not imply that half of the total habitations were left without any water service. Sources such as hand pump, open well and other sources exist. Lack of OHT is certainly a handicap for any village. The overhead tank source facilitates reduction of distance travelled, collection time, assured quantum and so on.

Table 4.7 : Water Supply Schemes

Area	Hand pump	Hand pump per 1000PP	OHT	CWSS	Others	OHT Capacity	Total number of stand post	Stand post per 1000 population	Total No. of HSCs	Population covered by HSCs
Wet										
Sum	2585		420	3	52	15839500	4550		8819	38090
Mean	4	6	1			24595	9	6.7	14	60
Range	1-9		0-3		0-1	500-100000	0-200		0-1800	0-6200
Mixed										
Sum	1914		393	4	98	11411000	4193		5889	30405
Mean	2	6	0.5			13071	9	7.9	7	37
Range	1-9		0-4		0-1	500-100000	0-129		0-451	0-3000
Dry										
Sum	1521		316	1	15	9007000	2494		5390	29078
Mean	2	5	0.5			14140	5	4.9	8	46
Range	1-9		0-4		0-2	500-100000	0-59		0-327	0-1600
Hill region										
Sum	717		169	1	25	6447000	1727		6235	33273
Mean	3	4	1			29041	4.8	5.3	28	150
Range	1-9		0-3		0-2	500-100000	0-104		0-350	0-1800
Total										
Sum	6737		1298	9	190	42704500	12964		26333	130846
Mean	3	6	1			17973	7	6.6	11	56.6
Range	1-9		0-4		0-2	500-100000	0-200		0-1800	0-6200

Source : TWAD re-survey 1999. OHT – Over Head Tank, CWSS – Combined Water Supply Scheme and HSC – House Service Connection.

Besides hand pump and overhead tanks, there exist other schemes. The Combined Water Supply Schemes (CWSS) and the other sources like open well, ring well and pipeline extension are in use in the district. The CWSS have been coming up in a big way in the district, and it covered only 36 per cent of the total habitations. A more detailed discussion on this will follow in the subsequent part of this chapter. Other sources like open well, ring well and pipeline extension covered about 8 per cent of the habitations.

4.2.4 Stand Posts and House Service Connections

The total number of stand posts in the district was 12,964, the average number of stand posts worked out to be 5.4 per habitation. In terms of coverage across different categories of regions, in wet area the average number was 9, in mixed 7.9, in dry region it was 4.9 and in hill region the average number being 4.8. The prescribed norm by the Rajiv Gandhi Drinking Water Mission is for every 150 populations one stand post is to be provided. For every one thousand population there were 6.6 stand posts for the district as a whole. When compared with the norms, for every 152 population one stand post has been provided by taking the district average. In wet region it was 148, mixed 127, in dry region 198 and in hill region it was 158. These average values do not mean to suggest that the state provision fulfilled the norms. Because still nearly 54 per cent of the habitations were not covered with OHT facilities. And therefore the above-mentioned average numbers stand posts referred to only those habitations where OHT and stand posts were provided (Table 4.7).

With respect to house service connections, the total number was 26,333, the district average worked out to be 11 house service connections per habitation. House service connections were the highest in hilly region and the least in mixed and dry regions. In terms of coverage of the total rural population it was 6.6 per cent.

4.2.5 Water Consumption

According to the TWAD census data, given the schemes and sources spread across different villages, the actual quantity of water made available to the prescribed level, viz., 40 litres per capita per day (lpcd) about to 43 per cent of the total habitations received less than 40 lpcd. Of which in dry region, more than 90 per cent of the habitations were deprived of access to water to the prescribed level. The availability of water measured in litre per capita per day refers to water drawn from over head tanks through stand posts and house service connections. However, water drawn from hand pumps are not considered in measuring lpcd. Besides, traditional water sources such as open well, river, spring, lake, ponds and agricultural well were the sources with which the households depend up on for water for domestic purpose.

4.2.6 Expenditure on Water Supply

A crucial component of economics of drinking water supply is the cost of provision of sources. Provision of water sources entails investment on various schemes, which involves installation of mechanical devices, digging of wells construction of over head tanks, laying of pipelines, quality testing and labour costs etc. Analysis of district level data on cost aspects yielded the following results.

For the district as a whole the total cost of installation of various sources starting from the 1972 to 1998 was Rs.178.28 crores at current prices. Appropriate Wholesale Price Index is used as deflators to adjust the prices for inflation. The per capita cost of installation of all sources at was Rs. 903.8. The cost of installing hand pump scheme in the last twenty-six years worked out to be Rs. 20.16 crores, which is 11.3 per cent of the total cost of all schemes. The cost per hand pump was calculated at Rs. 29933, and the per capita cost of hand pump was Rs.102 (Table 4.8) and (Figure 4.2).

Installation of Over Head Tanks (OHT), called power pump, costed Rs. 38.64 crores for the district as a whole, where the per capita cost of OHT showed Rs.196. As mentioned earlier, the OHT facilities were provided only to 46 per cent of the total habitations. The cost per OHT was Rs. 2,97,710. A rough estimate made by the TWAD officials showed the cost of providing one liter of water through OHT to be Rs. 9 at current prices.

Table 4.8 : Scheme-wise Installation cost.

(Rupees in lakhs)

Schemes	*No. of schemes*	*Installation cost*	*Cost per scheme*
Hand pump	6737	2016.64	0.299
Power pump	1298	3864.27	2.98
CWSS	9	10063.0	1118
Others [Pipeline extension, Open well, Ring well and Gravity schemes]	190	1884.7	9.9
	8234	17828.57	

Source: TWAD re-survey 1999.

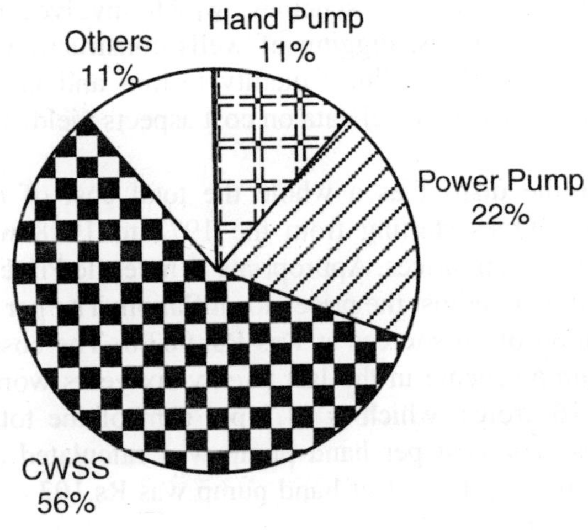

Fig. 4.2 : Schemes-wise installation cost.

Regarding other schemes such as open well, ring well, pipeline extension and of gravity schemes, the costs of installation of the same was Rs. 18.84 crores. The lion's share goes to pipeline extension to the extent of 99.2 per cent, while the rest of the schemes received the remaining amount.

Investment of water supply programmes across different regions in the district showed an interesting trend. Of the total cost incurred, the wet region, which covered 644 habitations, attracted the amount of Rs. 41.91 crore with a percentage of 23.6. Mixed regions, which covered 873 habitations, received the maximum amount of Rs. 113.71 crores and the percentage showed 63.8. In dry regions, which covered 637 habitations received Rs. 14.57 crores with a percentage of 8.17. In the hilly region, which covered 222 habitations, received Rs. 8.08 crores of amount as investment, which comprised 4.5 per cent. Even the per capita cost of investment did not vary much between wet, dry and hilly regions. However, the per capita cost showed a substantial difference between wet, mixed and dry and hilly region. But by looking at mixed regions the difference was abnormal. This is attributed to high cost programme under combined water supply schemes (Table 4.9) and (Fig. 4.3).

Table 4.9 : Area-wise Installation cost.

Area	*Total cost (Rs. in lakhs)*	*Per capita cost in Rupees*
Wet	4191.36 [23.5]	621.50
Mixed	11371.09 [63.8]	2141.30
Dry	1457.09 [8.17]	294.83
Hill region	808.11 [4.5]	296.11
Total	**17828.57**	

Source : TWAD re-survey, 1999.

4.2.7 Funding Agencies

Financing the water supply schemes has been done through numerous agencies and programmes. Water is being the state subject; the Minimum Needs Programme (MNP) promotes water supply schemes at the state level. As mentioned in the foregoing chapters the Accelerated Rural Water Supply Programme (ARWSP) has been initiated by the Central Government. Besides these two, national and international agencies such as Life Insurance Corporation (LIC), World Bank, EEC, DANIDA, UNICEF, DRP, Local bodies, WGDP, ITDP, DRDA and others contributed in the form of loans and subsidy towards rural water supply programmes (Fig. 4.4).

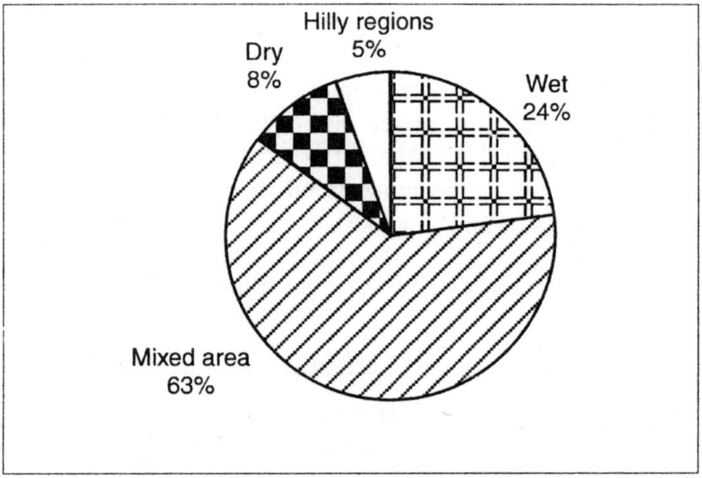

Fig. 4.3 : Area-wise Installation cost.

During 1972-98, among the agencies LIC topped the list in advancing the loan amount to the extent of Rs. 87.81 crores of the total and the percentage stood at 49.3. Next to LIC, the MNP contributed Rs. 29.26 crores and in terms of percentage it was 16.6. The ARP promoted the programmes to the extent of Rs.10.59 crores in percentage terms it was 5.9, the local bodies where the investment made was Rs.11.23 crores, comprised 6.97 per cent. The international agencies such as the World Bank, EEC, DANIDA and UNICEF put together extended loan amount of Rs. 93.67 lakhs constituting 0.58 per cent. Other agencies like WGDP, ITDPD and DRD contributed the least towards water supply programmes (Table 4.10).

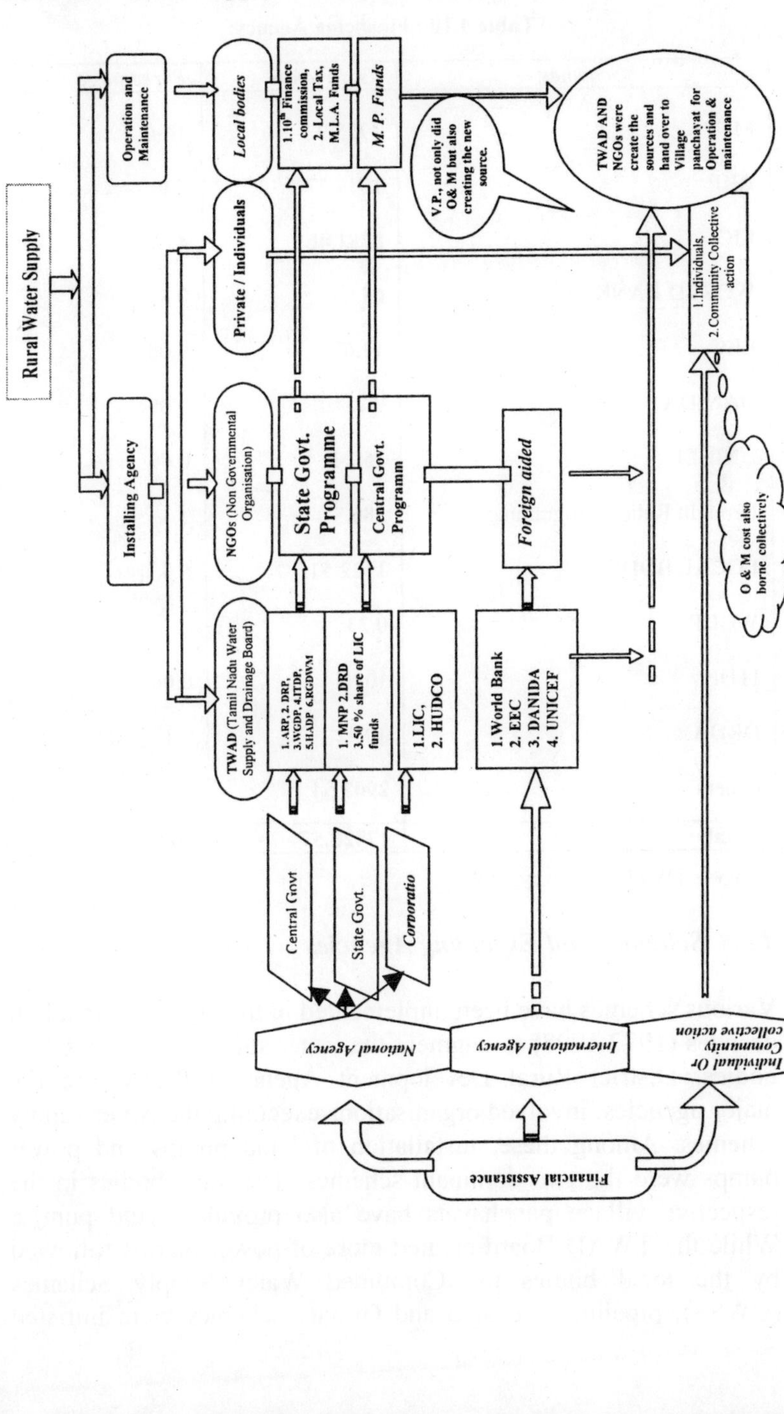

Fig. 4.4 : Financing of rural water supply.

Table 4.10 : Financing Agency.

Schemes	*Rs. In lakhs*	*Percentage*
MNP	2925.92	16.6
ARP	1059.27	5.9
LIC	8781.46	49.3
WORLD BANK	64.03	0.35
EEC	13.67	0.08
DANIDA	0.73	0.004
UNICEF	15.24	0.09
Drought Relief Programme	586.37	3.3
LOCAL BODY	1122.51	6.3
WGDP	0.23	
ITDP	10.85	0.06
DRDA	30.42	0.17
Others	2907.54	16.3
Total	**17828.57**	**100**

Source : TWAD re-survey, 1999.

4.2.8 Schemes and Executing Agencies

Various schemes have been implemented in the last two and a half decades (1972-1998) to augment the water supply. TWAD, Local bodies, District Rural Development Agency (DRDA) are the major agencies, involved organisations executing the water supply schemes. Among these, installation of hand pumps and power pumps were the two dominant schemes. The local bodies in the respective village panchayats have also provided hand pumps. While the TWAD Board created more of power pumps followed by the local bodies the Combined Water Supply Schemes (CWSS), pipeline extension and Gravity schemes were initiated by the TWAD. The DRDA concentrated more on installing hand pumps and a very few power pumps (Table 4.11).

Table 4.11 : Execution of schemes – Agency and period

Schemes	*Year of completion*			*Agency executed*			
	1960 to 1980	*1981 to 1990*	*After 1990*	*TWAD*	*Local body*	*DRD*	*Others*
Hand pump	275	3858	2594	3155	3256	179	147
Power pump	333	303	662	874	420	2	2
CWSS	-	-	9	9	-	-	-
Others [Pipeline extension Gravity schemes Open well Ring well]	25	34	131	129	29	-	32
	633 [7.6]	4195 [51.0]	3406 [41.23]	4167 [50.6]	3705 [44.99]	181 [2.2]	181 [2.2]

Source : TWAD re-survey, 1999.

4.2.9 Period of Installation of Schemes

Over the decades different water schemes had been initiated in the district. It may be relevant to discern the impact of major national and international missions with respect to rural water supply. Although the water supply schemes got started from the first five year plan onwards, they gained momentum after the declaration of International Drinking Water Supply and Sanitation Decade (1981-1990). More than 50 per cent of the existing schemes were initiated during this period. Subsequently, at the national level the Rajiv Gandhi Drinking Water Mission was started during 1986. These two missions had made a remarkable change in the implementation of rural water supply schemes in India and in the study state in particular. By comparing the different schemes, the hand pumps in particular showed fourteen-fold increase in its number only after 1981. However, the current strategy at the district level is to concentrate more on Combined Water Supply Schemes (CWSS) (Table 4.12).

Table 4.12 : Year of completion of the schemes

Area	*Year of completion*			*Total*
	1960 to 1980	*1981 to 1990*	*After 1991*	
Wet	212	1533	1315	3060 [37.16]
Mixed	160	1066	1183	2409 [29.26]
Dry	183	970	700	2013 [24.44]
Hill region	78	626	208	912 [11.07]
Total	**633 [8.7]**	**4195 [51.0]**	**3406 [41.3]**	**8234 [100]**

4.2.10 Combined Water Supply Schemes (CWSS)

This is a comprehensive programme, which envisages creation of source in specific spots and to provide water supply to more than one habitation. Besides, CWSS curtails water expenditure by means of not trying to circumvent the undue expenses in villages where the water level is abysmally low. Hence, the scheme depends largely on sub-surface water and in places with rich groundwater sources.

Under this the total investment made up to year 2000, was Rs. 100.44 crores at current prices. The TWAD board officials expressed the view that the total amount allotted has not been spent fully; only 30 per cent of the allotted amount was used for this purpose. Since the scheme is currently in progress, the officials concerned are likely to utilize the amount in due course of the period.

The scheme has so far covered 36 per cent of the total habitations with a population of 6,59,231, which constitutes 33.4 per cent of the total population. In terms of village panchayats the programme has covered 148 village panchayats, where the total number of village panchayats in the district is 408. There are 9 schemes under the CWSS operating in the study district now (Table 4.13).

Table 4.13 : Status of rural water supply through Combined Water Supply Schemes (CWSS)

Name of the scheme	*Coverage*			*Cost in Rs. in Lakhs*	*Covered popula-tion*
	Block	*Pancha-yat*	*Habita-tion*		
1. Lalgudi & Pullam-padi CWSS	Lalgudi & Pullampadi	28	43	200.056	45021
2. Allurpatti CWSS	Thottiyam	8	29	240.0	41584
3. Allakkudi CWSS	Thiruvaram-bur	1	8	124.25	16366
4. Biratiyur CWSS	Andanallur Manikandam	9	19	171.12	16366
5. Thirumara-yanapuram	Thottiyam	2	6	64.36	26445
6. Thempalam CWSS	Thathai-yangar pettai	11	24	652.00	39336
7. Thandalai	Musiri	11	26	321.24	29707
8. Sri Rama-samudram	Thottiyam	7	27	361.00	19545
9. Manaparai* water supply schemes	Manaparai & Marugapuri	71	674	6900.20	424861
		148	856	10000.44	65923

* Work in progress.

The per capita cost incurred by the CWSS worked out to be Rs. 510 for the whole district population. If users alone are considered then the cost was Rs. 1,526 per capita. Hence when compared to other schemes the CWSS has not been cost effective. The CWSS sounds expensive due to cost of installed pipeline to carry the water from the pumping main. The normal distance covered by CWSS ranges from one to 50 km.

One may expect economies of scale from the combined water supply scheme, than from a single scheme or a few schemes providing water supply to a large number of habitations. Other schemes usually provide a source in each village while CWSS chooses a few locations to install the facility. Hence, the cost per head ought come down, but calculation of per capita cost proved otherwise. The cost under CWSS is higher due to pipeline extension work, pipelines have to be installed for 25 to 50 kilometre distance to supply water and as a result the costs get escalated under CWSS. Therefore, CWSS is not cost effective, but this scheme facilitates those habitations with scarce local source. Hence though CWSS has been coming up well in the district this scheme has certain spillover effects, viz., the environmental conflicts. A discussion on this issue shall be included in the last part of this chapter under environmental dimensions of drinking water supply.

4.2.10.1 Significance of CWSS

This programme has certain merits also. The CWSS is an advanced one when compared to earlier schemes. Prior to CWSS, schemes like hand pumps and OHTs were created in locations where water availability was good. Households had to reach the sources to gather water and in that process they had to spend time and extra energy towards water collection. Under CWSS, water is provided mainly to those villages where there is dearth of water for domestic purposes. Under this households were able to save time and reduce the distance travelled to collect water. Above all the quality of water is reportedly better than the other sources, where CWSS has an elaborate system of treating the water to maintain the quality.

4.2.11 Sanitation Facilities

Sanitation by and large in the study district is poor. There were 3,91,209 houses in the rural areas of the district at the time of TWAD re-survey. Of which there were only 365 houses had dry latrine facility, comprising 0.09 per cent to the total. The NGOs had played a role in providing low cost latrines in the district to the extent of 1600 latrines across the district. In the hilly region, the latrine facility was almost nil. However the data showed a minimum number of facilities at least in Government colonies and housing quarters (Table 4.14).

Table 4.14 : Sanitation Facilities

Area	*Number of dry latrines*	*No. of low cost latrines*	*No. of pit latrines*	*Community latrines (No)*	*No. of septic tanks*	*Sludge drainage*	*No. of homes having sludge drainage facility*
Wet							
Sum	7	709	0	30	22010	50	80
Mean	0.01	1.10	0	0.05	34.18	0.08	0.12
Range	0-5	0-180	0	0-3	0-5000	0-50	0-75
Mixed							
Sum	144	780	10	53	2717	1992	2905
Mean	0.16	.89	0.01	0.06	3.11	2.28	3.33
Range	0-50	0-60	0-5	0-10	0-214	0-500	0-250
Dry							
Sum	214	111	3892	18	1364	0	5
Mean	0.34	0.17	6.11	0.03	2.14	0	0.01
Range	0-50	0-100	0-350	0-4	0-200	0	0-5
Hill region	0	0	0	0	0	0	0
Sum	0	0	0	0	0	0	0
Mean	0	0	0	0	0	0	0
Range							
Total							
Sum	365	1600	3902	101	26091	2042	2990
Mean	0.15	0.67	1.64	0.04	10.98	0.86	1.26
Range	0-50	0-180	0-350	0-10	0-5000	0-500	0-250

Source : TWAD re-survey, 1999.

Regarding the septic tanks and latrines, the scenario was very peculiar. Although the Government made certain provisions towards latrines by means of constructing septic tanks with less than 3 feet depth and 3 feet breadth, most of them became defunct quickly since they had not been connected with water facilities.

The point central to sanitation in the rural areas of the district is that be it dry latrine, septic tanks, low cost latrine, or pit latrines, they were found in those houses, which were constructed by the State Government in Government colonies and housing quarters. In total, only 8 per cent of the total number of houses had anyone of the forms of latrines.

In the wet villages, as expected, the number of septic tanks was comparatively higher. In dry villages pit latrines were large in number. The situation has been deplorable in SC and ST colonies and hill regions as the state provision was virtually nil in this region. The community latrines in Government colonies are in the rudimentary stage.

4.2.12 Regression Results

Regression analysis is used to identify the variables influencing per capita availability of water in the district. The water availability (lpcd) is taken as dependent variable. The chosen independent variables, included area (wet, mixed, dry and hilly region), hand pumps per one thousand population, per capita cost of installation, CWSS per one thousand, OHT per one thousand population, proportion of house service connection, quantity liter per minute and number of septic tanks (the water providing capacity of the source as stated by the board officials). Correlation matrices are used to choose the significant variables. Of the ten variables taken, correlation coefficients were significant for only nine variables.

$$Y= f(X_1+X_2 + X_3 + X_4 + X_5 + X_6) + U_i$$

Where
Dependent variable: litre per capita per day (lpcd)
Independent: Variables:

X_1 AREA	:	as a dummy variable (Wet, mixed, Dry and Hill)
X_2 HP1000P	:	Hand pump per thousand populations
X_3 SP1000P	:	Stand post per thousand populations
X_4 QINLPM	:	Quantity liters per minuets

X_5 CWSS : Combined water supply per 1000 population

X_6 SANISEPT : Water for personal hygiene

U_i = Error term

Firstly, about the area (dummy variable), the coefficient turned negative indicating an inverse relationship between per capita availability per day and the area. The negative sign implies that moving from wet to mixed, dry and hilly region the per capita availability goes on decreasing. This may be attributed to the higher number of sources in wet region and the relatively lower number of sources in mixed, dry and hilly regions. The other independent variable, OHT per thousand populations was positive but not significant, implying that the number of OHTs may be more in a habitation but the capacity of OHT lower. In other cases the number of OHTs may be few in number but the capacity may be higher. Regarding hand pumps per one thousand populations, the relationship showed negative and significant sign. This suggests that the availability of hand pumps per one thousand population are more in the wet region and the number goes on declining from moving to wet and dry, dry and hill region (Table 4.15).

Table 4.15 : Habitation level – Regression results

Variable	*Coefficient*	*T statistic*
AREA	-.411928**	-1.793
HP1000P	-.015215	-.370
SP1000P	.074377*	14.279
QINLPM	.027509*	12.013
CWSS	3.579388	1.367
SANISEPT	4.15311E-04	.218
(Constant)	**30.476520***	**44.056**
R Square	.22138	
N	2376	

* significant at 5 per cent level.

** significant at 1 per cent level.

Stand posts per thousand populations as an independent variable showed a positive relationship and remained statistically significant. The provision of stand posts is an offshoot of OHT facility. In the study district, as mentioned earlier the numbers of stand post provided were greater and the capacity of OHT were also more. In places where OHT capacity was higher the number of house service connections were also more.

Quantity of Litre Per Minute (LPM) is another crucial independent variable, which turned out to be positive in relationship with lpcd and statistically significant. The positive relationship envisages that in villages where the yielding capacity of the source is high the supply of water also be higher. In dry villages though the number of sources were moderate the yielding capacity in terms of lpm has been poor.

Two other variables such as Combined Water Supply Schemes (CWSS) and sanitary facility were positively related to water availability and turned out to be statistically not significant. The secondary data sources showed that there were large number of latrines and septic tanks existing in the study district. In reality septic tanks were not linked with water facilities and the latrines were improperly used. More discussion will follow while discussing the primary results in the subsequent part of this chapter. In regard to CWSS, the schemes as such were implemented in not many habitations. The R square value showed 0.22, which indicates that only twenty two per cent of the variations in the dependent variable has been explained by the variations in the independent variables.

5

ANALYSIS OF PRIMARY HOUSEHOLD SURVEY

Detailed primary household survey was conducted during May to October 2000 across the five selected villages. The response from the households was satisfactory. As indicated in the methodology, five villages were selected based upon the dry and/or wet status. The villages include, Athikudi, a wet area, Nagayanallur, Mullipadi, which are partially wet and dry (Mixed) Oothukuli a dry area and Thenpuranadu hilly region, where the concentration of scheduled castes and scheduled tribes is also high.

The composition of sample respondents included head of the household, in most cases male or female i.e., the spouse, or both husband and wife. Purposively, the households from scheduled castes and scheduled tribes were included mainly to study whether equity prevailed in water distribution.

The primary survey conducted for six months in the study villages aimed to address a host of issues pertaining to drinking and domestic use of water. They include the various types of sources created by the state agency and the existing traditional sources and performance of both these sources. The per capita household consumption of water is an important indicator both from the supply and demand side of provision of water. The question is whether or not the selected households have access to the prescribed norm of 40 litres per capita per day (lpcd) in rural areas. Distance travelled and time spent are other crucial theoretical variables involved in this context? Corollary to this is the role of women, who generally fetch water for domestic use. Another aspect is to find out the requirement of water for livestock maintenance,

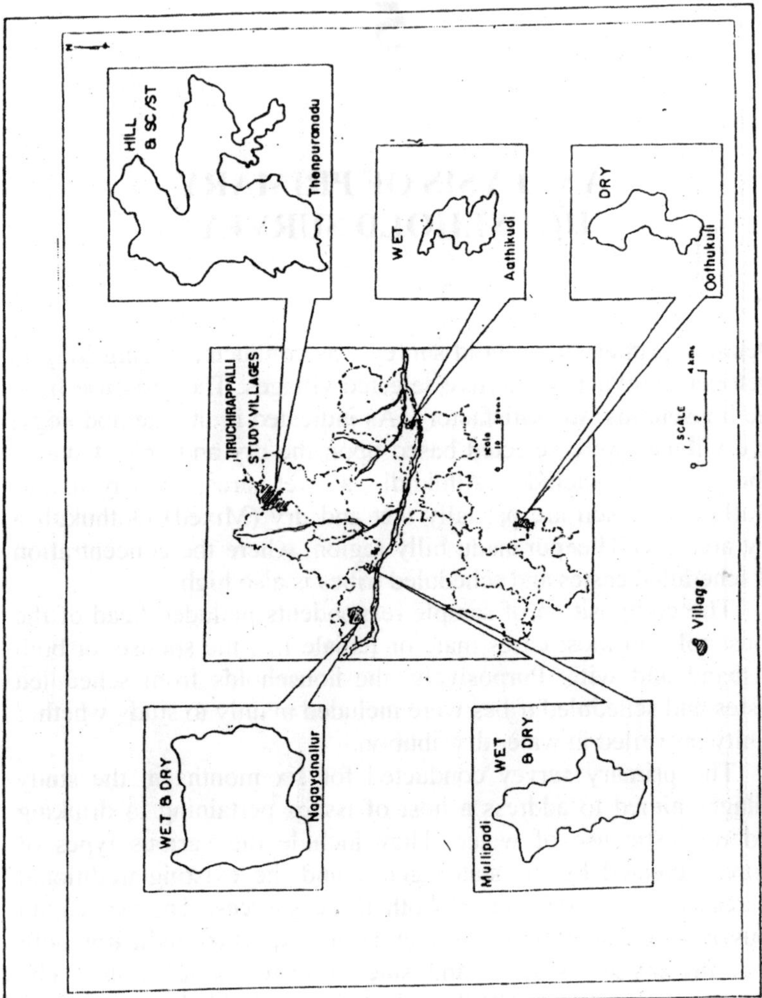

Map 2 : Study Villages.

whether the source available is adequate and if inadequate the extent of alternative sources available for the upkeep of livestock population. And, finally, the question of willingness to pay for improved water supply also formed a part of the analysis.

This chapter presents the case study results. A case-by-case presentation is warranted as each village is unique in its characteristics and the forces at work can better be explained only when each case is discussed separately.

I. CASE STUDIES

5.1 CASE STUDY-1

Athikudi, a village Panchayat, is located in Lalgudi taluk of Tiruchirappalli district. This is situated 24 km. away from Tiruchirappalli town. This village is chosen mainly because it is a wet village, close to Cauvery river delta. Athikudi comprises five habitations viz., Athikudi (main), Athikudi colony (Where lower community living, i.e. SC/ST), Natarajapuram, Vazhuthiyur, and Govinthapuram. The total population as per 1999 TWAD re-survey was 4945, with an average of 989 per habitation. The average distance between two habitations is 1.36 km. The average family size is 5. A sample of 64 households are chosen, which is 10 per cent of the total households in the village. This sample size constitutes 20 per cent of the total sample households of the study area (Table 5.1 & 5.2).

The village has two primary schools, four Anganwadis and two ration shops. The major communities of village are, *inter alia*, Naidu Kallar, Muthuraja and Pallar. The classifications of habitations are based upon the communities. Being a wet village, paddy and sugarcane are the major crops raised in the village all through the year. During summer bore well water is the prime source of water for irrigation. There are 8 brick industries located in the village. Labourers are brought from neighbouring districts, which increased the demand for water.

Of the total respondents in 53 per cent of the sample households have male as head of the household, 43.8 per cent of them have female and 3 per cent comprises both husband and wife. Of these, 39.1 per cent belongs to scheduled castes (SCs) and the remaining 60.9 are from other communities (Table 5.3).

Table 5.1 : Basic details of sample villages.

Name of the sample village	T.P. of 1999	SC/ST	T. No. of Houses	Thatched houses	LPCD	Cost of provision (in lakhs)	Hand pump	OHT/ Power pump	CWSS	Others	OHT capacity	No. of SP	No. HSCs	PP. covered by HSCs
Athikudi														
Total	4945	1100	1040	460	123	13.90	14	3	0	1	100000	19	15	80
Mean	989	220	208	92	24.6	2.78	3	1	0	0	20000	3.8	3	16
Range	370-1860	0-500	75-375	30-185	13-40	0.48-5.23	1-4	0-2	0	0-1	0-60000	1-13	0-15	0-80
SD	681	223.19	134.56	63.5	14.08	2.04	1	1	0	0	25248.76	5.22	6.71	35.78
CV	145.22		154.57											
Nagayanallur														
Total	6194	2019	1238	1025	405	277	30	6	4	1	194000	70	200	1000
Mean	516	168.25	103.7	85.42	33.75	23.08	3	0	0	0	16166.67	5.83	16.67	83.33
Range	168-1360	0-1360	34-275	31-267	15-40	0.20-240.92	1-6	0-2	0-1	0-1	0-64000	1-17	0-90	0-450
SD	341.04	393.35	68.17	65.27	8.88	68.68	1	1	0	0	20581.69	5.13	33.12	165.60
CV			151.34											
Mullipadi														
Total	3460	1437	692	522	270	18.42	12	5	0	0	150000	36	0	0
Mean	384	159.67	76.89	58	30.06	2.05	1	1	0	0	16666.67	4	0	0
Range	140-825	0-407	28-165	24-101	14.5-40	00-6.57	0-2	0-2	0	0	0-60000	1-13	0	0
SD	265.24	147.98	53.15	24.07	10.46	2.30	1	1	0	0	21794.49	4.15	0	0
CV	144.94		144.66											
Oothukuli														
Total	3095	485	620	152	297.50	10.19	13	1	0	0	60000	18	0	0
Mean	386	60.63	77.50	19	37.19	1.27	2	0	0	0	7500	2.25	0	0
Range	150-1805	0-375	30-362	8-52	25-40	.20-7.65	1-5	0-1	0	0	0-60000	1-11	0	0
SD	574.57	132.73	115.27	15.10	5.25	2.58	1	0	0	0	21213.20	3.54	0	0
CV	67.18		67.23											
Thenpuranadu														
Total	7130	6980	1423	739	495	11.40	31	1	0	2	70000	29	0	0
Mean	445.63	436	88.94	46.19	30.94	.71	2	0	0	0	4375	1.81	0	0
Range	120-750	120-750	25-150	15-80	25-55	0.14-4.12	1-4	0-1	0	0-1	0-30000	1-5	0	0
SD	187.33	174.39	37.52	20.6	9.17	0.98	1	0	0	0	8139.41	1.47	0	0
CV	237.88		237.00											

Name of the Panchayat	Total No. of HHs	No. of sample HHs	Water source		Mode of water supply	Status of Water Supply
			Earlier	Present		
Wet						
Athikudi	640	64*	Open well River	SP, HP, Own HP Agricultural power pump	Power Manual Manual Manual	Water availability is in abundance, but the water quality in some parts of the village is poor.
Mixed						
Nagayanallur & Mullipadi	1480+ 920	74** 46**	Open well, River & agri. Tank	HP, SP & CWSS River	Manual Power Manual	Composite characters with both mixed areas. Scarcity is acute during summer. Nitrate content is high in a few habitations. Adequate supply of water.
Dry						
Oothukuli	600	60*	*Oththu* (Spring)-	*Oththu,* HP & SP	Manual Manual Power	Quality of spring water is excellent, but the groundwater level is low and hence scarcity.
Hill						
Thenpuranadu	670	67*	*Kudavu*	SP# HP & *Kudavu*	Power Manual Manual	Traditional water source is the principle source. And the Modern sources are supplementary.

Note : * 10 % and ** 5 % of the sample HHs from the total HHs in study village. HHs: Households *'Oothu' 'Kodavu'* are the traditional sources, which people use for drinking in the sample villages of Oothukuli and Thenpuranadu respectively. HP – Hand Pump, SP – Stand post through Over Head Tank. SP# – Through OHT, from open well, CWSS – Combined Water Supply Schemes.

Table 5.3 : Social status of sample households.

Sample Village	*Type of Respondents*			*Caste*		
	Head of the HH male	*Wife of HH female*	*Both*	*SC/ST*	*BC/MB C/DNT/ OC*	*No. of sample households*
Wet Athikudi	34 [53.1]	28 [43.8]	2 [3.1]	25 [39.1]	39 [60.1]	64 (20.6)
Mixed Nagayaiya-nallur and Mullipadi	79 [65.8]	18 [15.0]	23 [19.2]	43 [35.8]	77 [64.2]	120 (38.6)
Dry Oothukuli	36 [60.0]	17 [28.3]	7 [11.7]	7 [11.7]	53 [88.3]	60 (19.3)
Hill & SC/ST Thenpuranadu	57 [85.1]	5 [7.5]	5 [7.5]	67 [100.0]	0 [0.00]	67 (21.5)
Total	**206** **(66.2)**	**68** **(21.9)**	**37** **(11.9)**	**142** **(46.3)**	**169** **(54.3)**	**311**

Note: Figures in parentheses are percentage of totals.
Source : Primary household survey.

Table 5.4 : Respondents' Occupation.

Sample Village	*Agriculture and labour*	*Private*	*Govt.*	*Business*	*Others*
Wet Athikudi	45 [70.3]	6 [9.4]	4 [6.3]	1 [1.6]	8 [12.5]
Mixed Nagayaiyanallur & Mullipadi	92 [76.7]	6 [5.0]	5 [4.2]	3 [2.5]	14 [11.6]
Dry Oothukuli	50 [83.3]	-	1 [1.7]	8 [13.3]	1 [1.7]
Hill & SC/ST Thenpuranadu	54 [80.6]	-	3 [4.5]	-	10 [14.9]
	241 [77.5]	12 [3.9]	13 [4.2]	12 [3.9]	33 [10.5]

Note : Figures in parentheses are percentage of totals.

Among the sample respondents, 70 per cent are agricultural labourers, agriculturists and land less labourers. About 9 per cent are engaged in non-agricultural activities. Government servants include 6 per cent, 2 per cent in business activities and 13 per cent is grouped under others (Table 5.4).

Table 5.5 : Distribution of landholding in the sample households.

Name of the Panchayat	*Total land holding (in acres)*					
	LLs	*0.1 to 1*	*1.1 to 2.5*	*2.51 to 4*	*4.1 >*	*Total*
Wet						
Athikudi SC/ST	18[28.13]	3[4.7]	3[4.7]	1[1.6]	0[0.0]	25(39.1)
OC	18[28.13]	3[4.7]	7[10.9]	5[7.8]	6[9.4]	39(60.9)
Total	36[56.0]	6[9.4]	10[15.6]	6[9.4]	6[9.4]	64[20.6]
Mixed						
Nagayanallur & Mullipadi SC/ST	26[21.7]	11[9.2]	4[3.3]	2[1.7]	0[0.0]	43(35.8)
OC	37[30.8]	21[17.5]	10[8.3]	4[3.3]	5[4.2]	77(64.2)
Total	63[52.5]	32[29.2]	14[11.7]	6[5.0]	5[4.2]	120 [38.6]
Dry						
Oothukuli SC/ST	2[3.3]	1[1.7]	3[5.0]	0[0.0]	1[1.7]	7(11.7)
OC	9[15.0]	14[23.3]	17[28.3]	5[8.3]	8[13.3]	53(88.3)
Total	11[18.3]	15[25.0]	20[33.3]	5[8.3]	9[15.0]	60[19.6]
Hill						
Thenpuranadu SC/ST	5[7.5]	8[11.9]	24[35.8]	12[17.9]	18[26.9]	67 [21.5]
Total	115 [37.0]	61 [19.6]	68 [21.9]	29 [9.3]	38 [12.2]	311

Source : Primary household survey, LLs: Land Less Labour. Figures in parentheses indicate percentages of total. OC: Other Community (Upper Caste), SC/ST: (Lower community).

Nearly 56 per cent of the respondents do not own agricultural land, 9.4 per cent own below one acre, 15.6 per cent own 1.1 to

2.5 acres, 9.4 per cent have 2.5 to 4 acres and above 4 acres by 9.4 per cent of the respondents. The average landholding in this village is 1.70 acres. The land value is Rs. 1,94,180 acre at current prices (Table 5.5) and (Figure 5.1).

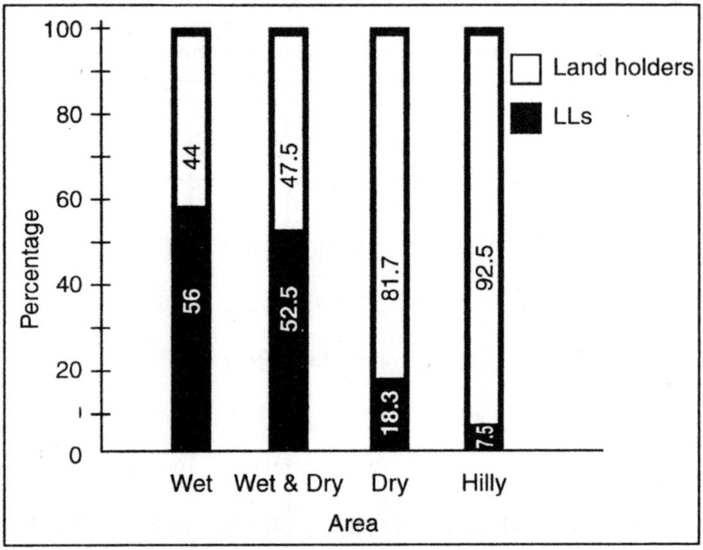

Fig. 5.1 : Landholdings of respondent.

With regard to type of houses in the village more than 70 per cent of the houses are other than thatched ones. Of this, 40 per cent have pucca terrace. Regarding floor of the houses, 67 per cent of them are other than soil; of this 64 per cent are made of cement and 1 per cent mosaic. The average value of house is Rs. 87,395 at current prices (Table 5.6).

The per capita income of the selected households is Rs. 875 month ranging from a minimum of Rs. 150 to a maximum of Rs. 6,167. The average agricultural income per annum was Rs. 24,000 (Table 5.7).

5.1.1 Sources of Water

For domestic use before the introduction of modern sources of water supply traditional sources such as open well and irrigation open well, canal and ponds were the dominant supply sources.

Table 5.6 : Status of house in the sample households.

Sample Village	Type of House						Type of floor				Present value of house and No. of rooms*					
	Thatched	Tiled	Terraced	Pucca	Others	Total	Soil	Cement	Mosaic	Others	Total	Mean	Range	N	Std Dev	CV
Wet	19	16	17	6	6	64	21	41	1	1	5418500	87395	500 – 600000	62	120044	137.36
	[29.7]	[25.0]	[26.6]	[9.4]	[9.4]		[32.8]	[64.0]	[1.6]	[1.6]	*112	2	1 – 10	62	2	100
	44	55	12	0	9	120	52	68	0	0	3685500	31772	1000 – 125000	116	26102	82.12
Mixed	[36.7]	[45.8]	[10.0]	[0.0]	[7.5]		[43.0]	[56.7]	[0.0]	[0.0]	*164	1	0 – 5	116	1	100
	9	33	14	3	1	60	12	47	1	0	2878000	48780	3000 – 200000	59	44081	90.37
Dry	[7.5]	[27.5]	[11.7]	[2.5]	[0.8]		[20.0]	[78.0]	[1.7]	[0.0]	*117	2	0 – 8	59	1	50
	8	30	3	0	26	67	39	25	0	3	1604500	23948	1000 – 150000	67	23117	96.53
Hill & SC/ST	[11.9]	[44.8]	[4.5]	[0.0]	[38.8]		[58.0]	[37.0]	[0.0]	[0.0]	*95	1	1 – 3	67	1	100
Total	**80**	**134**	**46**	**9**	**42**	**311**	**124**	**181**	**2**	**4**	**13586500**	**44692**	**500 – 600000**	**304**	**64680**	**144.72**
	[25.7]	**[43.1]**	**[14.8]**	**[2.9]**	**[13.5]**		**[39.9]**	**[58.2]**	**[0.6]**	**[1.3]**	***488**	**2**	**0 – 10**	**304**	**1**	**50**

Figures in parentheses are percentage of totals.
Source : Primary household survey.

Table 5. 7 : Income of the respondents.

(In Rupees)

Areas	*Income of res-pondent (p/m)*	*Average agriculture income (p/a)*	*Average income of households (p/m)*	*Per capita income of HHs.*
Athikudi (Wet)	3079	54837	3859	875
Nagayanallur& Mullipadi (mixed)	1220	55167	1768	405
Oothukkuli (Dry)	1344	00	1569	326
Thenpuranadu (Hill regions)	916	19435	2582	532

This tendency changed slowly and the households had started to use modern sources for cooking, drinking, washing, bathing and livestock maintenance.

For the Panchayat as a whole, own and Government sources such as hand pumps, power pumps (OHT: Stand Post and House Service Connection) exist in the village. The total number of hand pumps, power pumps and house service connections are 31, 4 and 113 respectively. Majority of households own private low cost hand pumps, which are accounted in the primary survey (See Plate 1).

For the sample households, hand pumps are as principal source for drinking and cooking needs to 73 per cent of the respondents. And 15.6 per cent of stand posts and 7.8 per cent of house connections are the principal sources of the respondents. As high as 97 per cent of the respondents depend on modern supply sources for drinking and cooking purposes. Seventy-three per cent of the sample households use hand pumps as the principal water source for drinking and other domestic needs. While, 15.6 per cent use stand post and 7.8 per cent possess house service connection for their needs. Hand pumps are the dominant principal source owing to better water quality (Table 5.8) and (Figure 5.2).

The respondents are reluctant to use water supplied through stand posts and house service connections, for drinking and cooking purposes. The reason is reportedly that water once stored in tanks, the colour and smell got changed, making it unsuitable for drinking purposes. The change in colour is attributed to iron concentration in the water. Therefore, the respondents prefer to draw from hand pumps and use at once for drinking and cooking. However, for other domestic purposes like washing, bathing and cleaning the respondents replied positively towards using stored water, supplied through stand posts and house service connections. In addition, people use the public source for bathing and washing cloths right at the source point itself (See Plates 2 & 3). Besides, there are numerous alternative sources such as canals, ponds, and agricultural wells in this village. For other than drinking and cooking purposes, residents of this village use alternative sources in summer from April to July.

Table 5.8 : Status of principal source of drinking and cooking water for households in the sample villages.

Area Sample village	*No. of households using as a principal source for drinking and cooking*						
	Hand Pump	*Stand post*	*HSCs*	*Tradi-tional*	*Open well*	*Agri. Source*	*Total*
Wet	47 [73.4]	10 [15.6]	5 [7.8]	—	—	2 [3.1]	64
Mixed	23 [19.2]	60 [50.0]	32 [26.7]	—	3 [2.5]	2 [1.7]	120
Dry	10 [16.7]	15 [25.0]	—	33 [55.0]	2 [3.3]	—	60
Hill region	4 [5.9]	43* [64.1]	—	7 [10.4]	13 [19.4]	—	67
Total	84 (27.0)	128 (41.2)	37 (11.9)	40 (12.9)	18 (5.8)	4 (1.3)	311
	Percentage of modern source			*Percentage of traditional source*			
Wet and Mixed	56.9			2.3			59.2
Dry and Hilly regions	9.3			31.5			40.8

Figures in parenthesis give percentages of totals.

* Open well, the traditional source of water being distributed through modern schemes. HSCs: House Service Connections.

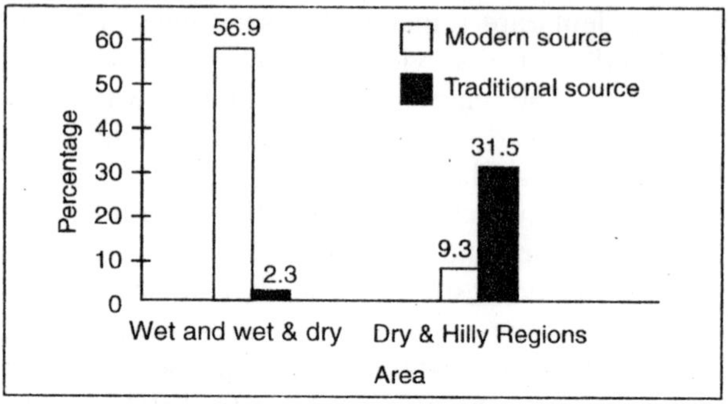

Fig. 5.2 : Principal source drinking and cooking.

Given the fact that both traditional and modern sources are plenty in the village, the current demand of the residents is for Cauvery water supply through house service connection. Historically, they had depended largely on traditional sources for drinking and cooking purposes. Once the hand pumps and power pumps were established, their job of fetching water became easier. With the installation of hand pumps and stand posts, they now seek Cauvery water, which is supposed to be tastier and colour less than the water they get routinely through the current sources.

5.1.2 Demand for Water

The present study considered a number of variables to discern the water demand at the domestic level. The chosen variables *inter alia* are drinking, cooking, bathing, washing cloths, utensil cleaning, livestock maintenance, personal hygiene, paddy par boiling, house cleaning, gardening and other needs. The average quantity of water used per household in Athikudi is 417 litres per day. Since in this village for purposes like bathing, washing cloths and even livestock maintenance the respondents freely use alternative sources directly. Hence, the exact quantity of water used for domestic purposes is difficult to measure.

For drinking and cooking purposes the average requirement per household per day is 36 litres, and 7.6 litres per capita per day (lpcd) respectively. The percentage of water requirement for drinking to the total water consumption per household is 8.65. For all domestic purposes the per capita consumption of water is 85.56 litres (Table 5.9). Out of the total quantity of water consumed, 24 per cent is used for bathing, 12 per cent for utensil cleaning, 15 per cent for washing cloth, house cleaning 3.1 per cent, 4.5 per cent for livestock maintenance and 23.8 per cent for other purposes (Table 5.10) and (Fig. 5.3).

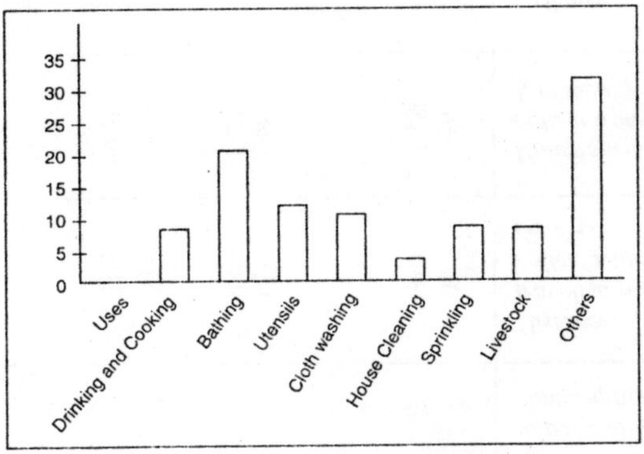

Fig. 5.3 : Usage-wise consumption

5.1.3 Distance and Time

Athikudi village is endowed with a large a number of sources created by the Government, Non-Governmental Organisation (NGO) (See Plate 4) and private sources. The distance travelled on an average by households is 10 metres, with a range of 1 to 40 meters from the house. And the time taken to fetch water is 56 minutes. These two variables viz., time and distance are crucial in the provision of water. The experience in this village with respect to time and distance may not be generalized for other villages. Because many sources are found in this village, one can find two to three sources in one spot. Besides NGOs also have provided adequate additional facility sources (Table 5.10).

5.1.4 Role of Women

Of the 64-sample households, females in 89 per cent of the households fetch water for domestic use, males in 1.6 per cent of the households and in 9.4 per cent of the households both the male and female collect water for domestic use. Alternatively, 29.7 per cent of female head of family renders service in bringing water,

Table 5.9 : Water consumption of sample households, distance and time of water collection

Area	Total consumption water by households P/D	Water for drinking and cooking purpose	Percentage of drinking water to the total by HHs	Per capita consumption water per head for all purpose (lpcd)	Lpcd for drinking and cooking	Percentage of per capita drinking water consumption to per capita consumption	Distance and Time		Average	
							Distance travelled p/d to collect water (in meters)	Hours spent to collect water (in Minutes)	Distance (in meters)	Time (in Minutes)
Athikudi										
Mean	416.9	36	8.65	85.6	7.6	9	10	56		
Range	70-1416			18-322			1-40	5-180		
Nagayanallur & Mullipadi									71.5	62
Mean	368.8	28	7.59	84.1	6.3	7	133	68		
Range	107-985			24-280			1-600	5-240		
Oothukuli										
Mean	434.2	28	6.55	78.6	4.9	6	1332	229		
Range	75-992			21-177			2-3100	60-360		
Thenpuranadu									776	153.5
Mean	245.6	26	10.6	56.4	5.8	10	219	78		
Range	97-521			22-125			2-900	15-200		
	366	30	8.3	76	6.15	8				

Table 5.10 : Consumption of water – Usage-wise.

Area		*No. of sample house holds*	*Consumption of water per household*	*Drinking and cooking*	*Bathing*	*Utensils cleaning*	*Cloth washing*	*House cleaning*	*Sprinkling at the entrance*	*Livestock*	*Others (ablution, vehicle cleaning gardening & paddy boiling)*
Athikudi Wet		64	416.9	36 [8.56]	99.6 [23.9]	50.4 [12.1]	62.5 [15]	12.9 [3.1]	37.1 [8.9]	18.8 [4.5]	99.2 [23.8]
Nagayanallur & Mullipadi Mixed		120	368.8	28 [7.59]	71.9 [19.5]	39.1 [10.6]	40.2 [10.9]	14.6 [3.9]	25.4 [6.9]	25.4 [6.9]	124 [33.6]
Oothukuli Dry		60	434.2	28 [6.55]	62.5 [14.4]	45.1 [10.4]	49.9 [11.5]	22.1 [5.1]	28.2 [6.5]	53.8 [12.4]	143.8 [33.1]
Thenpuranadu Hill & SC/ST		67	245.6	26 [10.6]	65.6 [26.7]	32.4 [13.2]	6.14 [2.5]	5.2 [2.1]	15.7 [6.4]	9.9 [4.0]	84.6 [34.5]
Total		311	366	30 [8.3]	77.2 [21.1]	42.4 [11.6]	36.5 [9.9]	13.1 [3.67]	26.3 [7.2]	25.5 [6.9]	114.6 [31.3]
Source of water consumption	**TWAD source**		223.4 [61.0]	20	42.9	32.7	15.4	10.5	19.5	3.6	78.8
	Other sources		142.6 [39.0]	10	34.3	9.67	21.1	2.6	6.5	21.9	35.8

Figures in parenthesis represent percentages of totals.

32.8 per cent are daughters including school going children and 37.5 per cent includes others, like, son and in-laws. Informal discussion with the respondents revealed that collection of water by women folk has been the tradition in rural areas. They consider that collection of water by male is a social taboo (Table 5.11).

Table 5.11 : Water collectors

Areas	*Female*	*Male*	*All members*	*Female head alone*	*Helping to female head in water collection*	
					Daughter (Including school children)	*Other (In laws, husband, son)*
Wet	57 [89.1]	1 [1.6]	6 [9.4]	19 [29.7]	21 [32.8]	24 [37.5]
Mixed	118 [98.3]	—	2 [1.6]	71 [59.2]	34 [28.3]	15 [12.5]
Dry	50 [83.4]	3 [5.0]	7 [11.7]	16 [26.7]	33 [55.0]	11 [18.3]
Hill region SC/ST	67 [100.0]	—	—	45 [67.2]	12 [17.9]	10 [14.9]
	292 (93.8)	4 (1.3)	15 (4.8)	151 (48.6)	100 (32.2)	60 (19.3)

Figures in parentheses are percentage of totals.

5.1.5 Livestock Maintenance

About 44 per cent of the sample households in the village rear livestock. The composition of livestock showed 50 per cent of cows, 8.6 per cent of bull and 41.4 per cent of sheep and goat. The average income from livestock per household per annum is Rs. 2,489 at current prices. The livestock average holding per household is 4.1 per cent. Requirement of water for livestock maintenance per household per day is 44 litres for drinking by livestock. The per capita requirement per day is 10.7 litres.

Among the sources available, modern sources cater 93 per cent of the water needs of livestock, and the rest is met through traditional sources. The number of trips made by households for collection of water for livestock showed 17.9 per cent for one trip, 43.93 per cent for two trips and 39.3 per cent for three trips. For livestock care taken within the households, female constitutes 36 per cent and the rest by male. It is to be noted here that the field survey in this village was conducted during summer season and as a result dependence on Government sources showed higher percentage and the number of trips made also was greater. Seventy-five per cent of the livestocks were taken to the source like agricultural well and pond for bathing of livestocks (Table 5.12).

Table 5.12 : Source and consumption of livestock

Source	*Athikudi*	*Nagaya-nallur & Mullipadi*	*Oothukuli*	*Thenpura-nadu*	*Total*
Livestock not available	36 [56]	48 [40]	18 [30]	27 [40.3]	129 [41.5]
Available	28 [43.8]	72 [60.0]	42 [70.0]	40 [59.7]	182 [58.5]
Open well	2 [7.1]	2 [2.7]	1 [2.3]	1 [2.5]	6 [3.2]
Hand pump	20 [71.4]	20 [27.8]	32 [76.2]	—	72 [39.6]
Stand post	5 [17.9]	26 [36.1]	8 [19]	3 [7.5]	42 [23.1]
HSCs	1 [3.6]	19 [26.4]	—	—	20 [10.9]
Irrigation & Traditional Source	—	5 [6.9]	1 [2.3]	36 [90.0]	42 [23.1]

Figures in parenthesis represent percentages of totals.

5.1.6 Water Quality and Health

As mentioned earlier, the ground water once drawn from the aquifer develops a red tinge within 15 to 30 minutes of time. (See Plates 5 & 6) As part of the study, the water sample was taken from this village and tested. The iron content of the water showed 4.34 mg/litre, while the maximum permissible limit is 1 mg/litres.

Other parameters like pH, calcium, magnesium, sodium, potassium, bi-carbonate, sulphate, fluoride, chloride, nitrate, TDS, total hardness and fecal-coliform showed the level within the permissible limit (Table 5.23). The water quality testing of the sample was done with the help of Geo-chemical sub-divisions, Ground Water Board, P.W.D., Tiruchirappalli, as part of the study. A detailed discussion is included, on water quality under environmental dimension of water supply, in the later part of the chapter.

Unsafe water causes health hazards. During the field survey it was observed that 60.9 per cent of the households were unaware of water-borne diseases. About 15.6 per cent suffered from typhoid fever, 4.7 per cent had diarrhoea and 18.8 per cent were affected with jaundice. The average cost of treatment per household per annum worked out to be Rs. 856 at current prices. On an average, the respondents travelled 7 km. to avail medical facilities. Nearly 52 per cent of the affected people approached Government hospitals for treatment, 28 per cent preferred private hospitals and 20 per cent depended on native medicines (Table 5.13).

5.1.7 Sanitation

About 75 per cent of the respondents do not have any toilet facility in the village; the remaining has access to lavatories built in Government housing colonies. However, even these provisions are seldom used by the people. Therefore, nearly 95 per cent of the respondents go for open-air defecation. The average use of water for sanitary purpose per household per day is 17 litres (Table 5.14). Irrespective of whether there is in-house latrine or open-air use, invariably males prefer to use water in lakes, ponds and river for ablution. Females although go for open-air defecation, but return home for use of water. In regard to distance covered for defecation purpose, it ranged from 50 to 500 meters. Female move about an average 107 meters and men about 255 meters from home for this purpose.

When asked about the reasons for not having latrines inside the house, the respondents expressed varied views for it. It includes lack of money, space and water, besides lack of willingness and fear of bad smell in the house. The response from them revealed their ignorance about personal hygiene and safe practices.

Table 5.13 : Water borne diseases and health impact.

Areas	*Do not affected in the year 2000*	*Water borne*			*Affected persons*			*Hospital*			*Average distance move for treatment (km.)*	*Average treatment cost per household Per annum*
		Typhoid	*Cholera & Diahorroea*	*Jaundice*	*Women*	*Men*	*Children*	*Private*	*Govt.*	*Native*		
Wet	39 [60.9]	10 [40.0]	3 [12.0]	12 [48.0]	3 [12.0]	12 [48.0]	10 [4.0]	7 [28.0]	13 [52.0]	5 [20.0]	7	856.4
Wet & Dry	92 [76.7]	12 [42.9]	5 [17.9]	11 [39.3]	7 [26.9]	9 [32.1]	12 [42.9]	13 [46.4]	9 [32.1]	7 [21.4]	8	2766
Dry	40 [66.7]	7 [35.0]	2 [10.0]	11 [55.0]	5 [25.0]	9 [45.0]	6 [30.0]	5 [25.0]	9 [45.0]	6 [30.0]	20	2330.3
Hilly region	40 [59.7]	16 [59.3]	4 [14.8]	7 [25.9]	11 [40.7]	7 [25.9]	9 [33.3]	7 [25.9]	20 [74.1]	—	24	1958
	211 [67.8]	45 [14.5]	14 [4.5]	41 [13.2]	26 [19.0]	37	37					1983

Figures in parentheses are percentage of totals.

5.2 CASE STUDY II

Mullipadi and Nagayanallur are the two village Panchayats possessing partially wet and partially dry land. These are located 46 km. and 60 km. away from Tiruchirappalli town respectively. The population in Nagayanallur as per TWAD re-survey was 6194 during 1999, and in Mullipadi was 3460. The SC & ST population in Nagayanallur was 2019 and in Mullipadi it was 1437. Nagayanallur comprises 13 habitations and Mullipadi consists of 5 habitations (Table 5.1).

The cropping pattern in Nagayanallur village Panchayat is worth mentioning here. In wetlands, crops such as paddy, banana and cotton are grown. And in dry lands crops like ragi, jowar, milet and groundnut are grown. The village has both well and canal irrigation. Similarly, in Mullipadi tank, bore well and canal irrigation is used in wet areas, where banana, paddy, cotton and *'korai'* (a type of grass used to make mats) are grown. Dry land cultivation in Mullipadi concentrate on jowar, millet and groundnut crops. There are 1930 houses in these two villages, of which, 1547 are thatched houses and the remaining are terraced or tiled or pucca houses.

Information from the TWAD board suggests that the fluoride content of the water in this block is high. The location of the villages nearby the river along with the soil composition has been attributed as reason. Mullipadi is situated close to river Cauvery and the Nagayanallur is located 15 km. away from the river. The mixed characteristics are common for these two villages.

For the primary survey, samples of 120 households were chosen by taking both villages together comprising 5 per cent each of the total households. Even the analysis is done for both villages together so as to represent mixed areas. The sample households constitute 38.6 per cent of the total sample size (Table 5.2). Among the total respondents in the two villages, males 15 per cent, female 19.2, both male and female head 65.8 per cent. The average family size of the sample households is 5. The scheduled castes and schedule tribes constitute 35.8 per cent of sample and the rest are other communities. The occupations of the respondents included agricultural, private and Government employment, business (small shops) and others (self-employment). Agriculturists, agricultural labourers and landless labourers constitute the majority of the respondents (Table 5.3 & 5.4).

Nearly 52 per cent of the respondents are landless labourers and the remaining hold land between 0.8 and 5.5 acres. Bore well, tanks and canal irrigation facilities are in these villages. The average agricultural land value is Rs. 24533 at current prices. Regarding the types of houses, majority are tiled followed by thatched houses. Cement flooring is the maximum followed by soil. The average value of houses is Rs. 31,772 at current prices (Table 5.5 & 5.6).

The average monthly income of the respondents is Rs. 1,220. The annual income from agriculture worked out to Rs. 55,167. The per capita income per household per annum was less than Rs. 3,230 for 55 per cent of the respondents (Table 5.7).

5.2.1 Source of Water Supply

Historically the inhabitants of the two villages had access to traditional sources such as open wells, irrigation tanks and river. Provision during the early seventies, through various schemes like hand pumps, power pumps and CWSS have come into use (See Plate 7). About 19.2 per cent of the respondents depend upon hand pumps as the principal source for drinking water (See Plate 8). Nearly 50 per cent of the respondents depend upon stand post and 26.7 per cent on house service connection for drinking water purpose. Improved facilities witnessed in mixed villages can be attributed to CWSS. As mentioned earlier, the CWSS mainly target areas, which are dry in nature and also villages close to river Cauvery.

In regard to traditional sources 4.1 per cent of the respondents are still depending upon open well agricultural well and pump sets for drinking water. More than 50 per cent of the respondents do not use agricultural source of water for drinking at the time of agricultural activities. About 33.3 per cent of them carry water from home for drinking purpose; only 13 per cent of them consume the water available in the agricultural fields for drinking purpose (Table 5.8).

For other than drinking use, they resort to river and agricultural pump sets for bathing and washing purposes. In some cases in Mullipadi, even modern sources like stand posts are utilized for bathing and washing purposes. In the other village viz., Nagayanallur both traditional and modern sources are used for other than drinking purposes.

Certain strange observations were made in these villages with respect to water use. In Nagayanallur water from modern sources meant for domestic use, are used for agricultural activities. This practice deprives the neighbouring village from getting access to drinking water. Another shocking feature is that water facilities available in SC and ST colonies are not utilized by other communities for drinking and cooking purpose by neighbouring habitations. In other words, other than SC and ST communities are unwilling to use water from the sources existing in SC and ST colonies.

5.2.2 Demand for Water

Total requirement of water per household per day for all purposes is 368.8 litres. For drinking purpose alone per household demand is 28 litres per day, which is 7.6 per cent of the total consumption. The per capita consumption for all uses per day is 84.1 litres and for drinking and cooking purposes it is 6 litres per capita per day. The percentage of per capita drinking and cooking water consumption to per capita total consumption is 7 (Table 5.9).

For other domestic uses, 19.5 per cent goes for bathing per day, 10.5 per cent for utensil cleaning, 11 per cent for cloth washing, 3.9 per cent for house cleaning and 6.9 per cent for house entrance sprinkling, 6.9 per cent for live stock maintenance and 33.6 per cent for other uses such as gardening and ablutions (Table 5.10).

More than 80 per cent of the respondents were satisfied with the modern mission source in terms of adequacy of water for drinking and cooking purposes. And the rest of them are households with no house service connections. They are devoid of adequate water supply owing to lack of house service connections.

5.2.3 Distance and Time

On average the respondents travelled 133 metres to collect water and the maximum distance travelled is 600 meters. The distance moved by them is mainly to get access to stand posts and Ground

Level Water Reservoirs (GLWR). The GLWR are located outside the habitations (See Plate 9). The time required on an average by a household is 68 minutes for water collection. This time duration implies collection of water from the modern sources for all purposes. It is observed that drawing water from stand posts takes lesser time than collecting water from hand pumps. Understandably the water collection from the house service connection takes the least time (Table 5.9).

As mentioned earlier, Nagayanallur village Panchayat consists of 13 habitations and Mullipadi village comprises 5 habitations, out of 18 habitations, 8 habitations are yet to be provided with OHT (See Plate 10) facilities and therefore, time consumed for water collection in 8 villages is higher than the other habitations. In some cases, even where OHTs are present, the households do not prefer such sources on the ground that the OHTs are located in places where people go for open-air defecation. Consequently, the households preferred to walk certain distance to collect water from hand pumps.

5.2.4 Role of Women in Water Collection

In regard to water collectors, women always play a vital role. In these two villages, it is found that women alone constituted 98 per cent of the total water collectors and water collection by all family members constituted 1.6 per cent. Of the 98 per cent of women collectors, women head alone figured 59.2 per cent, 28.3 per cent includes daughters and school going female children, and 12.5 per cent includes, in-laws and others (Table 5.11).

There is a legacy behind collection of water by women. Generally tendency on the part of agriculturists and agricultural labourers is leaving of home by male agricultural labourers in the early hours to do agricultural work. And female labourers join male members for agricultural work late in the morning. Women are virtually left with the collection of water and cooking work etc. as part of domestic assignments besides their agricultural work.

5.2.5 Livestock Maintenance

The total number of livestock population with the sample households in 276. Of which buffaloes and cows covered 38.4 per cent and the rest of them are goat, sheep and pigs. Nearly 40 per cent of the households do not own livestock. On average 3.8 per cent of livestock is maintained per household. The average income from livestock holding is Rs. 1,230 at current prices.

Requirement of water for livestock maintenance per household per day is 25.4 litres. The per capita requirement of water per day is 10.1 litres. Dependence on other than public source of water is to the extent of 8.6 per cent and 14 per cent of public sources (TWAD, Local bodies and DRDA) and the remaining from agricultural sources (Table 5.12).

With regard to care of livestock, 29.2 per cent are by women alone, 16.7 per cent of men and 52.8 per cent of all members of family.

5.2.6 Water Quality and Health Hazards

Apparently the quality of groundwater is deplorable in Mullipadi village Panchayat. During the field survey, small size worms were witnessed in the water (See Plate 11). In this village, seepage of sewage into drinking water pipes is witnessed and there are cases of diarrhoeal deaths in the recent years (See Plate 12 & 13). More than 75 per cent of the selected households responded negatively to water borne diseases. Of the affected population, 42.8 per cent were hit by typhoid, 14.3 per cent due to cholera and 39.3 per cent due to jaundice.

Children are more vulnerable to water borne diseases. Compared to men and women, men are reported to be susceptible to water borne diseases. For treatment, majority preferred private hospitals to Government hospitals. On average in mixed villages respondents have to travel 8 km. to get access to health services. The treatment cost per household per annum has been Rs. 2766 at current prices (Table 5.13).

5.2.7 Sanitation

The percentage of population owning a toilet inside/backyard of the house is 10. And the rest of the lot does not have a latrine at home. Average expenditure of construction of latrine worked out to be Rs. 4,023 at current prices. The average requirement of water per household per day for sanitation purpose is 15 litres and the per capita use is 3 litres (Table 5.14).

Given the fact that majority use open air for defecation, and for the question posed for the absence of latrines inside the house, the respondents replied more or less similar as in wet village viz., lack of space, inadequate money, strong preference for open air, and fear of smell etc. It is observed that mostly men move longer distance for ablution than women do.

Table 5.14 : Sanitation Facilities.

Areas	*Having toilet*		*Average cost for construction of latrine*	*Water used for cleaning (in liters)*	*Per capita water used (in liters)*
	No	*Yes*			
Wet	48 [75.0]	16 [25.0]	9343	17	3.4
Mixed	107 [89.2]	13 [10.8]	4023	15	3
Dry	58 [96.7]	2 [3.3]	6000	8	1.1
Hilly region	67 [100.0]	—	NA	—	
	280 [90.0]	31 [10.0]			

Figures in parentheses are percentage of totals.

5.3 CASE STUDY III

Oothukuli village Panchayat was chosen to represent dry area in the district. This is located 55 km. away from Tiruchirappalli town and the village comes under Marungapuri block of Manapparai taluk. Oothukuli consists of 8 habitations. According to TWAD Board re-survey 1999 the village population was 3095 and the SC and ST population was 485. The total number of households was 620 of which 9.7 per cent i.e., 60 households have been chosen for the primary household survey.

Oothukuli is primarily a dry village due to poor irrigation facility and the cropping pattern. Dry crops such as *cholam, kambu* and ragi are grown in this village. Besides agricultural activities, the inhabitants are engaged in gem-cutting business and agricultural work. Rainfall being the main source of irrigation along with irrigation tanks. The ground water table is so low that bore wells and agricultural open wells are not yielding adequate water for irrigation purpose. The situation would be worse during summer season.

For each habitation, on average there are 77 households. The lpcd has been 37. The expenditure incurred on provision of water supply by all agencies is Rs. 10,19,000. The average cost per habitation worked out to be Rs. 1,27,000 at current prices. The expenditure ranged between Rs. 1.20 lakh to Rs. 7.6 lakh. The number of hand pumps in the village is 13. There is only one OHT facility in this village. There is also GWSR in this village.

The capacity of OHT is 60000 litres. And OHT facility is available in only one habitation; the remaining 7 habitations are devoid of OHT facilities. There are 18 stand posts getting distributed in one habitation. This village Panchayat has no other TWAD schemes such as CWSS, pipeline extension and house service connections (Table 5.1 & 5.2).

Of the total 60 sample households, 60 per cent comprises male respondents, 28 per cent female and 11.7 per cent both male and female. Community-wise classification showed 88 per cent is other than SC, which includes, *Ambalakarar, Chettiar, Urralikounder*, washer men, and the SC population comprises 11.7 per cent (Table 5.3).

About 83 per cent of the respondents are engaged in agricultural activities and land less labourers, 2 per cent constitutes government employees and 13 per cent in business. Some of the respondents besides their agricultural activities are engaged in gem-cutting work. The average family size of the respondents is 6. And the average number of children is higher in this village (Table 5.4).

About 18.3 per cent of the respondents do not own any land. The remaining are landholders. Average landholding is 3.5 acres per household. And land value of dry land per acre is Rs. 20,391 at current prices (Table 5.5).

In regard to housing, 15 per cent of the houses are thatched, 55 per cent being tiled, 12.8 per cent terraced, and 15 per cent of pucca houses. The percentage of thatched houses in the rural areas has been on the decline across most villages. The reason may be due to housing colonies built by the government and the loan facilities extended by the state. Types of flooring are such that 20 per cent is soil flooring and the remaining are cement and mosaic. The average value of house is Rs. 48,780 at current prices (Table 5.6).

The average income of the respondents per month is Rs. 1,344 at current prices. And the average income of the family per month is Rs. 1,569. The per capita income of the household per month is Rs. 326 (Table 5.7).

5.3.1 Sources of Water Supply

Both traditional and modern sources are available in this village. But when compared to mission sources in Oothukuli, traditional source is predominant. More than 55 per cent of the respondents depend on spring (*Oothu*)*. (See Plate 14) as principle source for drinking and cooking purposes. This village differs from other sample villages with respect to dependence on traditional source. It is due to the fact that ground table is so low, so much that respondents complained of having dug 350 feet depth to get water. The problems would be severe during summer (Table 5.8).

Despite the low ground water level, water spring is present owing to nearby rock hills. The rock formation is such that flow of water sloping towards this village and hence spring yields water for the residents in this village. The spring is of two-fold viz., *temple oothu* and *maradi oothu.*

Both types are located in pond like source. Surprisingly, the SC and ST population (socially oppressed group) are not allowed to collect water from the spring directly during rainy season.

* There is an interesting story behind the name of the village Panchayat. In olden days, kings when they went for hunting in jungles, they had looked for water source for quenching thirst. Once it so happened, the king found a dog entering a bushy field and came out drenched. The king realized that there was some water source and when probed further they found a spring (Oothu) and from then onwards this place has been called Oothukuli (Oothu means spring and Kuli means pit).

During summer, the users prepare a number of sample pits within the pond for collection of water. Other than SC and ST community people are only allowed to use the water directly and the socially oppressed group of population can gain access to water only with the help of others.

The traditional source viz. Oothu is situated 2 to 3 kms. away from the village. However, modern sources are created within the habitation. About 58.3 per cent depends upon spring source for drinking and cooking. And the rest of the proportion are depending upon hand pumps and stand posts as principle source.

For other purposes such as bathing, and washing cloths residents used agricultural well water. And for cleaning utensils, cleaning house, sprinkling entrance, boiling paddy, livestock and ablution, residents used hand pumps, and stand posts (GLWR and OHT). Respondents are not satisfied with the public distribution system due to low yielding and low level of groundwater. Vegetation is poor due to lack of water for gardening.

5.3.2 Demand for Water

The total requirement of water for all purposes per household per day is 434.2 litres. For drinking alone, the demand for water per household per day is 28 litres. In percentage terms it is 6.6. The per capita consumption of water for all purposes per day works out to be 78.6 litres and for drinking and cooking it is 4.9 litres and in percentage terms it is 6. The percentage of water consumption for drinking and cooking declined from moving from wet to mixed and dry areas. The reason being in wet areas requirement of water for other purposes could not be captured as respondents resorted to direct spots such as river, agricultural pump sets for use. While in dry areas water use for other purposes could be gauged as the respondents bring home the water for use of all purposes (Table 5.9).

Regarding the break-up details of percentage of water used per day for different domestic purposes, for bathing it is 14.4, for utensil cleaning 10.4, for washing clothes 11.5, for house cleaning 5.1, for sprinkling house entrance 6.5, for livestock 12.4 and the rest goes for personal hygiene and paddy boiling etc. (Table 5.10)

5.3.3 Distance and Time

On average the respondents travelled 1332 metres to collect water for all purposes. The maximum distance recorded during field survey is 2.1 km. Distance travelled by the respondents in a dry village like Oothukuli is higher when compared to wet and mixed areas. The reason is scarcity of water in dry village. Even within the village, there is difference in distance to be moved to collect water, as closer the spring shorter the distance and *vice versa* (Table 5.9) and (See Plate 15).

Similar to traditional source, even for modern source, such as, hand pumps, the residents have to trek long distances. The reason is in dry villages hand pump sources can be located only in places where there is water resource.

Time spent for water collection in this village is 3.81 hours per household per day. The range is minimum of 1 hour to a maximum of 6 hours. Time duration is inclusive of waiting and filling time.

5.3.4 Role of women

Female participation in collection of water is significant in this village. About 83 per cent of women are engaged in this process (See Plate 16). Male comprise just 5 per cent. And 11.7 per cent of all members of family are involved in water collection.

It is equally important to discern the persons who help in water collection. For instance, in this village female children constituted 55 per cent in assisting water collection, 18.3 per cent of other family members and 26.7 per cent of female head alone collect water without any help from other family members (Table 5.11).

An interesting feature in this village is observed. That is, female children go to springs and slowly fill the pots and make them ready for carrying home. School going children, girl children in particular are engaged in this practice. School children are pressed into this job mainly to reduce the waiting time (See Plate 17). Detailed discussion on female participation, girl children in particular and associated environmental degradation are included under environmental dimensions of rural water supply in the later part of this chapter. It is heartening to notice females also collecting water even during night hours in this village (See Plate 18).

5.3.5 Livestock Maintenance

The total number of livestock holding by the sample households is 221. Nearly 70 per cent of respondents do own livestock. The composition of livestock is that 44.8 per cent of goat and sheep and 55.2 per cent of cow and bull. The average income from livestock per annum is Rs. 530 at current prices. The per capita consumption of water by livestock is 13.9 per day.

Dependence on traditional sources such as ponds, and tanks during summer for livestock maintenance is nil. Water drawn from hand pumps for livestock constitutes 76.2 per cent and 19 per cent of stand posts during summer.

The number of times the animals consume water varied between mixed villages. In a dry village like Oothukuli, the number of times the livestock's are fed with water is higher. In regard to up keeping of livestock, 26.1 per cent of women, and 38 per cent of men and 35.7 per cent of all members of family are engaged in the maintenance of livestock population (Table 5.12).

5.3.6 Water Quality and Health

Water quality during rainy season causes concern in this village. As water level in ponds gets increased on par with paddy fields. Respondents complained about the quality of water drawn from hand pumps. According to them the water drawn from hand pump is saline and tasteless and smells iron sometimes. In fact, they resorted to spring sources of water for drinking and cooking purposes mainly to avoid salt water and iron smell of water.

About 66.7 per cent of the respondents expressed that water-borne diseases have not affected them. The rest of them have complained about diseases such as diarrhoea, jaundice and typhoid. Children are more (45 per cent) affected, followed by male to the extent of 30 per cent and female by to the extent of 25 per cent. The treatment cost per annum towards water borne diseases is Rs. 2,330 at current prices. They travel a distance of 20 km. on average to have access to public health care (Table 5.13).

5.3.7 Sanitation

Sanitation facilities are equally deplorable in this village too. Nearly 96 per cent of the respondents do not have latrine within the premise. This implies that majority use open-air for defecation and a few use septic tanks.

Water required for personal hygiene works at to be one litre. Men move a distance of 580 metres on average and women move about 370 metres away from home for defecation purpose. As mentioned in other cases, male respondents used water available near by the open-air ground, while women return home for use of water for personal hygiene. The sources of water for personal hygiene are hand pumps and stand posts (Table 5.14).

5.4 CASE STUDY IV

Thenpuranadu, another village Panchayat, situated in a hilly region, is chosen as one of the sample villages. This is located in Thuraiyur taluk and Uppiliyapuram block of Tiruchirappalli district. This village Panchayat is chosen for two reasons. The first reason being concentration of scheduled caste and scheduled tribe population and the second reason is location of this Panchayat on a hill, 900 metres above the mean sea level. This is a reserved assembly constituency, situated 75 km. away from Tiruchirappalli town. There are about 16 habitations coming under this Panchayat.

As per the TWAD re-survey 1999 the village population was 7130. Of the total, 98 per cent belongs to SC and ST population. The lpcd was 31. Investments made towards water supply were Rs. 11.4 lakhs. There are 31 hand pump schemes, 4 OHTs, which includes 2 OHTs and 2 GLWSR. The total capacity of OHT is 70,000 liters, and there are 29 stand posts (See Plate 19) attached to it (Table 5.1).

Agricultural activities are carried out with the help of stream and well irrigation. Traditionally *jowar,* millet and *ragi* were cultivated in this village. But currently, at the time of field survey, it is observed that farmers cultivate more of commercial crops like *tapioca* and *fruits*. Cultivation of commercial crops brought in a remarkable change in the living standard of the farmers in the hilly region.

It is worth mentioning that farmers in this village are hardworking and dedicate themselves for agricultural activities. Another fact about agriculture in this village is that lands have not been transacted for the past several years. Joint family system is one of the reasons for absence of land transaction in this village.

A sample of 67 households is chosen in this village for primary survey, which comprises 10 per cent of the total households in the village Panchayat. Male constitutes 85.1 per cent of respondents, female 7.5 per cent and both male female 7.5 per cent. All the respondents belong to scheduled tribes (Tables 5.2 & 5.3).

About 80.6 per cent of the respondents depend on agriculture activities, 4.5 per cent employed in government service and 14.5 per cent in other activities, including agricultural activities. The landless labourers in the village are the least when compared with other sample villages. More than 90 per cent of the respondents are landholders. On average the respondents own 3.4 acres (Tables 5.4 & 5.5).

Regarding the type of houses, 11.9 per cent of houses fall under tiled, 4.5 per cent of terraced, 38.8 per cent of other categories, which include government-housing colonies. In regard to flooring, 58 per cent comes under soil, 37 per cent of cement flooring and 4.5 per cent of other categories. The value of house, at the time of field survey, is Rs. 23,948 (Table 5.6).

The average family size of the respondents is 5. The average income of the respondents per month is Rs. 916 at current prices and the average income of the household is Rs. 2,582 per month. The per capita income per month is Rs. 532. Households engaged in agriculture earned Rs. 19,435 per annum (Table 5.7).

5.4.1 Sources of Water

Both traditional and modern sources are in vogue in this village. Modern sources albeit are difficult to be installed in hill region like Thenpuranadu. Yielding capacity of hand pumps is low and as a result the modern source is less significant in this village. About 83.5 per cent of the respondents drew water from shallow open well (Plate 20) and of which, 64 per cent received water through modern distribution system from open well, 5.9 per cent depends on hand pumps. Further 36 per cent of respondents got water through manual lifting from hand pumps, open well, *'kudavu'* and streams (Table 5.8) and (See Plate 21).

Lakshmanapuram, one of the habitations in the village Panchayat does not have even a single modern source. This is a testimony that the state agency is yet to cover villages to provide at least a single source. Nearly 30 per cent of the respondents used agricultural wells for water for drinking. About 63 per cent carried water from home to the work place for drinking purpose.

5.4.2 Demand for Water

The demand for water per household for all domestic uses per day works out to be 246 litres, with a range of 97 to 521 litres. For drinking and cooking purposes the requirement per household per day is 26 liters and in percentage terms it is 10.6 to the total water requirement. The per capita consumption per day for all domestic purposes is 56.4 liters and for drinking and cooking purposes it is 5.8 litres and it works out to be 10 per cent of the total (Table 5.9).

Break up details of domestic use of water is worth mentioning. About 26 per cent of total water required is used for bathing, 13.2 per cent for utensil cleaning, 2.5 per cent for washing clothes, 2.1 per cent for house cleaning, 4 per cent for livestock maintenance, 6.4 per cent for sprinkling entrance and the remaining 45 per cent for other purposes, which include paddy boiling, ablutions and gardening (Table 5.10). The proportion of water used for house cleaning, livestock and washing clothes has been low because of the availability of substitute sources. In particular, water consumption by livestock is lower compared to wet and mixed villages. The reason is the location of cattle shed nearby the agricultural field.

5.4.3 Distance and Time

On average the distance travelled to fetch water from traditional sources is 219 metres, with a maximum of 900 metres. Traditional sources such as *kudavu* and open well are located downstream, while the inhabitants live mostly upstream. Hence, the distance trek to fetch water in hilly region is high when compared to wet village. The nature of landscape has a bearing on the quality of water as human wastes upstream gets carried downstream during rainy season and affect the quality of water (Table 5.10). The time required for fetching water from the traditional and mission sources is one hour and twenty minutes on average. Depending upon the type of traditional sources the time consumed varied among the respondents.

5.4.4 Role of Women

In this village women alone do the water collection. Of the total women collectors, 67 per cent constitutes female head of households, and the rest comprises daughter and daughter-in-law. It has been the traditional practice in this village that women bring water for domestic use (Table 5.11). The role played by women is significant not only with respect to fetching of water but also in community participation and participating in organized protest etc. for assured water supply.

5.4.5 Livestock Maintenance

The total number of livestock maintained by the respondents is 165. Of which, 67 per cent is cow and bull, 34 per cent of goat, sheep and pigs. The bull population is higher in this village mainly for ploughing purposes as mechanized ploughing is difficult in hill regions.

Nearly 60 per cent of the respondents own livestock and the income from livestock is Rs. 6,204 per annum per household. Water required for maintenance per cattle is 4.4 litres. Traditional source is a dominant source of water for livestock maintenance in the village situated in a hill region. The number of times the cattle is fed with water is once by 75 per cent of the respondents and the rest provide two times a day. In regard to livestock care, women comprise 52.5 per cent, 40 per cent of men and the rest by all members (Table 5.12).

5.4.6 Water Quality and Health

During rainy season, quality of water downstream in the village is poor. The water gets contaminated as the flow of water carries human excreta and other filth in the drain upstream. *Kudavu*, the traditional surface source is exposed to pollutants and mainly the drainage water flowing from upstream. The surroundings of the water schemes are deplorable, which pose a great threat to human health in this village (See Plate 22).

About 60 per cent of the respondents are reportedly unaffected by water-borne diseases. The rest of them are victims of water-borne health problems. Among the victims, 59 per cent being hit by typhoid, 15 per cent of cholera and jaundice and the rest are affected by diarrhoea. Gender-wise, women are affected more than men followed by children. Seventy-four per cent of the victims approached private hospitals for treatment and the rest of them resorted to government hospitals. On average they travel 24 kms. to reach hospitals for treatment. They spent about Rs. 1,958 per annum towards medical expenses (Table 5.13).

5.4.7 Sanitation

Invariably all the respondents use open air for defecation. The distance moved from home by male to the open site is 416 metres and female 278 metres. The quantity of water per head per day for personal hygiene is 3.6 liters. The source of water for this purpose is stand posts to the extent of 60 per cent, 5 per cent uses hand pumps and the rest use the sources available nearby the defecation site (Table 5.14).

The fact remains that there are latrines available (Government built housing colonies) in this village, but those latrines were seldom used. Surprisingly most of the latrines located within the houses were converted into either as kitchen or storeroom (See Plate 23). The reasons for not constructing lavatories are lack of money and space, and unwillingness for a latrine inside the house.

5.5 Seasonal Variations in Access to Water for Drinking and Cooking Purposes

The general notion of water scarcity during summer period and relative water abundance during rainy season can be verified with the help of seasonal variations in consumption of water among selected households. Excepting dry village, in all other categories the mean values of litre per day per household showed a difference on the lower side between summer and non-summer periods. It can be inferred that water scarcity *per se* prevailed in dry village when compared to other categories. The field observations made by the authors also confirmed this view. An interesting observation is that in wet, mixed and hilly regions the availability of supplementary sources facilitated the households a direct accesses and use. While the dry village has been less endowed with supplementary sources and hence the mean of consumption in non-summer months showed a relatively lower values for wet, mixed and hilly regions (Table 5.15).

Table 5.15 : Seasonal variation.

(Litre per day per household)

Consumption of water	*Drinking and Cooking*	
	May to October	*November to April*
Wet		
Mean	36	33
Range	10-72	5-120
S.D	16	24
N	64	64
Mixed		
Mean	28	26
Range	6-60	5-90
S.D	11	15
N	120	120
Dry		
Mean	28	32
Range	6-65	10-120
S.D	12	20
N	60	60
Hilly region		
Mean	26	20
Range	8-60	8-72
S.D	11	12
N	67	67

N: Sample size.

5.6 Source, Usage and Consumption by Area

The respondents do not depend solely upon single scheme for all uses for various purposes. The data set out in Table 5.16 showed lots of variations across regions in this regard. Although the state norms primarily aimed at providing water to cater to all the domestic needs such as cooking, drinking, bathing, cloth washing and utensil cleaning and other uses, but the actual usage is the other way around. In wet village as many as 48 per cent of the respondents resorted to public modern as principal source for cooking and drinking. In addition, in the same wet village, nearly 44 per cent, respondents depend upon the modern schemes installed by themselves privately for cooking and drinking purposes. For other purposes such as bathing and washing etc., the respondents in the wet village resorted again to own modern schemes. It may be recalled here the higher concentration of modern schemes promoted by the state in wet villages, in the foregoing chapter. Hence, the per capita consumption in wet village is bound to be higher than the other category.

The mixed region (wet and dry) displayed a different picture. The modern public schemes provided water for all the domestic purposes in this category of villages. More than 90 per cent of the respondents depended upon the above said modern public schemes for drinking and cooking purposes. Even for other uses, about 76 per cent of the respondents relied upon the same modern public schemes. This is due to the combined water supply, a scheme, which came in a big way in these study villages. In dry village, the observation was made during summer season. The traditional schemes remained a major source for drinking and cooking purposes to about 60 per cent of the respondents. On the other hand, the respondents depend largely on modern schemes for other domestic purposes such as bathing and washing. However, the quantity received for other purposes was less, owing to culture* of the respondents in dry area.

---

* Normally the people in dry area take both once in a week, as observed during the field visit. Even the number of times they collect is relatively lower than the other categories of villages.

Table 5.16 : Matrix between source, usage and consumption by area.

Usage	*Drinking and Cooking*						*Bathing*						*Cloth Washing*						*Utensils Cleaning*					
Consumption	*OTS*	*OMS*	*PMS*	*PTS*	*PS*	*%*	*OTS*	*OMS*	*PMS*	*PTS*	*PS*	*%*	*OTS*	*OMS*	*PMS*	*PTS*	*PS*	*%*	*OTS*	*OMS*	*PMS*	*PTS*	*PS*	*%*
Wet 0	-	-	-	-	-	-	1	-	1	8	5	23.4	-	-	1	6	6	20.3	-	-	-	-	1	1.6
1 to 20	-	12	2	-	2	25	-	-	-	-	-	-	-	2	5	-	-	10.9	-	7	3	-	1	17.2
21 to 40	-	10	13	-	3	40	-	4	1	-	-	7.8	-	8	3	-	-	17.2	-	8	16	-	1	39.1
41 to 60	-	6	15	-	-	32	-	1	1	1	-	4.7	-	3	3	-	-	9.4	-	15	5	-	-	31.3
61 to 80	-	-	1	-	-	1.6	-	2	1	-	-	4.7	-	3	-	-	-	4.7	-	1	1	-	-	3.1
81 and above	-	-	-	-	-	-	1	22	13	2	-	59.4	1	16	7	-	-	37.5	-	3	2	-	-	7.8
N	-	28	31	-	5	64	2	29	17	11	5	64	1	32	19	6	6	64	-	34	27	-	3	64
%	-	43.8	48.4	-	7.8	100	3.1	45.3	26.6	17.2	7.8	100	1.6	50.0	29.7	9.4	9.4	100	-	53.1	42.2	-	4.7	100
Mixed 0	-	-	-	-	-	-	5	-	-	19	10	28.3	5	-	-	22	13	33.3	-	-	-	-	-	-
1 to 20	1	-	42	-	1	36.7	-	-	-	-	-	-	-	-	12	-	1	10.8	1	-	34	1	1	30.0
21 to 40	-	-	59	1	4	53.3	-	-	2	-	-	1.7	1	-	10	1	2	11.7	4	1	46	2	-	45.5
41 to 60	1	-	11	-	-	10.0	-	-	15	1	1	14.2	-	-	15	1	1	14.2	-	-	24	1	-	20.8
61 to 80	-	-	-	-	-	-	1	1	11	1	-	11.7	-	1	7	-	-	6.7	-	-	2	-	-	1.7
81 and above	-	-	-	-	-	-	3	-	45	1	4	44.2	3	-	21	1	3	23.3	-	-	1	1	1	2.5
N	2	-	112	1	5	120	9	1	73	22	15	120	9	1	65	25	20	120	5	1	107	5	2	120
%	1.7	-	93.3	0.8	4.2	100	7.5	0.8	60.8	18.3	12.5	100	7.5	0.8	54.2	20.8	16.7	100	4.2	0.8	89.2	4.5	1.7	100
Dry 0	-	-	-	-	-	-	1	-	1	5	18	41.7	1	-	-	3	14	30.0	-	-	-	-	-	-
1 to 20	-	1	4	13	-	30.0	-	-	3	-	1	6.7	-	-	8	-	1	15.0	-	-	11	-	-	18.3
21 to 40	1	-	13	18	1	55.0	-	-	5	-	-	8.3	1	-	8	-	-	15.0	1	1	24	1	1	46.7
41 to 60	-	-	4	4	-	13.3	-	-	1	-	-	1.7	-	-	6	-	-	10.0	-	-	14	1	-	25.0
61 to 80	-	-	-	1	-	1.7	1	-	23	1	-	41.7	-	-	16	1	1	30.0	-	-	2	-	-	3.3
81 and above	-	-	-	-	-	-	-	-	-	-	-	-	-	-	-	-	-	-	-	-	4	-	-	6.7
N	1	1	21	36	1	60	2	-	33	6	19	60	2	-	38	4	16	60	1	1	55	2	1	60
%	1.7	1.7	35.0	60.0	1.7	100	3.3	-	55.0	10.0	31.7	100	3.3	-	63.3	6.7	26.7	100	1.7	1.7	91.7	3.3	1.7	100
Hilly 0	-	-	-	-	-	-	-	-	2	1	-	4.5	3	-	-	44	5	77.6	-	-	-	-	-	-
1 to 20	-	-	20	9	-	43.3	-	-	3	-	-	4.5	-	-	4	1	-	7.5	-	-	17	5	-	52.8
21 to 40	-	-	23	10	-	49.3	-	-	11	3	-	20.9	-	-	3	2	1	9.0	-	-	30	8	-	56.7
41 to 60	-	-	3	2	-	7.5	-	-	13	7	-	29.9	-	-	1	1	-	3.0	-	-	2	2	-	6.0
61 to 80	-	-	-	-	-	-	-	-	9	1	-	14.9	-	-	1	1	-	3.0	-	-	2	-	-	3.0
81 and above	-	-	-	-	-	-	-	-	12	5	-	25.4	-	-	-	-	-	-	-	-	-	1	-	1.5
N	-	-	46	21	-	67	-	-	58	17	-	67	3	-	9	49	6	67	-	-	51	16	-	67
%	-	-	68.7	31.3	-	100	-	-	74.6	25.4	-	100	4.5	-	13.4	73.1	9.0	100	-	-	76.1	23.9	-	100

OTS : Own Additional Source, OMS : Own Modern Source, PMS : Public Modern Source, PTS : Public Traditional Source, PS : Private Source, N : Number, % = percentage to the total.

(Contd. Table)

(Contd. ...)

Usage	House Cleaning						Ablution						Sprinkling at Entrance						Livestock					
Consumption	OTS	OMS	PMS	PTS	PS	%	OTS	OMS	PMS	PTS	PS	%	OTS	OMS	PMS	PTS	PS	%	OTS	OMS	PMS	PTS	PS	%
Wet 0	-	5	-	-	-	7.8	(10)-	2	-	-	-	18.8	-	-	-	-	-	-	(37)-	-	-	-	-	58.7
1 to 20	-	24	23	-	2	76.6	-	17	9	-	-	40.6	-	16	11	1	-	43.8	1	17	3	-	-	33.3
21 to 40	-	4	3	-	-	10.9	1	15	9	-	-	39.1	-	13	13	1	-	42.2	-	2	1	-	-	4.8
41 to 60	-	1	2	-	-	4.7	-	1	-	-	-	1.6	-	8	1	-	-	14.1	-	2	-	-	-	3.2
61 to 80	-	-	-	-	-	-	-	-	-	-	-	-	-	-	-	-	-	-	-	-	-	-	-	-
81 and above	-	-	-	-	-	-	-	-	-	-	-	-	-	-	-	-	-	-	-	-	-	-	-	-
N	-	34	28	-	2	64	1	35	18	-	-	64	-	37	25	2	-	64	38	21	4	-	-	64
%	-	53.1	43.8	-	3.1	100	1.6	54.7	28.1	-	-	100	-	57.8	39.1	3.1	-	100	60.3	33.3	6.3	-	-	100
Wet & Dry 0	-	1	3	-	-	3.4	(2)-	-	-	-	-	(2)1.7	-	-	-	-	-	-	(47)-	1	-	-	-	40.3
1 to 20	-	-	84	3	2	76.1	1	12	34	1	-	40.0	3	-	74	2	-	65.8	2	33	21	1	2	49.6
21 to 40	4	-	14	-	-	15.4	1	10	28	-	-	32.5	-	1	28	-	-	24.2	-	5	5	-	-	8.4
41 to 60	-	-	4	-	-	3.4	2	3	17	-	2	20.0	-	-	5	2	1	6.7	-	-	-	1	1	1.7
61 to 80	-	-	-	-	-	0.9	-	1	2	-	-	2.5	-	-	3	-	-	2.5	-	-	-	-	-	-
81 and above	1	-	-	-	-	0.9	-	-	3	-	1	3.3	-	-	1	-	-	0.8	-	-	-	-	-	-
N	5	1	106	3	2	117	4	26	84	1	3	120	3	1	111	4	4	120	49	39	26	2	3	119
%	4.3	0.9	90.6	2.6	1.7	100	3.3	21.7	70.0	0.8	2.5	100	2.5	0.8	92.5	3.3	0.8	100	41.2	32.8	21.8	1.7	2.5	100
Dry 0	-	-	-	-	-	-	(2)-	-	-	-	-	3.3	-	-	-	-	-	-	(17)-	-	1	-	-	30.0
1 to 20	1	1	38	-	1	69.5	1	-	10	-	1	20.0	-	16	17	-	-	55	-	14	4	1	1	31.7
21 to 40	-	-	14	-	-	23.7	-	-	25	-	-	41.7	1	4	17	-	1	38.3	1	13	4	-	-	30.0
41 to 60	-	-	2	-	-	3.4	-	-	15	-	-	25	-	-	1	-	-	1.7	-	3	-	-	-	5
61 to 80	-	-	1	-	-	1.7	-	-	3	-	-	5	-	1	-	-	-	1.7	-	1	-	-	-	1.7
81 and above	-	-	1	-	-	1.7	-	-	3	-	-	5	-	-	2	-	-	3.3	-	1	-	-	-	1.7
N	1	1	56	-	1	59	1	-	56	-	1	60	1	21	37	-	1	60	18	32	9	1	1	60
%	1.7	1.7	94.9	-	1.7	100	3.3	-	93.3	-	1.7	100	1.7	35.0	61.7	-	1.7	100	30.0	53.3	15	1.7	1.7	100
Hilly 0	-	-	2	-	-	3.1	(2)-	-	-	-	-	3.0	-	-	-	-	-	-	(26)-	-	-	1	1	75.8
1 to 20	-	-	53	8	-	93.8	-	-	38	8	-	68.7	-	-	53	7	-	89.6	1	-	3	-	-	21.2
21 to 40	-	-	-	2	-	3.1	-	-	15	2	-	25.4	-	-	4	-	-	6.0	-	-	-	-	-	3.0
41 to 60	-	-	-	-	-	-	-	-	2	-	-	30	-	-	1	1	-	3.0	-	-	-	-	-	-
61 to 80	-	-	-	-	-	-	-	-	-	-	-	-	-	-	-	-	-	1.5	-	-	-	-	-	-
81 and above	-	-	-	-	-	-	-	-	-	-	-	-	-	-	-	-	-	-	-	-	-	-	-	-
N	-	-	55	10	-	65	2	-	55	10	-	67	-	-	58	9	-	67	27	-	3	1	1	66
%-	-	-	84.6	15.4	-	100	3.3	-	82.1	14.9	-	100	-	-	86.6	13.4	-	100	40.9	-	4.5	1.5	1.5	100

OTS : Own Additional Source, OMS : Own Modern Source, PMS : Public Modern Source, PTS : Public Traditional Source, PS : Private Source, N : Number, % = percentage to the total.

The hilly regions displayed a peculiar scene nearly one-third of respondents used traditional schemes for drinking and cooking, the rest of them received traditional source of water through modern distribution system for the same. For other purposes, particularly for washing cloth they utilized the small stream water, the rest of the purpose were served by water from the modern distribution systems.

5.6.1 Hypothesis Testing-II

The per capita consumption of water is a crucial policy variable. Modern scheme promoted by state agencies, aim at achieving maximum results in terms of coverage targeted villages but still the uncertainty prevails over the question of provision of water for domestic use in general and for cooking and drinking in particular. In other words, whether or not all the regions received potable water for drinking and working purposes in equal proportion. Therefore, it may be necessary to test this hypothetical situation to ascertain the distribution across the selected villages. Here, for this purpose, two groups are classified with wet and mixed as one group and dry and hilly region as the other.

5.6.2 Null Hypothesis

There is no significant difference between the stated two groups with respect to per capita consumption for cooking and drinking purposes.

5.6.3 Alternative Hypothesis

There is significant difference between the stated two groups with respect to per capita consumption for cooking and drinking purposes.

The 't' test results confirmed that the null hypothesis gets rejected. This implies per capita consumption of water in wet and mixed region is higher than the dry and hilly region. The mean difference showed 7 litres for the first category and 5 for the next category, statistically significant at 5 per cent level. The reason for this is interesting. Modern schemes facilitated higher physical water sources in wet and mixed region and relatively less in the other category. In addition, the yielding capacity of water is greater in wet and mixed region, while the yielding capacity of water is deplorably low in dry and hilly region (Table 5.17).

Table 5.17 : 't'-test results – Per capita consumption of water.

't'-tests for independent samples of ZONE Zone-wise				
Variable	Number of Cases	Mean	SD	SE of Mean
PERCONSU Per capita consumption of water				
Wet & Mixed region	184	6.7157	2.673	.197
Dry & Hilly	127	5.3384	1.939	.172

Mean Difference = 1.3773

Leven's Test for Equality of Variances : F=14.905 P = .000

't'-test for Equality of Means					
Variances	t-value	df.	2-Tail Sig.	SE of Diff.	95% CI for Diff.
Equal	4.97	309	.000	.277	(.832, 1.923)
Unequal	5.26	308.21	.000	.262	(.862, 1.892)

5.7 Regression Results – Household Demand

Theoretically a large number of variables are at force in determining the quantity of water consumed for all domestic purposes. The list includes family size, value of house, total landholdings, irrigated land, average income, agricultural income, female education, occupation, principal source, distance and time. It may not be necessary that all the variables shall have its influence in all the regions uniformly. A certain set of variable may be dominant in same regions, while certain other is more influencing in other regions. This can be an hypothetical situation as to which type of variable exerts its influence significantly as a determinant factor is a matter to be taken for hypotheses testing.

5.7.1 Hypothesis – III

The family size, landholding, per capita income, female head education, occupation, house value, area (wet, mixed, dry and hill), cooking trip per day, distance and time are the key determinants of consumption of water.

At the house hold level, twelve variables have been identified, which include area as a dummy variable for area were numbered as 1, 2, 3 and 4 for wet, mixed, dry and hilly region respectively. The other independent variables included family size, value of house, total landholdings, irrigated land, average income, agricultural income, female education, occupation, principal source, distance and time. Correlation matrices were applied to understand and shortlist the number of variables, which influence the per capita water consumption at the household level. Of the twelve variable, area, family size, value of house, cooking per day, female education and occupation were chosen (i.e.) were considered for running the regression against per day water consumption per households as these variable exhibit a high percentage of correlation.

$$Y = f(X_1+X_2+X_3+X_4) + U_i$$

Where,

Y: Average consumption water per household per day

X_1 = Area (dummy variable: Wet, mixed, dry and hilly regions)

X_2 = family size

X_3 = Present value of House and Plot

X_4 = Number of times cooking per day

U_i = Error term

The regression analysis brings forth the following results. Factors like area, family size, cooking per day and value of house turned out to be significant ($P < 0.05$). The R square value turns at to be 0.211. This shows that 21 per cent of the variations are explained by the variations in the independent variables. Here, area has been used as a dummy variable in order to capture the variations among the rural region (Table 5.18).

Table 5.18 : Regression Results – Household Demand.

Variable	*Coefficient*	*T statistic*
X_1: Area	-7.266677*	-3.238
X_2: Familsize	-6.537346 *	-6.020
X_3: Prevalue	1.51476E-04*	4.091
X_4: Cookperd	17.324082*	3.376
(Constant)	**86.937886**	**7.187**
R Square	**.21182**	
N	311	

* Significant at 5 per cent level.

To understand the implications of the results a detailed discussion is necessary. In the case of area, as indicated in the methodology, four categories were made, such as wet, mixed, dry and hill region. Negative value of coefficient was found with area factor. This implies that per capita consumption goes on declining in wet, to mixed, dry and hill region. This negative trend is due to high level of per capita consumption in wet area, slightly lower in mixed area, further low level in dry area and the lowest in the hilly region. The secondary source of information from the TWAD Board also supported this view. Even the availability of sources such as the number of power pumps, hand pumps, and house service connections also varied in this order across four categories. Besides, the field survey witnessed more number of own/private sources in wet regions where compared to other categories.

Another crucial factor, which is inversely related to water consumption, was the family size. As family size increases the resultant total consumption goes up but the per capita consumption comes down. This is due to water requirement for other domestic uses, which does not vary regardless of the number of persons in a household. For instance, water used for cooking, house cleaning, upkeep of livestock, washing cloths and bathing may not increase commensurately with the increase in family size. Earlier study on this aspect by Reddy (1999) lends support to this view. Further for bathing and washing cloths some of the respondents use sources other than public services. This relationship pertains to the quantity of water collected for the domestic use. However the quantum of water used for activities like bathing, washing cloths, and cattle could not be quantified at source points like river, pond, canals and stream.

The variable, cooking per day, which refers to the number of times water is used for cooking at the household level, has come out positive and statistically significant. The positive sign explains that the increase in frequency of cooking per day leads to increase in water consumption. During the field survey it was observed that in wet villages 64 per cent of the sample households cooked twice a day and 22 per cent used water thrice a day for cooking. In dry villages this frequency was less and in hilly region 91 per cent of the households cooked twice a day. In mixed village, 85 per cent of the households cooked twice a day.

Informal discussion with the households revealed certain facts about their pattern of cooking. Households expressed that due to water quality, the food (rice) prepared out of this water not lasts for more than 8 hours and, hence, they increased the frequency of cooking per day. Besides, the rice obtained from ration shops also does not stay for longer hours if cooked once a day. Therefore, they had to cook more than once a day.

The present value of house as a variable came out positive and significant at 5 per cent level. This implies that higher the value of house, greater the level of consumption of water. Being an economic indicator, this variable was correlated with average income of respondents and due to multicollinearity problem; the income variable has been dropped from the regression analysis.

The positive relationship between the average consumption of water for domestic purpose and the present value of house established the fact that wherever house value was higher, the water consumption also was greater. However, it can never be generalised that consumption of water increases along with increase in present value of house.

5.8 Factors Affecting Willingness to Pay

An earnest attempt is made to find out the willingness to pay (WTP) by the households towards sustainable water supply in all the study villages. As part of questionnaire, questions relating to WTP were included. The questions posed mainly with the focus to elicit information on willingness to pay for additional quantity and for good quality of water provision.

Athikudi : Willingness to pay for house service connection per household per month is Rs. 5. And for the water quality improvement the respondents expressed their willingness to pay an average of Rs. 4 per month per households.

Nagayanallur and Mullipadi : On average, the willingness to pay for improved quality of water by the respondents per household per month is Re. 1, whereas, is Rs. 5 for increased quantity of water. Among the total respondents 73.3 per cent of them expressed willingness to pay for additional water provision, extension of distribution time and house service connection. And the rest of them are unwilling to pay any money for provision of water.

Otthukuli : The willingness to pay for improved water supply is higher in this village when compared to other sample villages. On average per household the willingness to pay is Rs. 9 per month for improved water supply, additional supply of water and house service connection. And for improved quality of water the respondents are willing to pay Re. 1 per month per household.

Thenpuranadu : About 85 per cent of the respondents are willing to pay for improved water supply per household per month. For additional water supply the willingness to pay per household per month is Rs. 7 and for the quality improvement it is Rs. 3 (Table 5.19).

Table 5.19 : Willingness to pay for improved rural water supply

Areas	*Ready to pay*		*Amount per month per household*	
	Yes	*No*	*Time extension HSCs*	*Quality*
Wet	34 [53.1]	30 [46.9]	5	4
Mixed	88 [73.3]	32 [26.7]	5	1
Dry	57 [95.0]	3 [5.0]	9	1
Hill	57 [85.1]	10 [14.9]	7	3
	236 [75.9]	75 [24.1]	6	2

Figures in parentheses are percentage of totals.

Regression analysis is used to understand the factors influenceing WTP. The dependent variable in this case is willingness to pay for improved quantity and quality per month per household (WTP_{QQ}). While the independent variables included Area (wet, mixed, dry and hilly as a dummy variable), total land (farm size in hectare), family size, water collection time, distance travelled, household annual income the social status, (1 for SC & ST and 2 for others) and present value of house (Table 5.20).

Table 5.20 : Regression Results – Willingness to Pay.

Variable	*Coefficient*	*T statistic*
$AREA_{1 to 4}$	0.326651	0.130
TOTLAND	3.047671*	4.284
FAMSIZE	0.888548*	0.836
WTCOTIME	6.998567	1.830
DISTRAVE	0.006042	1.165
TOINCOH	0.001136	1.220
SSCAST	10.591693*	2.144
(Constant)	-15.394569	-1.200
R Square	0.16971	

* Significant at 5 per cent level.

$$Y = f(X_1+X_2+X_3 + X_4 + X_5\ X_6 + X_7) + U_i$$

Where,

Y: WTP_{QQ}: Willingness to pay for improved quantity and quality of water.

Independent Variable:

$X_1 = AREA_{1 to 4}$	Dummy Variable (Wet, Mixed, Dry and Hilly)
X_2 = TOTLAND	Household total land (Firm Size in hectare)
X_3 = FAMSIZE	Family Size
X_4 = WTCOTIME	Water Collection Time
X_5 = DISTRAVE	Distance Travelled
X_6 = TOINCOH	Household Income (annual)
X_7 = SSCOMM	Social Status (1- SC/ST and 2 - Other Community)
U_i = Error term	ands

Of the eight variables, only three variables turned out to be statistically significant and positive, they include water collection time, social status and farm size. The implications are interesting. As water collection time increases, the WTP also increases across all the households. In regard to social status variable, the households belonging to backward castes are willing to pay higher amount than the schedule caste households are. Regarding farm size, larger the agricultural landholding, the higher will be the WTP.

The other variables such as area, distance travelled, family size and household income were not statistically significant in relation to WTP. However, these four independent variables were positively correlated with WTP.

5.9 Source/Health Matrix

The preparation of source-use matrix (Table 5.21) based on primary survey information is useful in understanding the health implication owing to consumption of water through traditional and modern sources. As stated earlier, more than 50 per cent of the respondents replied negatively to queries relating to health impact of unsafe water. In the wet village, the incidence of water-borne diseases such as typhoid, cholera and jaundice were high where the modern sources have been predominant.

In the mixed villages, the incidence of water-borne diseases was lower compared to other category of villages. Can this be attributed to the house service connections? The number of house service connection has been very high in these villages when compared to other categories.

In dry village the dependence on traditional source is high, particularly for drinking and cooking purposes. Jaundice has been the major water-borne diseases being reported. While in the hilly region, the incidence of water–borne diseases was higher when compared to wet, mixed and dry villages. The predominant source of water for drinking and cooking has been traditional.

The water-borne diseases caused by the use of modern sources are relatively lower than the use of traditional sources. In terms of percentage, the former worked out to be 28.6 and the traditional sources caused nearly 38.9 per cent. It may be worth mentioning that modern/mission sources supplied by the state are safer (as claimed to be) when compared to the traditional sources.

Table 5.21 : Source and Diseases Matrix– Area wise

Diseases	*Sources*		
	Modern	*Traditional*	*Percentage to the total*
Wet			
Not affected	39 (60.9)	—	60.9
Typhoid	10 (15.6)	—	15.6
Cholera & Diarrhoea	3 (4.7)	—	4.7
Jaundice	12 (18.8)	—	18.8
Mixed			
Not affected	90 (75.0)	2 (1.7)	76.7
Typhoid	11 (9.2)	1 (0.83)	10.0
Cholera & Diarrhoea	5 (4.2)	—	4.1
Jaundice	11 (9.2)	—	9.2
Dry			
Not affected	15 (25.0)	25 (417)	66.7
Typhoid	2 (3.3)	5 (8.3)	11.7
Cholera & Diarrhoea	1 (1.7)	1 (1.7)	3.3
Jaundice	5 (8.3)	6 (10.0)	18.3
Hilly			
Not affected	31 (46.3)	9 (13.4)	59.7
Typhoid	11 (16.4)	5 (7.5)	23.8
Cholera & Diarrhoea	2 (2.9)	2 (2.9)	14.8
Jaundice	4 (5.9)	3 (4.5)	25.9

Figures in parentheses indicate percentage to total.

Among the sample villages, the incidence of water-borne diseases is greater in hilly region compared to the other sample villages. This is mainly due to the open-air defecation by the people living upstream area while the sources are located downstream area. During the rainy season there is a possibility of mixing of this with the drinking water resulting in water-borne diseases. Despite the fact that they used to boil the water for drinking purpose, the incidence of diseases was felt in large number in this village.

Among the water-borne diseases found in the villages, jaundice had affected many when compared to other health problems. There was inhibition on the part of the respondents in revealing diseases like diarrhoea.

The information furnished in Table 5.22 is confined to the cases reported with the government hospitals and hence the total picture on water-borne diseases in the district cannot be captured with the help of this data alone. Because data on cases reported with the private nursing homes were not accessible for the present study. The available data showed a higher percentage of worm infection related diseases. Amoebiasis was the next major water related health problem, followed by acute diarrhoeal diseases, typhoid and jaundice.

The district scenario, with respect to water-borne diseases does vary from the field survey results. For instance, the district level data showed a very low percentage of incidences of jaundice, but the survey results showed the other way in terms of larger cases of jaundice. A possible reason could be under-reporting of cases with the health centres and the other crucial reason is the tendency of the people to take to native medicines towards treating jaundice. Similarly, the respondents owing to shyness and inhibition towards admitting such facts did not reveal the diarrhoea and cholera diseases.

Table 5.22 : Water-borne diseases in the study district (Rural) 2000.

(In persons)

Water-borne diseases	*Adult*		*Child*		*Total*
	Male	*Female*	*Male*	*Female*	
Acute Diarrhoeal Diseases	2946	2926	1911	1846	9629 [21.8]
Amoebiasis	4925	5051	1990	1881	13847 [31.4]
Worm infection	4463	4615	5552	5298	19928 [45.2]
Typhoid Fevers	436	131	83	52	702 [1.6]
Jaundice	14	7	1	1	23 [0.1]
	12784 [28.9]	12730 [28.8]	9537 [21.6]	9078 [20.6]	44129

Figures in parentheses indicate percentage to total.

Source : Deputy Director of Health Service, Rural District, Tiruchirappalli.

5.10 Community Participation in Tiruchirappalli District

People's participation in the provision of basic necessities is gaining prominence in the recent years. Community Participation (CP) may manifest in various forms. The users, beneficiaries themselves form a group either to create a source or to organize themselves to operate and maintain sources created by the State. The role applied by Non-Governmental Organizations (NGOs) in this realm is another facet of CP. Yet another mode is state induced community participation, that the State Government would bear partially the financial requirements. Participation may also be in the form of agitations and protests against the delay or negligence in the implementation of water supply programmes. In certain other cases, a few individuals, preferably economically well-off people join together to render service in this sector. In this way the concept of community participation is getting shaped and eventually evolving a system by involving the maximum members, users in the decision-making processes.

Kerala and Karnataka have exemplified as model states by demonstrating the participation of people towards rural water supply. Field survey experience of the study villages with respect to community participation in Tiruchirappalli district can be presented in the following manner.

In Athikudi village Panchayat, a fully wet area Cauvery and Coleroon river delta, the NGOs called *'Sevai'* have created a number of additional hand pumps. The hand pumps installed by them are technically superior to the state installed hand pumps. Besides these, they gave training to local people for operating and repairing the hand pumps. A peculiar form of participation has been observed in this village. Users by organizing themselves extended the pipelines from the main distribution line and created stand post closer to their houses. This sort of illegal practice is in vogue in all the sample villages.

In Nagayanallur village Panchayat, a village having both mixed characteristics, the NGOs role has been a worth mention. They provided hand pumps in three habitations, of which two were operational at the time of survey. The provision made is perfect in construction of platform and a small tank to store water for washing purpose.

Interestingly, an upper caste group in this village organized themselves in consummating an overhead tank facility and installed house service connections for about 60 households. They mobilized fund from economically well off people to meet the capital investment of OHT. A member has donated land required for construction and another member donated the well. And for operation and maintenance they collect Rs. 50 per month from the users and operate successfully. The water supplied through public sources has been used for washing cloths and livestock maintenance.

Another habitation in Nagayanallur village is called Karung Kadu, where people use open well for drinking purpose and for lifting the water up; households in this habitation have collectively procured an electric motor pump. They collected Rs. 10 per household per month towards operation and maintenance.

Oothukuli village Panchayat, a dry village, where spring is the main traditional source, there has been no community participation towards water supply. NGOs played little role in this village in creating sources. When enquired about streamlining the spring source, the residents were reluctant that the state would disturb the traditional source in the process of constructing platforms or hand pumps.

Thenpuranadu, a village Panchayat, situated in a hill area, where there was no sign of NGOs service. However, people's participation in this realm is significant. In Nachilipatti habitation, which comes under Thenpuranadu, the entire population of the habitation organized themselves in mobilizing funds towards digging an open well in their habitation. The residents handed over the open well to the TWAD Board; the board then invested money in fixing motor, pipelines and the whole distribution system. Even till date the distribution system from the open well has been successfully functioning.

On the whole, the participation by the people towards water supply is not homogeneous across the villages. However, the common feature is rendering their labour in one form or the other towards creation of sources. In regard to the role played by NGO, their service has been significant in wet villages than in dry villages. This can be due to cost factor. The cost of providing additional sources may be cheaper in wet villages than in dry villages. And finally community participation has become indispensable as the state would initiate and implement water supply programmes only if the representations come collectively from a group or a user's association.

5.11 Discussion

Analytical description of four categories of villages has been presented in preceding section of this chapter. Looking at villages separately on a case study basis helped in understanding the problems at the grassroots level. The magnitude of the problem certainly varied across villages, therefore, it is necessary to highlight the pattern, the commonalties and dichotomies between the villages.

Behaviour of the socio-economic and environmental variables in the realm of rural water supply by taking all the sample villages and all sample households warrant a thorough discussion.

In the sample study villages, on the whole, there are two distinct sources, which serve the purpose of provision of water. They are traditional and modern (mission) sources. Modern sources, in particular, remained a dominant source of drinking water. Dependence of mission sources in all the four categories of villages for drinking purpose is evident. About 60 per cent of the respondents depended on modern sources for drawing water for drinking purposes. For other domestic uses such as bathing, washing cloths etc. other than TWAD sources were relied upon.

Prior to mid-1970s, dependence on traditional sources in the study district had been high. After the introduction of modern sources by 1974, preference turned slowly towards schemes like hand pumps and power pumps. Modern sources are established in large numbers in villages where water is abundant, while traditional sources are still in vogue in villages where scarcity of water is acute.

Among the traditional sources, spring, *Kodavu,* open well, stream and river waters served as sources for drinking purpose. River water is resorted to mostly during power failure. While the modern sources such as hand pumps and power pumps are prominent sources, of which power pumps in terms of OHTs and stand posts served the purpose more than hand pumps.

Utility of hand pumps for drawing water for drinking purpose is very high in a wet village due to two reasons. Large number of hand pumps available in wet village, which includes private owned hand pumps also. And the second reason is the quality of water. It gets changed quickly after the withdrawal. Hand pumps are handy for respondents to draw water as and when required by them. Low cost of hand pumps also is responsible in this context. The number of hand pumps goes on declining moving from wet to mixed, dry and hilly villages. This is due to the problem of lifting the water through hand pumps from the ground level.

Comparatively, contribution of modern sources is significant in wet and mixed categories of villages than dry and hilly villages. Combined water supply schemes and house service connections are higher in wet and mixed villages than the other categories.

Although modern sources are predominant across the sample villages, still traditional sources continue to serve where mission sources failed to deliver the good.

Distance and time, the two policy variables behaved in the following manner. Time and distance are more towards collection of water from traditional source than the modern sources. Even the waiting time too varied between these two. Waiting time is higher for traditional sources; spring in particular than the modern sources. However, among the mission sources, time and distance are more for hand pumps. The time consumed is variant and high during summer for traditional sources. Distance and time are positively correlated but the time taken is influenced more by duration of waiting. The present study found out a negative correlation (r = -0.3224, significant at .01) between average income of household per month and the distance travelled to fetch water. This suggests that higher the income lower the distance and *vice versa.* Glaeser (1995), found a '*low correlation*' between income and distance travelled to fetch water, in his study on housing of the rural poor in Tamil Nadu.

Another crucial policy variable is per capita consumption of water (lpcd). By looking at the total sample households' consumption of water, all the households are provided with 76 lpcd on average. This is certainly above the Government norm of 40 lpcd. However, caution needs to be exercised in analyzing the household survey results. The consumption level of 76 lpcd does not imply the total water provision by the state (TWAD) alone. The quantum consumed viz., 76 lpcd does include privately owned plus the puolic sources. To be accurate, 51 lpcd is being provided by the state. Hence, it cannot be construed that the state has fully covered all the habitations in providing water supply.

Across the classified categories of villages, the scenario is different. Sample villages with wet and mixed characteristics received water to the prescribed norm through public source, while villages with dry and hilly characteristics received water less than the prescribed norm.

Interestingly, the actual consumption of water for drinking and cooking purposes it is estimated as 6.2 litres per capita per day, of which, 4.2 litres being drawn from the public source.

By looking at the consumption level of all the sample households, the average consumption of 311 households was 366 litres per day. Of which, 61 per cent of water has been drawn from the public sources. The remaining 39 per cent from other sources such as own source, traditional source and agricultural sources for all purposes. The percentage contribution by the TWAD sounds higher due to the fact that the household survey was conducted during summer. The proportion of public service varied across uses and categories of areas such as wet, mixed dry and hilly regions. The average consumption of water per household for all domestic uses is high. However, in other categories water uses for bathing, washing, and livestock are done directly' at the source point itself and the respondents were not in a position to give the exact quantity of water used. Though the total quantity per household looked higher in dry areas, the per capita consumption however is lower in dry village and the least in hilly region.

But the per capita consumption of water per day has been close to prescribed level for all the respondents. Here the per capita income is less correlated with per capita consumption of water. It is important to recognize the variable, which is associated with income viz., house value. House value is positively correlated with per capita consumption. Type of houses, flooring, number of rooms in the house, house value are more crucial in determining water consumption than income per se.

It may be relevant to mention here that the poorer section of the population pay higher price for domestic water use than the rich (Dick and Mendoza, 1996). The implication is the indirect cost incurred by the poor in spending additional time and the distance travelled to fetch water.

Women as collector and user of water merits attention. Among the total respondents, more than 95 per cent comprised women in the collection of water for domestic use. Even assistance to water collection is predominantly by female children. Female education does play a role in water consumption. Participation of women is no rhetoric but evident in their participation in protests and agitation in seeking regular water supply in rural areas.

Rural water supply is comprehensive, which includes provision of adequate water for livestock maintenance. More than half of the respondents possessed livestock in one category or the other. The average consumption of water per livestock per day is estimated at 10 litres. Contrary to expectations, livestock population is found higher in dry village rather than in wet village. To the question whether water scarcity results in decline in livestock population in rural areas, the study could not find convincing evidence to answer the question posed. The fact remains that demand for water at the rural household level is positively correlated with water required for livestock maintenance.

Health hazards due to contaminated water consumption are a serious matter of concern. Lack of awareness of the linkage between health and unsafe water notwithstanding, more than half of the total respondents replied negatively about the water-borne diseases. Typhoid being the highest, followed by jaundice and cholera are the water-borne diseases reported in all four categories of villages. Village located in a hill is observed to be the worst hit by water related health problems. Among the victims, children are more susceptible to such diseases, followed by male and female adults. The majority of them are found approaching private hospitals for treatment. On average, the households spent Rs.1,983 per annum towards medication due to unsafe water.

Sanitation facility forms an important aspect in the discussion on water use at domestic level. As mentioned in the preceding chapters that 90 per cent of the respondents do not own a latrine inside the house premise and hardly 10 per cent owns inside the house. Even those owning seldom use the same for the purpose it is intended. Therefore, open-air defecation is the traditional practice still in vogue. Water required for ablution purpose is imminent. Female, among the respondents reportedly returned home for using water for personal hygiene while male found water for such purpose nearby the defecation site.

Nearly 75 per cent of the total respondents are willing to pay for improved water supply. For quality improvement and extension of distribution time the willingness to pay by house-hold per month is Rs. 8, however this amount is one-fourth of the amount required to be paid as tariff for house service connection.

Besides socio-economic and policy variables, a plethora of other aspects may directly or indirectly influence rural water supply. The over all impression of the respondents in regard to provision of water is satisfactory to fifty per cent of the total respondents. And the rest of them felt not satisfactory with respect to public sources. Consumption of mineral water in rural areas is minimum in the study villages about 33 per cent used mineral water sold in packets (not in bottles).

II. ENVIRONMENTAL DIMENSIONS OF DRINKING WATER SUPPLY

Water is essentially a renewable natural resource, which has no substitute. It provides life-sustaining amenity to human beings. The environmental aspects of drinking water can be described only in the backdrop of socio-economic sphere. The reason is that besides natural cyclical changes in environment of water, human intervention makes tremendous changes in the ecosystem in general and water sources in particular. One such instance is depletion of ground water resource, which is due to excess extraction by human beings. Secondly, degradation of quality of water for drinking and cooking purposes caused by human activities *ipso facto* discharge of effluents rendering water un-potable. Thirdly, the nexus between gender and environmental degradation is a matter of current concern. The vulnerability of women and female children in particular undergo hardship, which is aggravated further under degraded environmental conditions. Fourthly, the dominance of modern approaches over the traditional practices is worth reckoning. Evidences support that the traditional practices of water supply have been slowly vanishing. Traditional wisdom once lost is lost forever. And, finally, the environmental conflicts arising out of the use of environmental resources, is equally an important environmental factor in this context. A few of the above-mentioned frontier issues are taken up for investigation in the light of the information obtained from the study villages.

5.12.1 Drinking Water Quality

Environmental quality of water is an extremely important facet of drinking water supply. The WHO statistics show that most of the diseases in developing countries are related to unsafe water supply. The quality of water is as important as provision of adequate water supply, since the latter satisfies the quantity while the former ensures its potability. In India drinking water gets contaminated due to a host of reasons, starting from a rapid growth of population, industrialization, urbanization and excess use of chemicals etc. In rural areas, improper maintenance of hand pump sites and open-air defecation cause havoc on water quality besides other reasons.

The popular notion goes that potable water is visually clear, tastes sweet, is free from unpleasant flavours and odors, cook food well and quickly. Conversely, bad water or water unfit for drinking is that which is visually unclear, has a tinge of colour with a salty, metallic taste or smell and in which grains/pulses take a long time to cook. Seldom the general public realizes that it is germ free water that ensures safety. In fact there is a large area of public ignorance about how health is affected by consuming unsafe drinking water. In the absence of factual knowledge, misconceptions, and vague guesses are used to explain the relationship between quality of drinking water and health.

As part of the present study, water quality testing is done with the help of the Ground Water Board, Public Works Department of Tamil Nadu and the National Facility for Marine Cyanobacteria (NFMC), Bharathidasan University, Tiruchirappalli, India.

Water samples were collected* from 20 points (locations) across the five sample villages. Samples were drawn from both surface and ground water. Under surface water spring, *Kudavu*, river and stream waters were taken for quality testing. While ground water sources include hand pump and stand posts. The names of villages and the particulars regarding sources are furnished in Table 5.23.

Testing for the following parameters assessed the water quality of the samples: they include Electrical Conductivity (EC), *p*H, Calcium (Ca), Magnesium (Mg), Sodium (Na), Potassium (K), Biocarbornate (HCO_3), Carbonate (CO_3), Sulphates (SO_4), Chloride (Cl), Nitrate (NO_3), Fluoride (F), Total Dissolved Solids (TDS), Total Hardness (TH), and faecal coliform.

If the values of the parameters are within the Maximum Permissible Limits (MPL) then the water is considered suitable for human consumption. Conversely, if it exceeds the MPL then water quality is deemed to be unsuitable for consumption. By looking at the results of the sample water quality parameters excepting Ca, Cl, Mg, TDS, TH and faecal coliform all the others are within permissible level. Further, only one sample water drawn from groundwater from Oothukuli village showed values exceeding the maximum permissible limits. In this context microbial contamination that occurs due to improper waste disposal, lack of sanitation, faulty construction of well and lack of source protection are the major contributory factors for water-borne diseases (WHO, 1993) and in poor communities most such cases go unnoticed. This is a case with modern sources of water.

---

* Water samples have been collected under the strict instructions of the Groundwater Board. Glass bottles were used as containers, duly sterilized and used Separate containers for biological, physical and chemical parameters. Water samples for Quality testing were brought in containers kept in ice box within six hours after the Collection.

Water quality standards are compiled from Indian Standard Institution (ISI), Indian Council of Medical and Research (ICMR), World Health Organisation (WHO) and the Central Public Health and Environmental Engeneering Organisation (CPHEEO). It is to be mentioned that standards for certain parameters are not accessible. Maximum permissible limit is taken as a measure for the analysis.

Table 5.23 : Water quality results of the samples.

		EC	pH	Ca	Mg	Na	K	HCO_3	CO_3	SO_4	Cl	NO_3	F	TDS	TH as $CaCO_3$	Feacal Coliform	(Fe) Iron
WHO			*6.5-9.5*	*200*	*150**					*400*	*1000**	*100*	*1.0-1.5*	*1500*	*600**	*100mg1*	
ISI			*6.5-9.2*	*200*						*300*			*1.5*	*1500*		*100mg1*	*1mg/li*
ICMR			*6.5-8.5*	*200*						*400*		*50*	*2.0*	*1500*		*100mg1*	
Site name	**Source & Depth#**																
Athikudi	HP (Sh. bore well)	1320	7.1	100	49	113	18	409	0	132	167	16	0.21	800	450	< 2	**3.4**
	HP (Sh. bore well)	650	7.2	50	21	55	5	226	0	48	67	12	0.37	371	210	< 2	
	OHT (deep bore well)	480	7.4	40	16	53	3	250	0	27	39	0	0.23	303	165	< 2	
	OHT (deep bore wel)	410	7.6	34	13	35	4	195	0	19	32	1	0.35	236	140	< 2	
Oothukuli	Oothu1 (surface)	120	7.1	10	6	9	0	61	0	7	7	4	0.17	74	50	**120**	–
	Oothu2 (surface)	120	7.1	14	4	9	0	61	0	6	7	4	0.14	750	50	**110**	
	OHT (deep bore well)	540	7.5	42	19	53	2	299	0	29	13	23	0.64	331	185	20	
	HP (deep bore well)	7910	7.2	**400**	**131**	1058	219	616	0	265	**2283**	12	0.39	4776	**1240**	< 2	
Mullipadi	OHT (CWSS, I. Well)	640	7.6	38	21	51	5	189	0	35	71	7	0.41	323	180	70	–
	HP (deep bore well)	970	7.2	46	17	104	98	500	0	35	46	31	0.55	627	185	40	
	OHT (deep bore well)	1410	7.4	100	28	170	9	323	0	70	234	96	0.53	869	365	< 2	
	River (surface)	560	7.6	36	19	64	5	244	0	26	60	7	0.45	339	170	**230**	
Nagayanallur	HP (deep bore well)	2050	7.5	104	88	230	2	342	0	46	326	415	0.37	1382	**620**	20	–
	HP (deep bore well)	1930	7.5	176	22	267	27	494	0	101	277	310	0.47	1427	530	70	
	HP (deep bore well)	640	7.7	42	29	58	7	384	0	12	7	32	0.90	379	225	< 2	
	HP (deep bore well)	1690	7.5	74	41	271	9	445	0	101	262	149	0.73	1130	335	20	
Thenpuranadu	Kodavu 1 (surface)	240	7.0	18	11	18	2	110	0	6	18	12	0.13	140	90	60	–
	Kodavu 2 (surface)	150	7.2	12	9	7	0	79	0	5	7	2	0.14	82	65	< 2	
	OHT (Open well)	600	7.4	38	40	30	9	207	0	23	85	28	0.13	357	260	60	
	Stream water (surface)	120	7.8	6	9	14	0	61	0	11	7	11	0.09	89	50	70	

Source : Water samples colleted from study village and tested by Assistant Director Geochemistry Sub-division, Ground Water Board P.W.D., Tiruchirappalli 20. # Deep bore well more than 250 meter. Shallow bore well less than 40 meters. * CAHEEO - Central Public Health and Environmental Engineering Organisation. EC: Electrical Conductivity, Ca : Calcium, Mg : Magnesium, K : Potassium, HCO_3 : Bicarbonate, CO_3 : Carbonate, SO_4 : Sulfate, Cl : Chloride, No_3 : Nitrate, F : Fluoride, TDS : Total Dissolved Solids, TH: Total Hardness, Fe: Iron and Feacal Coliform.

The total hardness (TH) of sample water from Nagayanallur showed a value of 620 mg/lit. As mentioned earlier, information on the standards for parameters like sodium potassium, bicarbonate and carbonate are not available, even from the Ground Water Board official.

In regard to biological parameters, the surface water carries more of faecal coliforms than the groundwater. At the same time surface water source viz., spring water is free from physical and chemical contamination. Presence of faecal coliform is the unique problem more in surface source than in the groundwater source. The high fecal coliform level in the dry village is due to two reasons. The first one being, during rainy seasons the water level of ponds and agricultural paddy fields will be similar. Consequently, water stagnated in the paddy fields percolate into spring and into the ponds contributing to the high coliform level. Secondly, rainwater carried the excreta and, contaminates the source. Hence in poor communities diarrhoea and dysentery have become a part of life.

Iron concentration was 3.4 mg/litre for one of the samples drawn from groundwater source in Athikudi village. Excess iron concentration is a major problem faced by this village. As discussed in the case study I, due to high concentration of iron the colour of water changes within fifteen minutes after collection. Further incidences of diarrhoeal diseases due to unsafe water are recorded in this wet village.

Contaminated water is hazardous to human health, as majority of the diseases in rural areas are water-borne. Our field survey carried questions on the prevalence of water related health problems and sought responses from the households. Of the 311 households, 67 per cent of them responded negatively to water-borne diseases. Others reported to have suffered from water related diseases like, diarrhoea, cholera, typhoid, gastro-enteritis and jaundice. When cross-checked with the health officials of Government Hospitals, Primary Health Centers, in this area (i.e.) Athikudi (Anbil), Marurngapuri, Musiri and Chengattupatti, about the lower incidence of water-borne problem, the officials gave a different version that more than 60 per cent of the people suffer from water-borne diseases.

The Health officials confirmed cases like gastro-enteritis in all the five villages. The problem of gunie worm has been reported in the hilly region (Thenpuranadu). Higher incidence of typhoid, and cholera has been reported in Thenpuranadu (Hill). In wet village, cases of jaundice are reported in large number. Therefore, it can be construed that there is absolute lack of awareness on water related health problems among the respondents.

Invariably, in all the sample villages, partial breakage of water pipelines and mixing of sewage with drinking water lines have been witnessed during the field survey.

Regarding their practices of treating water before consumption, 26.4 per cent does not take any measure, 7.4 per cent use boiled waters throughout the year. The practice of boiling water is prominent in hilly region, Thenpuranadu where more than 60 per cent boiled water especially during winter and more at the time of sickness. When asked for the reasons they accepted that water couldn't be consumed without boiling in a cold place like theirs.

One-third of the total respondents filter the water at home. Interestingly, they use white cloth for filtering and in majority of cases part of their saree is used for filtering purpose (See Plate 24).

In hilly village, cloth is used to filter off dust, small worms and insects, which are visibly present in water. More than 99 per cent of the respondents never used any on-line treatment of water like aquaguard machines, except very few.

To sum up, a careful perusal of water quality, parameters indicate that most of the variables albeit did not exceed the maximum permissible level, the biological parameters are problematic in surface water sources, while physical and chemical parameters are problematic in groundwater sources.

The response from the households with respect to water quality and the health impacts thereof is lukewarm. As a result, the causal relationship between health and the quality could not be established in this study.

5.12.2 Depletion of Ground Water Resources

Groundwater depletion can lead to destruction of the sustainability of fragile ecosystem. The Azrag Oasis in Jordanian Badia is a unique case representing this feature. The Azrag, a Ramsar, wetland spread over 7500 hectares, has attracted a large number of rare and unique aquatic and terrestrial species and became a renowned place for migratory birds. But the human intervention leading to over extraction of groundwater resulted in total drying up of wetland, causing drastic fall in water table and drying up of natural springs. The ultimate result was deterioration of ecosystem with a threefold increase in salinity.

Groundwater depletion is a universal problem. The magnitude and extent of the problem vary between countries and even within the state. The economics of groundwater envisages that permanent reduction in groundwater tables increases both the capital and the operating costs of water supply (Dhawan, 1987).

Groundwater is the most valuable, renewable, but highly vulnerable resource. Hence the fall in water table and the attendant deterioration in water quality are matters of serious concern (Moench, 1994).

5.12.2.1 Groundwater Level in Tiruchirappalli District

Secondary source of information on groundwater levels in the district were collected from the Groundwater Board, Tiruchirappalli. The data were available for the period of 1971 to 1999. The Board maintains this information collected from 59 samples bore and open wells.

The Groundwater data for 28 years were classified and three monthly moving averages have been calculated. The decadal average for the year 1971–80 showed water table at 6.5 metres below the Ground level. For the next decade, 1981–90 the level was 8.5 metres and for the year 1991 to 1999 the groundwater level showed 7.6 metres, as can be seen from Table 5.24. Increasing value from 6.5 metres to 8.5 metres shows the reduction in water table.

It is to be mentioned that fluctuations of groundwater level over the three decades are obvious, as can be seen from Figure 5.4. The fall in water table was high during 1976, 1982 and between 1984 and 1992. The reduction was steep during 1996.

The data were analyzed for seasonal variations. During October, November and December, the water level had been better, close to ground level. This is due to North-East monsoon rain. The enhanced water table sustains up to March. But during summer months, April, May, June and July, the water table showed the lower levels.

Table 5.24 : Ground water level* in rural Tiruchirappalli district.

(In metres)

Year	1971	1972	1973	1974	1975	1976	1977	1978	1979	1980	Decadal water level
Water level	5.01	5.32	4.76	6.73	8.48	8.12	10.09	5.92	5.48	4.09	6.4
Year	1981	1982	1983	1984	1985	1986	1987	1988	1989	1990	
Water level	6.64	4.63	8.89	6.50	8.06	8.97	11.13	9.44	11.93	8.93	8.5
Year	1991	1992	1993	1994	1995	1996	1997	1998	1999	2000	
Water level	11.34	8.08	7.48	5.55	7.16	7.77	8.78	5.97	5.83	-	7.5

* Ground water level (table) measured from the ground level in meters.

Source : Ground Water Board, Tiruchi.

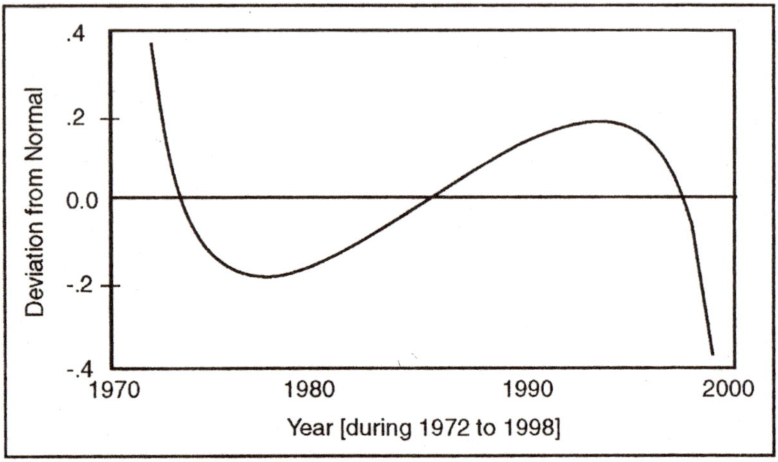

Fig. 5.4 : Ground water level.

Reiterating the fact that groundwater is the major source of irrigation, this study has found that in the rural districts 61.9 per cent of groundwater drawn is used for agricultural purposes, that was drawn through 46,963 energised agricultural pump sets. Of the total power consumption, 71 per cent went for agricultural activities. This is one of the causes of depletion of groundwater level. A study (Narayanamoorthy, 1996) conducted at the National and state level revealed that Flat Rate system and free electricity policy has aggravated in groundwater depletion.

Groundwater sources also met 80 per cent of the drinking water needs in the sample villages, through hand pumps and power pumps. As a whole, 6737 hand pumps and 1298 OHTs is the rural district depend on ground water source exclusively.

Observations made during the field survey revealed certain interesting insights. When asked about the reasons for depletion of groundwater, the response was inadequate frequency of rainfall. Further, the respondents explain that most rains occurred in a few days at irregular intervals. Incessant rains for a few days resulted in flash flood making storage of water difficult and floodwaters join the sea ultimately. Another reason expressed by the respondents is over extraction of groundwater, besides lack of replenishment of water due to rocky soil. About 35 per cent of the respondents felt that the water scarcity is due to groundwater depletion, 47 per cent obtained that the reason was surface water

Plate 1 : Hand Pump (low cost).

Plate 2 : Public 'Utility'.

Plate 3 : Public Source used for washing purpose.

Plate 4 : NGOs – Hand Pump Scheme (Thara Pump)

Plate 5 : Transparent water during collection

Plate 6 : Turbid water after 30 minutes of collection

Plate 7 : Infiltration well inside the river

Plate 8 : Hand Pump – Indian Mark II

Plate 9 : Ground Level Water Reservoir (GLWR)

Plate 10 : Over Head Tank

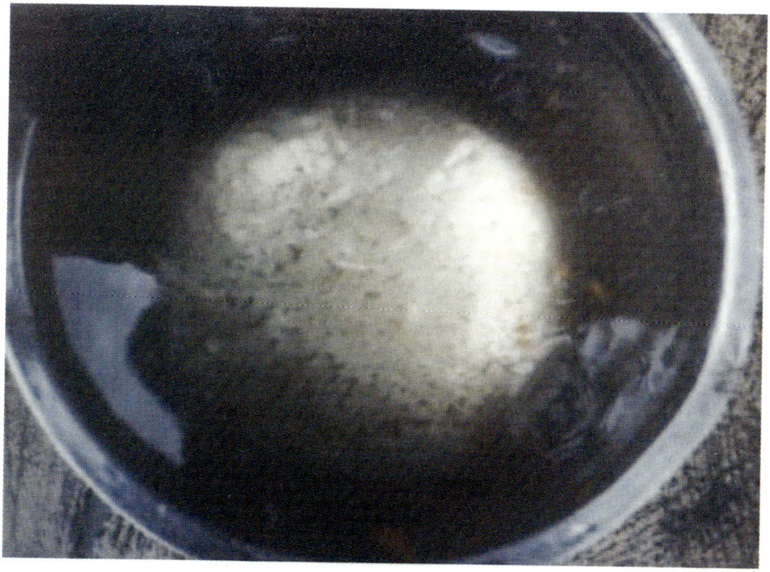

Plate 11 : Worms from ground water source

Plate 12 : Mixing of sewage with drinking water

Plate 13 : Collection of water containing sewage

Plate 14 : 'Spring' – a traditional source.

Plate 15 : Women treks a long distance.

Plate 16 : Water collection from the spring.

Plate 17 : School going children used for water collection.

Plate 18 : Water collection during night.

Plate 19 : Stand Post.

Plate 20 : Shallow Well

Plate 21 : 'Kudavu' – a traditional source.

Plate 22 : Unhygienic condition around the stand post.

Plate 23 : Latrine converted into kitchen.

Plate 24 : Filtering of Water.

scarcity and 3.2 per cent felt both the factors are responsible for depletion of groundwater resource.

Water resources although limited, have multifarious uses for different sectors viz., Industry, agricultural and domestic. Environmental conflicts arise mostly between agriculture and domestic uses. According to Mätzger and Moench (1994: p. 33),

> "Given steady increases in drinking water demands, conflicts are likely to erupt between agricultural users – whose livelihoods may depend on access to irrigation – and the populations depending on drinking water."

Drinking water schemes, which are designed to provide water supply to remote areas where sources are scanty, and places where creation of water is difficult are the root causes of conflicts. The main aim of the Combined Water Supply Scheme (CWSS) is to locate areas where water resources are plenty and establish supply through, power pumps, extension of pipelines to provide house service connection to distant places with scant water sources.

In this process water is carried to a large number of villages through pipelines from one particular huge scheme. Here conflicts arise between two groups of people claiming their stake. One group comprises people who live in the village, where pumping station and collector well are established, from which water is distributed to the targeted villages. The other group consists of people belonging to '*way-side villages*', across whose villages the pipelines are extended. The wayside villagers claim that water needs to be provided to them also, without which they would not allow the pipelines to be passed through their villages. People belonging to the village where pumping station is established also oppose the idea of installing pumping stations and collector wells in their village. They argue that such pumping stations would jeopardize the groundwater potential and ultimately affect their farm operation. Besides these, there were a number of protests and agitations against irregular and inadequate water supply to their villages.

An attempt has been made to collect the available information on conflicts from the TWAD Board records and daily newspapers. Instances of such occurrences can be presented as follows:

(a) The Perambalur the combined water supply scheme was about to be initiated at a cost of Rs. 26.4 crores to cater to the needs of one lakh population, covering 55 wayside villages during 1987. While the pumping station got installed in Coleroon river, which is 40 kms. away from Perambalur. The farmers of Thandenkorai, Esanakkorai and other ten villages opposed the scheme tooth and nail on the ground that groundwater would be depleted and their agriculture would be hit adversely. Consequently the TWAD officials had to suspend the scheme (*The Hindu*, 2000).

This incident has been cross-checked by the researcher during field visits. The farmers expressed the view that during the past one decade they had access to groundwater at 30 feet depth during rainy seasons, while in summer they had to draw water from 500 feet depth in the above said areas. They also expressed apprehension that lowering of water table could adversely affect their agricultural activities (Table 5.27).

(b) Another instance is from Sekkanam village Panchayat of Tiruchirappalli district. There is a small dam across Ponnani river situated near Sekkanam. With an investment of Rs. 48 lakhs a pipeline extension was made to provide rural water supply. These pipelines did cross the Mughavanur village Panchayats where the residents also sought water to their village and protested against the scheme to an extent of filing a case in the court against the TWAD Board.

(c) In Manachanallur block, Iyyampalayam village Panchayat, Arayeepallam habitation – an OHT was installed in 1999. This facility is expected to serve both Arayeepallam and Thambayipannai habitation. The residents of former village declined to extend the facility to the latter village. The host village refused because of insufficiency of water supply for themselves.

Many a village such as Nadupatti, Kadapamarathupatti, Chinna Karuppur, Mpudupatti, Valmal palayam, Thiruchendurai, Andanallur, Ammankudi, Maniakurichy, Ammasamuthiram,

Puruthakudi, and Keelakundupatti had protested against inadequate supply of water.

The foregoing section gives an overview of conflicts in the district. These types of environmental conflicts are not isolated cases in the study district alone but happen sporadically in the state as a whole. It can be inferred that farmers and active water users in villages are no longer insensitive to problems that affect them directly or indirectly.

5.12.3 Environmental Degradation and Gender

A careful perusal of current literature on environment suggests that there is a direct linkage between population growth, poverty and environmental degradation. Indeed environmental degradation and population could mutually influence each other in a vicious circle. Increased populations exert pressure and degrade the fragile environment and a ruined environment in turn induces more population growth. This vicious circle is well explained by Maler (1997: p. 263) in the following manner:

> "If environmental degradation increases the demand for workers, as it seems reasonable to expect, then fertility will also increase. For example, if land becomes overgrazed, cattle may have to be moved long distances, which will require more workers; if local water sources are polluted or depleted, more people will be needed to fetch water; and if deforestation reduces the local supply of firewood, more workers will be required to collect the same amount of wood as before. Thus there is an apparently vicious circle that affects mainly the poor: environmental degradation increases population, which increases degradation, and so on. An improved environment would reduce fertility thus improving the environment further."

Dasgupta and Maler (1995)* also shared a similar reasoning and developed further theoretical arguments. According to them,

---

* Filmer and Pritchett (1996: 4).

> "The children are devoted to that part of family income which is derived from the exploitation of natural resources for which the primary cost is in the time required to collect the good. Hence, as the implicit price of those goods goes up, the marginal value product of children relative to adults rises. Parents then may have the incentive to have more children in spite of the worsening environmental conditions, and in spite of the fact that an additional child might further worsen these conditions for all other families."

The behavioural part that creates a vicious circle is worth probing. Increased scarcity of common property natural resources such as water, firewood and grazing land, could make the parents to realize and place higher value for children. This is due to the practice of children gathering natural resources for the family.

Demographers are of the view that *environmental poverty* and female literacy are positively correlated. One such indicator of *environmental poverty* is the time spent by rural households on procuring basic necessities such as water, fuel and fodder from nearby local environment. The legacy in our country is that women and children are more vulnerable to the impacts of environmental poverty. A study conducted by the World Bank in 1997 highlighted another facet, viz., the number of female children and proximity to environmental resource base. Their study further confirmed "families living in areas in which distance from firewood source is greater have more children" (Agarwal, 2000).

The implications are profound as other factors such as women literacy and fertility rate are involved in understanding this issue. To reiterate the hypothesis initiated by Dasgupta and Maler, further state that children are not only treated as offsprings to provide old age support but also as enhanced *workforce*. Empirical evidences proved this hypothesis to be true with respect to a few countries under certain circumstances, and Thoane (1997) established that the economic value of children to households' was the determining factor of fertility.

The present study too made an observation pertaining to environmental degradation and burden of women and female children. This phenomenon is prevalent in one of the study villages viz., Oothukuli, a village Panchayat in Manapparai Taluk of Tiruchirappalli District. This village is basically a dry village where the percentage of total irrigated area is just twenty per cent and the ground water level is deplorably low. Interestingly, the village is endowed with springs, and in local language it is called '*Ootthu*' more than ninety per cent of the household depend solely on this traditional source for drinking and cooking needs. Notwithstanding the fact that the TWAD Board did create certain sources like hand pumps and stand posts, the households were found to be still using these sources for domestic purposes other than drinking and cooking.

A chain of six to seven spots of springs each formed like a pond are located at a distance of two to three kilometers away from the main village. Water from the springs ooze slowly, accumulate and get collected in a small pit (Width: 3 feet; depth; 1-2 feet). The local people themselves make these pits.

During summer season, it takes about one hour to collect a bucket of water, which is roughly eighteen liters. It is disheartening to notice that female children were exclusively pressed into the service. Carrying pots and buckets to fetch water, the female children had to walk 2 to 3 kilometre distance from their habitation to reach the springs. They flock around the spring and start collecting water until their containers are full. After the collection by the children, accompanying adult female members carry the filled pots to their respective houses. During field trips the authors observed that children at times had to wait for 6 hours for their turn to gather water. Even during late night children had to wait and collect water. The *modus operandi* is to use a piece of cloth, preferably a portion of the dress they wear, to filter the water. The water appears slightly turbid, more so during winter; the children use a small vessel to lift the water and fill their containers (See Plate 14).

During rainy seasons the problem of water scarcity is understandably not acute. Since structures where the springs are located, are filled with rainwater. Then the households have had easy access to water. As a result the time spent, and waiting time would be lower than during summer seasons.

School going female children visit the ponds after the school hours to collect water, while school dropout female children visit the spots even during day time to do the gathering during summer season.

5.12.3.1 Hypothesis Testing IV

As mentioned in the foregoing sections of the analysis and discussion chapter, the primary household survey has been conducted in five villages, and the data were as classified as villages in wet, mixed, dry and hilly region. An earnest attempt has been made to test whether there is a nexus between environmental degradation and burden on children in the sample villages. The sample households interviewed in dry area was 60, while in wet it was 64, in mixed areas it was 120 and in hilly region it was 67.

Among the four categories of villages, the average family size is larger in the dry area when compared to wet, mixed and hilly region. Incidentally, on an average the number the female children are higher in the dry area. Distance travelled and time spent to collect water also showed a marked difference in dry area when compared to other regions (Table 5.25).

The typical sample village, categorized under dry is Oothukuli village Panchayat, situated in Manapparai taluk of Tiruchirappalli district. This taluk is the most dry area in terms of area irrigated, rainfall, cropping pattern and more importantly by the groundwater level.

A hypothesis was framed to test whether the relationship between environmental degradation in terms of depletion of natural resource viz., the ground water level and the burden of women in general and female children in particular, is true or false.

The following are the null and alternative hypotheses:

Null hypotheses H0:	There is no significant difference in the number of female children found in fetching drinking water between a dry village and other regions.

Table 5.25 : Degradation and the burden of women and female children.

Area	*Family size*	*Children*	*Female children as water collectors*	*Total distance travelled per day collect water (Metres)*	*Time spent for water collection per day (in minutes)*	*Drinking Water Source*
Aathikiudi						
Total	331	89	49	646	36.05	SP, HP, NGOs source Thara pump, Agriculture pump set, and HSCs.
Mean	5	1.39	1	10	56	
Range	2-14	0-6	0-5	1-40	10-180	
SD	3	1.45	1	11	31	
Nagayanallur & Mullipadi						
Total	565	144	67	15957	81.10	SP, HP, CWSS, Source, River, Community participation source of OHT.
Mean	5	1.20	1	133	68	
Range	2-10	0-4	0-3	1-600	2.4	
SD	2	1.10	1	156	41	
Oothukuli						
Total	360	123	91	79927	137.36	SP, HP, Oothu, agriculture source.
Mean	6	2.05	2	1332	2.29	
Range	2-18	0-7	0-5	2-3100	60-360	
SD	3	1.4	1	850	96	
Thenpuranadu						
Total	314	91	43	14672	52	Open well, HP, SP, Kodavu and stream water.
Mean	5	1.36	1	219	78	
Range	2-9	0-4	0-3	2-900	15-120	
SD	2	1.29	1	238	48	
Grand Total						
Total	1570	447	250	111202	306.51	All source mentioned above.
Mean	5	1.44	1	358	99	
Range	2-18	0-7	0-5	1-3100	10-360	
SD	2	1.31	1	626	85	

Alternative hypotheses H1:	There is significant difference in the number of female children found in fetching drinking water between a dry village and other regions.

Analysis of variance was used to test the hypothesis. Specifically Duncan test is applied to test the difference in variations between one village and the rest three villages.

The ANOVA results suggest that there is a significant difference in variation between two means. This implies that the variation of the number of female children engaged in carrying water in dry area against the other areas is significantly different. Hence the null hypothesis gets rejected that there is no significant difference between female children found in dry area and in other areas. Duncan test at 5 per cent level of significance can be seen from Table 5.26.

Table 5.26 : ANOVA –Hypothesis testing

Variable: Number of female children by variable Areas

Source	D. F	Sum of Squares	Mean Squares	F Ratio	F Probability
Between the groups	3	39.5730	13.1910	16.49	.0000
Within the groups	307	245.4624	0.7996		
Total	310	285.0354			

Multiple range tests: Duncan test with significance level .05
The difference between two means is significant if MEAN (J)-MEAN (I) >= .6323 * RANGE* SQRT [1/N (I) + 1/N (J)] with the following value(s) for Range:

(*) Indicates significant differences which are shown in the lower triangle

Mean	Area	Grp 2	Grp 4	Grp 1	Grp 3
.5583	Grp 2				
.6418	Grp 4				
.7656	Grp 1				
1.5167	Grp 3	*	*	*	

Grp 1 Wet
Grp 2 Mixed
Grp 3 Dry
Grp 4 Hill

Table 5.27 : Instances of water conflict.

Name of the schemes	*Type of problems*	*Beneficiary villages (No.)*	*Problem village*	*Cost of scheme (in Rupees)*
Perampallur CWSS	Ground water reduction (Farmers oppose)	55 village Panchayats (one lakh people)	Thandankorai, Esanakorai, And others ten habitation	26.4 crore
Sekkanam Water supply schemes	Way side villagers' right	Karungulam	Mukavannur, Karaipatti, periyamaniyampatti, periyakarai patti, kalathupatty, and dom road	48 lakhs
Ayerampallam CWSS	Way side village rights. Scarcity	Ayerampallam	Thampayeepallam	—

Here the implication is profound. We may have to exercise caution and it is unwise to construe that wherever female children are found more in number carrying water, the environmental degradation is high. However, in the study village, in Oothukuli the phenomenon was witnessed by the authors during the field visits. Also it is not possible to generalize this scenario for other places.

5.12.4 Treating Traditional Water

Traditional sources of water such as open-well, river, lake, pond, spring and *kodavu* may not provide protected or safe water as much as modern sources. Nevertheless, the means of providing protected water from traditional sources do exist. For instance, in the hilly region, is was observed that open deep well continues to serve as a source for providing water for the village. But the distribution methods viz., pumping and distribution through pipelines are modern. In this case, there is overlapping of traditional and modern sources, where water (traditional sources) is treated before distribution.

In another case, the local people of Oothukuli village never allowed any state intervention to streamline the existing traditional source of water supply. There were allegedly scared that the government intervention would jeopardise the system in vogue. The underlying point is local resistance towards treatment of traditional water sources towards providing safe water.

Ultimately the user associations are found to be effectively taking initiatives towards treating the traditional sources of water as safe water. The user groups not only use the water but also preserve the same by a way of discouraging the people in using drinking water source for other purposes.

5.13 Water Institutions

As stated in the third chapter of the present study, institutional treatment to water problem is gaining currency in the recent period. In fact, it is important that the actual implementation of any programme depends largely on the institutional mechanism, which is at work. In reiterating the points made earlier that water institutions *per se* comprise laws, policies and administrative machineries. The fact remains, water as state subject, a host of policies, schemes and programmes have been introduced from time to time. And the RGNDWM (1986) and the National Water Policy (1987) are the milestones in this context. It is important to understand this as supply side institutions. The discussion, on various central and state schemes, was made elaborately in the preceding chapters.

It may be worthwhile to discern the water institutions with respect to user groups representing demand side. In this context user groups, who organize themselves either in creating schemes or operating and maintaining the existing water schemes on a continuous basis, are treated under user participation as institutions.

The institutional framework in vogue is the creation of schemes by the State Government through TWAD Board and handing over the responsibility of operation and maintenance with the local Panchayats. Excepting the piped house service connections, all other schemes are provided free of cost. No cost recovery is made for rural water supply.

Water institutions in the study villages manifested through user groups in the following manner. The users, beneficiaries themselves form a group either to create a source or to organize themselves to operate and maintain sources created by the state. Yet another mode is state induced water institution, that the State Government would bear partially the financial requirements. Participation may also be in the form of agitations and protests against the delay or negligence in the implementation of water supply programmes. In certain other cases, a few, preferably economically well off people join together to render service in this sector.

Some of the functional characteristics of water institutions in terms of user groups in the study villages can be summarised as follows:

In Athikudi village Panchayat, a fully wet area Cauvery and Coleroon river delta, the NGOs called 'Sevai' have created a number additional hand pumps. The hand pumps installed by them are technically superior to the state installed hand pumps. Besides these, they gave training to local people for operating and repairing the hand pumps. A peculiar form, of participation has been observed in this village. Users by organizing themselves extended the pipelines from the main distribution line and created stand post closer to their houses. This sort of illegal practice is in vogue in all the sample villages.

In Nagayanallur village Panchayat, a village having both mixed characteristics, the NGOs role has been worth a mention. They provided hand pumps in three habitations, of which two are operational at the time of survey. The provision made is perfect in construction of platform and a small tank to store water for washing purpose.

Interestingly an upper caste group in this village organized themselves in consummating an overhead tank facility and installed house service connections for about 60 households. They mobilized fund from economically well off people to meet the capital investment of OHT. A member has donated land required for construction and another member donated the well. And for operation and maintenance they collect Rs. 50 per month from the users and operate successfully. The water supplied through public sources has been used for washing cloths and livestock maintenance.

Another habitation in Nagayanallur village is called Karung Kadu, where people use open well for drinking purpose and for lifting the water up, households in this habitation have collectively procured a electric motor pump. They collected Rs. 10 per household per month towards operation and maintenance.

Oothukuli village Panchayat, a dry village, where spring is the main traditional source, there has been no community participation towards water supply. NGOs played little role in this village in creating sources. When enquired about streamlining the spring source, the residents were reluctant that the state would disturb the traditional source in the process of constructing platforms or hand pumps.

Thenpuranadu, a village Panchayat, situated in a hill area, where there was no sign of NGOs service. However, people's participation in this realm is significant. In Nachilipatti habitation, which comes under Thenpuranadu, the entire population of the habitation organized themselves in mobilizing funds towards digging an open well in their habitation. The residents handed over the open well to the TWAD Board, the board then invested money in fixing motor, pipelines and the whole distribution system. Even till date the distribution system from the open well has been successfully functioning.

On the whole, the participation by the people towards water supply is not homogeneous across the villages. However, the common feature is rendering their labour in one form or the other towards creation of sources. In regard to the role played by NGO, their service has been substantial in wet villages than in dry villages. This may be due to cost factor. The cost of providing additional sources may be cheaper in wet villages than in dry villages. And, finally, community participation has become indispensable as the state would initiate and implement water supply programmes only if the representations come collectively from a group or a user's association. The fact remains that the realization on the part of the people about the strength and the effectiveness of community participation is relatively lower in Tamil Nadu when compared to the State of Karnataka. Across the country the community participation is gradually proving to be a powerful tool in achieving the provision of safe water.

5.13.1 Tariff Estimation for Rural Water Supply

Pricing of rural water supply primarily aims at achieving sustainable rural water supply. Mobilisation of financial resource is necessary to achieve this. The responsibility of the state lies in creating the required sources in villages and leaving the responsibility of operation and maintenance with the Panchayats.

Designing appropriate tariffs for water help to achieve twin objectives: pricing forbids wasteful use of water and reduces the quantity of water that is wasted and contributes to protect the environment. Secondly, it facilitates revenue collection, in turn enables meeting O&M costs and recovers initial capital investment.

For an overall management of water resource to achieve sustainable utility, appropriate pricing policies are instrumental for effective demand management. This in fact, is an offshoot of the provision of agenda 21 of the United Nations Conference on Environment and Development (United Nations, 1997b).

The provision of potable water in rural areas on a sustainable basis is feasible only with replacement of expired sources and creation of new sources to meet the demand. This exercise entails expenditure not only on the part of the state but also from the users. User finance instills a sense of commitment on the part of users besides reducing wastages. For the select five villages estimation of the recovery rate required to cover operation and maintenance and quality control of water and calculation of the tariff rate have been carried out in the following manner.

Information on the capital cost, the amount of expenditure made each year for the creation of source and installation of required equipments, was obtained from the TWAD Board. The data on yearly expenditure on capital investment was available for ten years i.e., form 1989-90 to 1998-99. The cumulated capital cost is calculated by summing up yearly capital expenditure for ten years. In estimating the replacement cost, the capital expenditure of each year was adjusted for change with appropriate price index. The replacement cost, therefore, is $\sum_{i-110}^{10} \frac{I}{}$ where I is the capital expenditure adjusted with price index. The operation and maintenance cost obtained from the respective village Panchayats ranged from 0.5 to 5 per cent. However, the Rajiv Gandhi Drinking Water Mission through ARWSP and MNP prescribed that operation and maintenance cost be 6 per cent of the capital cost. Hence the present estimation also considered 6 per cent for the same and calculated per annum cost of O&M by dividing it by 10 (ten) years. A newer dimension is added in this cost estimation, that is the water quality improvement cost. In consultation with the TWAD officials, the quality improvement cost was taken to be 3 per cent of the total capital cost and incorporated in the estimation accordingly for each year (Table 5.28).

Here the tariff is estimated by taking all types of modern schemes and its costs of implementation. The water charge has to be recovered from all the users in order to cover replacement cost and to operate and maintain the sources on a continuous basis. It is left to the policy-makers to decide whether the rate can be collected along with property tax from the rural property owners.

By summing up the replacement cost, O&M cost and quality improvement cost the recovery cost per year was arrived. Next by dividing the recovery cost by the population in the respective village the annual per capita tariff per head was obtained. Ultimately tariff per capita per head per annum was thus arrived.

5.13.2 Calculation of Water Tariff for House Service Connections

The block rate pricing method with increasing rate is applied here. The data collected from Nagayanallur, one of the study villages is taken as a case to illustrate tariff estimation.

Number of house service connection	:	200
Population covered	:	1000
Water supplied per capita	:	82 litres
	:	82000 litres
Rounded off to	:	100000 litres
Capital cost	:	Rs. 240.72 lakhs
O&M cost (6% of capital cost)	:	Rs. 14.44 lakhs
Period of the project	:	15 years
O&M cost per year	:	14.44/15
	:	0.96 lakhs
Cost per month	:	0.08 lakhs
Quality control cost (1 % of the total cost)	:	2.40 lakhs

Table 5.28 : Tariff estimates of rural water supply – for all users.

(In Rupees)

Name of the village	*Cumulated capital cost 1990 to 1999*	*Replacement cost per annum*	*Operation & maintenance*	*Quality control cost*	*Recovery cost per annum*	*Per capita tariff per annum*
1	2	3	4	5	6	7
Athikudi	13,80,000	637341	82800	41400	761541	15.40
Oothukuli	9,88,410	.434658	59304	29652	523614	16.91
Mullipadi	18,42,000	870593	110520	55260	1036373	29.95
Nagayanallur	36,28,000	1484533	217680	108840	1811053	29.23
Thenpuranadu	17,57,000	905723	105420	52710	1063853	14.92

Quality control cost per year	:	0.16 lakhs
Per month	:	0.013 lakhs
Total cost to be recovered	:	0.08 + 0.013
Per month	:	0.093 lakhs (9300 Rupees)
Monthly Tariff required towards recovery (For an average family size of five)	:	47.7 Rupees

The assumptions set are in order:

1. Source of water created, pumped up to the Over Head Tank and distributed only to the houses with pipeline connections facility.
2. Each user has paid Rs. 2000 as deposit for getting house service connection.
3. Each user has a single source of pipe connection, which is metered to gauge the amount of water drawn.
4. The scheme got started during 1999-2000, with an investment of Rs. 240.72 lakhs.
5. As per the primary household survey, 82 lpcd has been provided to through this facility.
6. Tariff rates are calculated assuming each person gets 100 lpcd and family-size being 5 and drawing 500 litres per day for their domestic use.
7. The life-term of the scheme is for 15 years. The O&M cost are taken as 6 per cent of the capital cost and quality control cost as 1 per cent of capital cost.
8. The monthly tariff rate is calculated only for recovering the operation and maintenance cost and the quality control cost.
9. One lakh litres supplied per day is split up into various blocks of 20,000 litres, 20,000 litres, 25,000 litres 25,000 litres and 5000 litres. The remaining 5000 litres is assumed to be lost during transit.
10. First block of 2000 litres being provided free of cost, the subsequent quantum is charged at Rs. 2.5 per 1000 litres, Rs. 4.5 per 1000 liters for the next block and so on (see Table 5.29).

Table 5.29 : Tariff Estimates for House service connection

(In Rupees)

Block No.	*Quantity supplied (litres)*	*Rate per 1000 litres (Rs.)*	*Revenue per day (Rs.)*	*Revenue per month (Rs.)*	*Cumulated revenue per month*	*Per capita tariff per day*	*Per capita tariff per month*
1	2	3	4	5	6	7	8
1	20000	0	0	0	0	0	0
2	20000	2.5	50	1500	1500	0.05	1.50
3	25000	4.5	112.5	3375	4875	0.113	3.39
4	25000	5	125	3750	8625	0.125	3.75
5	5000	6	30	900	9525	0.03	0.90
							9.54

In recovering Rs. 9,300, the total cost to be recovered to operate and maintain the house service connections per month, the estimated tariff as shown in Table 5.29 may be applied. For every successive block, i.e. starting from the first block 20,000 litres to the fifth block of 5,000 litres attract tariff as indicated in column 7. The cumulative revenue per month reaches Rs. 9525, (which is close to Rs. 9300, can be seen in the fifth row and six column of the above table) when 95,000 litres of water are distributed. In this way, the per capita tariff per month viz., Rs. 9.54 is arrived.

The Eighth Five Year Plan as a strategy gave water a status on par with other resources. Subsequently the constitutional Amendment Act of 1992, entrusted the Panchayati Raj Institution to shoulder the responsibility of operation and maintenance of rural water supply. The Panchayati Raj Institutions are empowered to raise appropriate user charges to strengthen their financial base. The rural water supply systems create assets in the form of bore well, overhead tanks; stand posts and hand pumps etc. The sustenance of these assets depends largely upon the financial position of the village Panchayats. Due to inadequacy of funds for operation and maintenance, many water supply schemes were non-functional for some periods.

Estimation of water tariffs made in this study has great deal of implications. The first set of tariff aimed at all the users of public sources such as hand pump and stand posts. The estimated tariff for all users ranged from Rs. 15 to 30, at current prices, per capita per annum. It may work out to be Rs. 75 to 150 per household per annum. Now the problem is collection of the tariff from the actual users. Since this is a public source, the tariff amount can be collected along with house tax, similar to that of urban areas. In the case of house service connections, the estimated tariff showed Rs. 47.7 per household per month at current prices. In reality, the actual tariff now in vogue is rupees 30 per household per month. Although proposed tariff is certainly higher than the actual rate in practices, but the enhanced rate includes quality control cost.

Now in India 'user pay principle' is the current paradigm, which all the states are trying to invoke towards mobilizing funds for sustainable provision of public utilities. The users may no longer expect the state to provide and to take care of operation and maintenance. However, the fact remains that states have so far succeeded in making partial and total provision of water sources.

It becomes the responsibility of the local bodies to operate and maintain, unless the local panchayats could get same return through tariff collection, the village panchayats will not be in a position to ensure continuous water supply. It is in this context, the water tariffs are relevant.

In addition, potable drinking water as a merit good qualifies state intervention in ensuring minimum level for all inhabitants. There is justification for water tariffs in rural areas that the actual users gain participation in water provision by paying water tariffs. As merit good is associated with integrating the state's role in provision and the users role in sharing the cost in certain proportions through tariff.

There a number of arguments in support of water tariffs under user pay principle. The amount of money spent by the households for health care per annum showed a minimum of Rs. 850 to maximum of Rs. 2,760. In the event of failure of modern public sources, the users shall have to resort to unsafe sources resulting in health problem, which involve medical expenditure. By complying to the users pay principle, the user can save the expenditure which would otherwise be spent on health care.

Apparently, collection of rural water tariff appears to be an imposition of tax on rural households in general and poor in particular. The whole exercise is to mobiles fund from the users as tariff and this process instills a sense of commitment on the part of the users. Eventually, the tariffs collected will help achieving sustainable rural water supply. Even the rates are nominal and the rural households shall be in a position to internalize this cost as evidenced through their willingness to pay for better service. Incidentally, the expenditure made by households on other items exceeded multiple times higher than what is expected under water tariffs. For instance, expenditure during festival time used to be very high. It is only the mindset of the users to pay towards water tariff that matters here.

The solution to this problem lies in the mindset of the users to share the cost of the schemes. User financing is increasingly reckoned as a potential source of raising resources to make good the deficit in the budgetary provisions towards rural water supply. The economic rationale lies in treating water as 'not a free good'. Water resources need to be optimally allocated among the competing uses.

6

SUMMARY OF FINDINGS AND CONCLUSION

In the foregoing chapters the objectives set out in the introductory part, have been realised both with the help of secondary and primary household survey as well. This chapter intends to make a thematic presentation of the actual outcomes that have forth come in the study. Thematically this study is fourfold. Firstly, the macro picture at the nation as a whole, and the district profile arrived with the help of the secondary source of information, formed the basis of the subsequent exercises carried out in the study. Secondly, the actual behaviour of household, with respect to water for domestic uses as captured through household survey, represented the demand aspect of the question in the hand. Thirdly, the environmental implications of water provision from the points of view of groundwater depletion, water quality, health and environmental conflicts, remained a crucial facet of the study. And, finally, the institutional mechanism which operationalies the water provision is of great significance in this context.

6.1 Pattern of Rural Water Provision in India and in the Study District

The analysis of the NSSO data from 54th round unfolded the overall scenario of various schemes as sources in the country as a whole. Evidences support the view clearly the dominance of modern/mission schemes proving to be a major principal source of water over the period. Consequently, the traditional schemes had lost its significance as principal source in rural India. However, traditional schemes still remained as major supplementary sources of water for rural habitats. An hypothesis testing carried out in this study proved this argument.

On the quality front, even the modern schemes attracted a substantial number of complaints from the users particularly with the tube-well and hand pumps. Contrary to the principal of modern schemes i.e., providing water on a continuous basis even during summer season. The NSSO data brought to light the plight of households who depend on modern schemes, suffering from water scarcity during summer season. A large-scale use of earthen containers was reported in states like Haryana, Rajasthan and Gujarat. In states like Tamil Nadu, Kerala and Assam and a widespread use of plastic containers was reported and among them Tamil Nadu ranked first in plastic containers. The reason may be why the Tamil Nadu state is seriously contemplating to introduce an Act banning the use of plastics in the state. However, the act is yet to be implemented and still waiting for the legislative approval. In the case of water quality treatment by the users, less than 5 per cent reportedly adopted scientific methods, while 75 per cent not doing any treatment and the rest of them took to some conventional modes like using plain cloth for filtering and so on.

In the process of preparing a profile of rural water supply in the district at the habitation level based on the re-survey (1999) information collected by the TWAD Board, the analysis of the data showed the modern sources provided include hand pumps and power pumps (OHT, public fountain, and house service connection). Ninety-five per cent of the habitations have access to hand pump facility. Forty-six per cent of the habitations have been covered with power pumps and 8.4 per cent has pipelines extended from other sources. Even though more 90 per cent of the habitations were covered by hand pump scheme, but the provision of hand pumps as against the Government norm has not been fulfilled in 73 per cent of the habitations. The concentration of OHT facility is higher in wet villages. The capacity of OHT has been lower as against the Government norm in all the habitations. In dry villages the number of stand posts provided per 1000 population is below the norm. Combined Water Supply Scheme (CWSS) is the latest water supply programme under implementation. Of the total capital invested in the district, 56 per cent goes to CWSS. In terms of coverage of habitations, CWSS could cover even remote villages where water scarcity is acute, with potable water. However, CWSS is not cost-effective. Of the total schemes, about 51 per cent of them were installed during 1981-90, which is the International Drinking Water and Sanitation Decade. Regression results suggested that variations per capita water per day supplied has been explained by independent variables such as area, stand posts per 1000 population, and yielding capacity at 5 per cent level of significance. The R square has been 0.22.

The installation cost per scheme worked out to be Rs.0.29 lakh for hand pumps, Rs. 2.89 lakhs for power pumps and Rs. 1118.1 lakhs for CWSS at current prices. In sum, the cost of provision of public water has been significantly higher more so with CWSS. In financing the water supply schemes 49.3 per cent of the total cost was borne by LIC extended loan. The state contributed 16.6 per cent through MNP, 6.3 per cent by the local body and 5.9 per cent by the Central Government; others to the extent of 16 per cent towards various schemes in the district. The contributions made by international agencies have been less than one per cent of the total. With respect to cost, the provision of water supply is skewed more towards wet, and mixed villages than the other categories. Execution of water supply schemes were more by TWAD Board followed by local bodies, District Rural Development Agency (DRDA) and others.

The hard fact is that only less than 10 per cent of the houses had in-house latrine facilities. Despite this, 99 per cent of households used open-air defecation. This may not have direct link with rural water provision, but indicates the over all insufficiency of water for all purposes.

6.1.1 Household Demand for Water

The findings that emerged from the analysis of primary household survey are as follows dependence on modern/mission sources had started only after 1970s and remained as a major source at present. Wet village received more number of schemes than the other category of villages. Mixed villages enjoyed more of combined water supply schemes. Dry village received relatively less public utility facilities and depended largely on traditional sources. Hilly region has been served by traditional source through modern scheme of distribution of water. Major modern schemes identified in the study villages included hand pumps, power pumps (OHT, CWSS, GLWR), public fountain, house service connection, and agricultural bore-well while, the traditional sources are spring, *kudavu*, stream, river, pond and open well. Among the modern schemes, power pumps are dominant from which respondents drew water for domestic purposes. Hand pumps are more widely used in wet village. House service connections are not given in dry and hilly regions.

The mean distance travelled to fetch water in wet and mixed villages was less than 100 metres and time taken being 62 minutes. In dry and hilly regions the mean distance was 775 metres and spent on an average four hours towards fetching water for domestic purpose. The time spent for fetching and waiting time for traditional source ranged a minimum of one hour to a maximum of 6 hours during summer. The total water drawn for domestic purposes per household is estimated to be 366 litres. Of which, water utilized for drinking and cooking purposes is 30 litres per household and it constitutes 8 per cent of the total consumption only. The lpcd is 76 litres, and for drinking and cooking purposes it is 6.1 litres. The per capita consumption by livestock is estimated as 10 litres per day.

A causal relationship is established between per capita water consumption per household and independent variable such as area, cooking per day, and family size and value of house. These four variables turned out to be significant at 5 per cent level. The value of R square is 0.21. Area and family size showed negative relationship while, value of house and cooking per day showed positive sign. Willingness to pay is positive with 75 per cent of the respondents. On an average, the amount of money that they are willing to pay is Rs. 8 per month per house for improved water supply. Among the total respondents, the percentage of women water collectors constituted 93.8, inclusive of female school going children.

6.1.2 Environmental Implications

Water quality results confirmed 25 per cent of the total water samples tested showing values above the maximum permissible limits. Of which surface water samples contain higher faecal coliform levels while in ground water samples total hardness, iron, TDS, chloride, magnesium and calcium levels were found above the permissible levels. On health front, contrary to the responses of the respondents, the health officials confirmed higher percentage (above 60 per cent) of occurrence of water borne diseases in the sample villages. Typhoid being the highest, followed by jaundice and cholera were the water borne diseases prevailed in the villages. Ninety per cent of the total respondents owned no latrines. Even those who are all having, not preferring to use the latrines rather than going for open-air defecation. The decadal growth rate of depletion of groundwater showed that it was 6.4 metres during 1971-80, it had declined to 8.5 metres during 1981-90 and from 1991-99 the level showed 7.5 metres. Fall in groundwater will have adverse impact on rural water supply. Hypothesis testing with the help of Analysis of variance (ANOVA) confirmed that there is direct relationship between environmental degradation in terms of depletion of natural resource and the burden of women in general and female children in particular in collecting water.

Environmental conflicts in the district unfolded a new dimension. As against the general tendency that increasing number of bore-wells resulted in depletion of groundwater thereby affecting drinking water source, the newer phenomenon observed is that combined water supply scheme meant for augmenting drinking water provision allegedly depleting the groundwater potential thereby damaging the water meant for the agricultural activities.

6.1.3 Institutional Mechanism

Two separate tariff rates for rural water supply based on the primary survey information have been worked out: (a) a rate ranged between Rs. 22 and 44, as per capita per annum for recovering replacement cost and O&M cost for the all the study villages, and (b) a rate Rs. 48 per household per month for recovering O&M cost and maintaining quality for those having house service connections.

6.2 Suggestions for Policy Improvements

Policy prescription towards rural water provision is yet to gain momentum. The National Water Policy of 1987 has not emphasised adequately to drinking water provision. But the need of the hour is to ensure potable water supply to all. This has been the agenda right from the center on the top to local village panchayats to the bottom. Increasing realization of water-borne diseases due to consumption of unsafe water, makes it all the more necessary to prioritize drinking water and accord utmost importance to drinking water provision.

No doubt, efforts have been made at the Central and State levels from time to time to cover all the habitations with adequate water provision. The Rajiv Gandhi Drinking Water Mission stood as a testimony to this. But any effort made in a piece meal fashion may not fetch the desired results. A holistic approach to policy-making is mandatory at this level. It means policy exercise may consider efficiency, equity and sustainability and give equal weightage to all the three components. In this way the target group gets assure of not only the quantum prescribed but also the quality being ensured. The present study made in this backdrop makes the following suggestions towards improving the present policy and strategies.

1. Comprehensive Water Supply Schemes (CWSS), which is in vogue in the study district needs certain modifications. The present system of CWSS poses a host of problems. For instance, in the event of a failure of CWSS in one particular location, the impact will be on all the users from various different locations, which are connected under CWSS. Similar is the case of water quality. Therefore, the present CWSS system should be allowed to function not in isolation of the existing systems, be it a traditional or a modern.
2. The norms, set out by the State Government, the TWAD Board, are the offshoot of the Gandhi Drinking Water Mission. As estimated in the present study, water required for drinking and cooking purposes alone ranged from 5 to 8 litres per capita per day lpcd. The current norm viz., 40

lpcd followed may be inappropriate as the actual quantity requirement for all domestic purposes was more than 75 lpcd.

3. The use of potable water is not warranted for certain domestic purposes such as house cleaning, gardening and other uses. However, the actual practice is to use the potable water for all the purposes. The feasible solution lies in protecting and maintaining the traditional schemes thereby encourage households to resort to traditional schemes for purposes other than drinking, cooking and bathing.
4. On confirming the fact through field survey, the deplorable conditions of traditional schemes, particularly the operation and maintenance part in all the selected villages, it is suggested that it is imperative to invoke all the traditional practices like irrigation tanks, percolation ponds, by means of watershed management and water harvesting. This is a solution for sustainable water use and practice in the long run.
5. In India, the access to safe water is declared as a fundamental right. This necessitates and reaffirms the state's responsibility in ensuring this. The policy suggestion here is a need for a change in the mindset of the users, who should come forward to participate in the programme and to share the expenses involved collectively.
6. It is observed that there is a disparity in the provision of schemes across villages. Wet villages enjoyed more water supply schemes than the dry and hilly regions. The state provision shall be holistic and balanced if more schemes are diverted towards dry and hilly regions. Even the NGOs have a greater role to play in dry and hilly regions, where there is a dearth of schemes and sources.
7. Hand pumps and stand posts are basically mechanical appliances, requires proper maintenance to avoid breakdown. These appliances are subjected to all sorts of handling by all sections of rural people, and hence they are bound to breakdown. Consequently, the users are forced to resort to unsafe sources. The only solution to

this is to operate efficiently and ensure proper and regular maintenance. Lack of operation and maintenance cost has been the major cause of failure of most of the state created schemes and sources. Inadequate finance is the offshoot of operation and maintenance problem. Improper tariff system is the reason for paucity of funds besides dismal budgetary allocation. To ensure the schemes to be sustainable in long-term necessary, funds need to be generated. The user pay principle may sound relevant in this context. The users shall be able to pay for maintenance. This calls for rationalizing the water tariff. Estimates made by the present study suggests that Rs. 48 can be fixed as a monthly tariff rate per household with house service connection instead of the present tariff of Rs. 30. The revised tariff can take care of quality of water plus operation and maintenance cost. Other users without house service connection may be charged between Rs. 22 and Rs. 44 per capita per annum. This rate ensures recovery of capital, operation and maintenance and quality of water. The tariff may be incorporated with the property tax as is practiced in most urban areas.

8. There is no gain saying the fact that water sources meant for drinking purpose are contaminated and causing health hazards. Human and mechanical failures are the major causes for the prevalence of water-borne diseases. Mixing of sewage with drinking water owing to leakage of water pipes is the dominant cause for the incidence of gastro-enteritis, which affected all the study villages. Special attention needs to be paid towards the safety of pipelines and this single measure may have a tremendous effect ensuring health care in the rural areas.
9. Controversies over traditional *vis-à-vis* modern sources are continuing over the last two decades. Modern schemes *ipso facto* mission sources have an edge over traditional sources in the recent period. However, traditional sources are handy wherever modern source fail. Even in some cases, modern technology is applied to distribute water by drawing water from traditional sources. The traditional sources are to be conserved and preserved. The current

concept of *rainwater harvesting* needs to be popularized in rural areas. Modern schemes should supplement traditional water sources but not supplant the latter.

10. Supply based strategy of rural water supply has proved unsuccessful in the past. Still 44 per cent of the habitations remained partially covered with respect to provision in the district. Demand driven approach is the need of the hour. Investment decisions on water supply should be demand responsive.
11. There is a need for an enactment of an act on safe drinking water. As of now, there is no separate act towards achieving safe water in India. In view of the fact that more than 80 per cent of the diseases are water-borne, a full-fledged act may bring in double dividend in achieving safe water quality on the one hand and health care on the other.

6.3 Conclusions

Water as a renewable natural resource, which incidentally has no substitute, gets allocated across sectors like agriculture, industry and domestic use. Although the domestic sector requires less than 10 per cent of the total in developing countries, one-fourth of the rural population is deprived of access to potable water. Even where provided, the distribution and water quality problems continue to persist. Water being the state subject, concerted efforts have been undertaken at the central and state levels since early seventies. India, as signatory to the United Nations resolution on International Drinking Water Supply and Sanitation Decade 1981-90 had pledged its full support to the action plan under the Decadal programme. The launching of the "Rajiv Gandhi National Drinking Water Mision-1986" for rural water supply is a break-through and brought in many changes in the implementation of water supply schemes in rural areas. In this backdrop, the present study made an attempt to understand the implications of rural water supply programmes at Tiruchirappalli district of Tamil Nadu. This is achieved by conducting case studies of five villages under four categories with a sample of 311 households to enable to discern the actual problems at the grassroots level and to suggest measures for improving the existing system.

At the national level, the recovery of working expenses towards rural water supply has been zero as evidenced by gross receipts in states like Tamil Nadu, Karnataka, Madhya Pradesh and Tripura. This necessitates the rationalization of tariff rates for rural water supply in India. The rural water supply scenario in Tamil Nadu is no different from other states in terms of coverage of habitations. However, the state had the reputation of having started the Tamil Nadu Water and Drainage Board first in the country in the early seventies. The state budgetary allocation towards water supply has been gradually increasing from 41 per cent in 1992-93 to 71 per cent in 1997-98. While, the central assistance through ARP declined slowly from 36 to 22.6 per cent between 1990-91 and 1999-2000.

Tiruchirappalli, the study district is situated at the central part of Tamil Nadu, where the rivers Cauvery and Coleroon flow through. The water supply schemes implemented in the district are of twofold, hand pump and power pump. The schemes depended entirely on groundwater resources. While a newer project called Combined Water Supply Scheme (CWSS) has been a recent phenomenon in the district in the last one decade. The CWSS depends only on sub-surface water through infiltration well and gallery.

The wet villages of the district enjoyed a higher number of schemes, fulfilling the Government norms of hand pumps and stand posts; here the NGOs played a greater role when compared to other category of villages in the district. The dry and hilly villages received scant attention from the TWAD Board, as 90 per cent of the villages under this category did not fulfil the Government norm.

Historically, traditional surface sources of water had remained a major source for rural population for domestic purposes including drinking and cooking. After the advent of modern schemes people slowly started drawing from mission sources, which depended on ground water. Now, the advanced schemes like CWSS draw water from sub-surface water sources to cater to the needs of the area where there is dearth of water resource. The point to reckon with is switchover from groundwater to sub-surface sources as the former is depleting rapidly and the slowing down of yielding capacity. So far, between 1972 and 1999, the state had invested Rs. 1.8 billion towards this sector. The total investment made showed a declining trend moving from mixed to wet, dry and hilly region.

In financing the schemes, LIC loan was the maximum followed by MNP and local bodies. During the period of Rajiv Gandhi Drinking Water Mission, the maximum number of schemes was initiated. The TWAD Board has provided the highest number of major schemes, power pumps and CWSS in particular. The CWSS being a unique project of rural water supply in the district has already covered 36 per cent of the total habitations and the state is pinning its hope on this scheme to cover the remaining problem villages in the district.

Primary households survey results unfolded many interesting features on economic and environmental dimensions of rural of rural water supply. In wet and mixed villages the modern schemes dominated the traditional source, while in dry and hilly region the traditional sources served as principal sources and modern schemes are only supplementary sources as far as drinking and cooking purposes are concerned. By looking into usage of water for all domestic purposes, TWAD Board and local body sources contributed more than 60 per cent, while the rest goes to traditional plus own sources.

On an average, the selected households consumed 76 lpcd; of which, the TWAD Board provided 61 per cent and the remaining is met through traditional sources. Drinking water consumption constituted 3 per cent of the lpcd. Distance and time are the minimum in villages where the modern sources are predominant. Longer distance and time are associated where traditional source of water is availed. The legacy of women as water collectors has not changed; women continue to bear the burden of fetching water for domestic use in rural areas of the district.

Water quality results confirmed the presence of faecal coliform level over and above the permissible level in surface water, while the physical and chemicals parameters exceeded the tolerance limits in groundwater sources. Health hazards owing to contaminate water though is prevalent, majority of the households are unaware of the linkage between unsafe water and water-borne diseases. Notwithstanding the Governmental efforts towards construction of latrines in housing colonies, as high as 90 per cent of the households continue to use open air for defecation. Less than 10 per cent of the houses had any one form of the latrines. Even those owning seldom use the same for the purpose intended. Open-air defecation continues to be the practice in the rural district.

Community participation is limited to the extent of bearing minimum expenses of maintenance of machines and labour service to expedite the scheme executions.

Two sets of regression results confirmed a causal relationship firstly at the habitation level between water availability (lpcd) and area, stand post per thousand population and quantity litre per minute and secondly, between water consumption per household and area, cooking per day, value of house and family size.

Environmental dimensions of rural water supply brought forth by the study revealed depletion of groundwater natural resource to the extent of 1.1 metre, during 1971 to 1999. The spin-offs of environmental degradation in terms of depletion of groundwater resources on females including female children are evident in Oothukuli village. And, finally, the environmental conflicts arising over depletion of groundwater between agriculturists and domestic sector owing to the implementation of CWSS, add a newer dimension to water conflicts.

As part of an outlining alternative strategy, estimation of tariff rates for rural water users with and without house service connections were done separately. Inculcation of user pay principle will help achieve sustainable use of existing schemes.

To conclude, the status of provision of drinking water at the national, state and district levels have been unsatisfactory. Despite efforts from National and International Forums, on an average sixteen per cent of the rural habitations remained uncovered. Even where provided, the problem of O & M continued to persist. This study confirms that the implementation of water provision schemes is skewed towards wet and mixed villages, while arid and hilly regions have received less attention. This is evident with respect to creation of physical assets such as hand pumps and OHTs, capital investment made, lpcd, distance travelled and so on. Traditional sources of water continued to be handy in villages where the Government schemes played a lesser role. In regard to water quality, surface water sources were susceptible to biological contaminants, while the groundwater being affected by chemical and physical contaminants. As against the contention of the state, that modern sources are safer and the conventional sources are unsafe, the findings of our study are not in line with the Government's stand on quality of water.

The policy implications that have been forthcoming pleaded for *demand responsive* decision-making in the provision of rural water supply rather than supply oriented. The latter proved to be a failure owing to uneven distribution across the categories of villages in the study district. More investment is needed in dry and hilly regions of the district where the existing schemes are small in number, while the demand for domestic use is higher in these two categories of villages. Finally, the user pay principle needs to be invoked for rural water supply too. As against the arbitrary water tariff, a rate, which ensures continuous operation and maintenance plus good quality, has to be tried to achieve sustainability in rural water supply.

BIBLIOGRAPHY

Abdalla, C.W., B.A. Roach and D.J. Epp (1992). 'Valuing Environmental Quality Changes Using Averting Expenditures: An Application to Groundwater Contamination', *Land Economics*, May, Vol. 68 (2), pp. 163-169.

Adrian, H.G and E.M. William (1981). 'Price Elasticities for Water: A Case of Increasing Block Rates: Comment', *Land Economics*, May, Vol. 52 (2).

Agarwal, A. (1997). 'Water and Sanitation', *Down to Earth*, Sep. 15, Vol. 6(8).

Agarwal, A. (1999a). 'Promising water', *Down to Earth*, Sep. 15, Vol. 8(8).

Agarwal, A. (1999b). 'Safe drinking water' *Down to Earth*, Vol. 8 (3), June 30, 1999.

Agarwal, A. (1999c). 'Disasters in the making? Groundwater contamination in India is verging on disastrous proportions, especially with regard to mercury', *Down to Earth,* August 31, Vol. 8 (7).

Agarwal, A. (2000). 'Beyond the Billion', *Down to Earth*, June 30, Vol. 19 (3), pp. 30-36.

Agarwal, A. and Narain, S. (1997). *Dying wisdom, State of India's Environment - A Citizen's Report*, Centre for Science and Environment. New Delhi.

Alberini, A. (1995). 'Testing Willingness-to-Pay Models of Discrete Choice Contingent Valuation Survey Data', *Land Economics*, Vol. 71 (1), pp. 83-95.

Alexander, A.P. (1994). 'Why Don't Households Connects to the Piped Water System? Observations from Tunis, Tunisia', *Land Economics*, May, Vol. 70 (2), pp. 189-196.

Alexander, H.R. (1987). 'Status of the International Drinking Water Supply and Sanitation'. In F. W. Montanari, Terrence P. Thompson, Terrence P. Curran Walter Sankin, (eds.), 'Resource mobilization for drinking water and sanitation in developing nation', American Society of Civil Engineers. 345 east 47th street, New Delhi.

Asit, K.B., M. Jellall and G.E. Stout (1993). '*Water Resource Management: Water for Sustainable Development*' (ed.) in the Twenty-first Century, Oxford University Press, New Delhi.

Balachandra, K.K. (1994). 'Water, Sanitation and Health', *Kurukshetra,* March, Vol. XLII (6).

Bandyopadhyay, J. (1987). 'Political Ecology of Drought and Water Scarcity: Need for an Ecological Water Resources Policy', *Economic and Political Weekly,* December 12, Vol. 22(50).

Bhat, G.K. and A. Revi (1995). 'Water Crisis in Earthquake–Affected Areas of Marathwada', *Economic and Political Weekly*, July 22, Vol. 30 (29).

Bhatt, Y.K. and S. Ganapathy (1996). 'Community participation in rural water supply utthanmahiti experiment', proceedings of a National Seminar on Rural Water Supply and Sanitation, held at Center for Development Studies, Thiruvananthapuram, June, 20-22, (Unpublished).

Bijlani, H.U. (1998). 'Safe Water and Sanitation–The Future Outlook and Action', *Nagarlok*, Dec. Vol. 30 (4).

Billings, B.R. and D.E. Agthe (1981). 'Price Elasticities for Water: A Case of Increasing Block Rates: Reply', *Land Economics*, May, Vol. 57(2).

Biswas in Cox, W.E. (1987). 'The role of water in socio-economic development, Studies and reports in hydrology', UNESCO.

Brown, P. (1998). '*Global warming an civilization service*', University Press (India) Limited, Hyderabad.

Chaddha, D.K. (1999). 'We have enough water, we only need proper water management', *Down to Earth*, Vol. 8(3), June 30.

Chakravarthy, S. and K.S. Biswas (1997). 'An Approach to Rural Drinking Water Supply in India', Water Resource Journal, Sep, ST/ ESCAP/SER.C/ 194, pp.16-21.

Chatterji, D. (1997). 'Economic Evaluation of Urban Water Supply Schemes' *Economic and Political Weekly*, Vol. 32 (26).

Choe, K., D. Whittington and D.T. Lauria (1996). 'The Economic Benefits of Surface Water Quality Improvements in Developing Countries: A Case Study of Davao, Philippines', Land Economics, November, Vol. 72 (4), pp. 519-37.

Clark, R.M. and R.G. Stevie (1981). 'A Water Supply Cost Model Incorporating Spatial Variables', *Land Economics*, Vol. 57(1), February.

Daniels J.I., D.W. Layton, M.A. Nelson, A.W. Olivieri, R.C. Cooper, R.E. Danielson, W.H. Bruvold, R. Scfield, D.P.H. Hsieh and S.A. Schaub (1987). 'Organoleptic Water Quality: Health and Economics Impacts', In F.W. Montanari, Terrence P. Thompson, Terrence P. Curran Walter Sankin, (eds.), 'Resource Mobilization for Drinking Water and Sanitation in developing nations', American Society of Civil Engeneers, 345 east 47th street, New Delhi.

Dasgupta and Maler (1995). Poverty, Institutions, and the Environmental Resource Base, Handbook of Development Economics, Amsterdam: North Holland.

Davis, J., G. Garvey and M. Wood (1993). '*Developing and Managing Community Water Supplies*', Oxford Publication, 274 Banbury Road, Oxford.

Desai I.P. (1973). Water Facilities for the Untouchables in Rural Gujarat, Indian, Council of Social Science Research, New Delhi.

Development Promotion Group (DPG) (1999). Water and Sanitation. *News Review,* April-Sept.

Dhawan, B.D. (1987). 'Management of Groundwater Resources Direct *Versus* Indirect Regulatory Mechanisms', *Economic and Political Weekly*, Vol. 22 (30).

Dick, R.M. and M. Mendoza (1996). 'Alternative Water Allocation Mechanisms – Indian and International Experiences', *Economic and Political Weekly*, March 30, p. A-25.

Durgaprasad P. (1996). 'The synergistic relationship between water, health and development', *Kurukshetra*, Oct.-Nov., Vol. XLV (182).

Economic and Social Commission For Asia and the Pacific (1997). 'Guidebook on Private Sector Participation in Water Supply and Sanitation', United Nations, New York.

Filmer, D. and L. Pritchett (1996). 'Environmental Degradation and the Demand for Children', Policy Research Working Paper. 1623,The World Bank.

Ghosh, G., Mazumdar, K., Dubeey, A. and Ghander, J. (1995). *'Water Supply in Rural India – Policy and Program'*, Ashish Publishing House, New Delhi.

Glseser, B. (1995). 'Housing, Sustainable Development and the Rural Poor – A Study of Tamil Nadu', pp. 124-129, Sage Publications, New Delhi.

Golladay, F.L. and S. Katsu (1982). 'The Role of Prices in Management of Water Resources, Water for Human Consumption', Vol. 2. International Water Resources Association (IWRA), Selected papers prepared for the IV World Congress of the International Water Resource Association.

Gomez, C. (1987). 'Experience in predicting willingness to pay on water projects in Latin America', in F.W. Montanari, Terrrence P. Thompson, Terhence P. Curran Walter Sankin, (eds.). 'Resource Mobilization for Drinking Water and Sanitation in Developing Nations', American Society of Civil Engineers, 345 east 47th street, New Delhi.

Government of India (1987). *'National Water Policy*, Ministry of Water Resources', Government of India.

Government of India (1999). *'Guidelines for Implementation of Rural Water Supply Programme'* Rajiv Gandhi National Drinking Water Missions, Ministry of Rural Areas and Employment.

Government of India (2000). *'Annual Report 1999-2000'*, Ministry of Rural Development, Delhi.

Government of India (2000). *'Economic Survey'*, Ministry of Finance, Economic Division', New Delhi.

Government of Tamil Nadu (1994). *'Tamil Nadu State Water Policy'*, IWS, Chennai.

Government of Tamil Nadu (1999). 'Tamil Nadu state-water vision exersion 2025', Public Works Department, Water Resource Organisation.

Goyal V.C. (1997). 'Water-wise in Uttarakhand', *Down to Earth*, Vol. 5 (22), April 15.

Gupta S.K. and P. Sharma (1997). 'Pure Stuff', *Down to Earth*. Vol. 5 (17), Jan 31.

Hansen, L.G. (1996). 'Water and Energy Price Impacts on Residential Water Demand in Copenhagen', *Land Economics*, February, Vol. 72 (1), pp. 66-79.

Harou, P., A. Markandya., L. Bellu and Cistulli (1998). 'Environmental Economics and Environmental Policy' — A Work Book, Prepared by the EDI — World Bank and The Commission of the European Communities.

Hewitt, J.A. and W.M. Haneman (1995). 'A Discrete/Continuous Choice Approach to Residential Water Demand under Block Rate Pricing', *Land Economics*, May, Vol. 71 (2), pp. 173-92.

Hoek, W.V., F. Konradsen, J. Ensince., M. Mudasser and P. Jensen (2001). Irrigation water as a source of drinking water: is safe use is possible? Tropical Medicine and International Health, 6 (1) pp. 46-54.

Hoque, B.A., A.A. Shafiul., J.T.A. Chowdhury, U.K. Chowdhury and M.M. Hoque (1998). 'Surface Water Pollution Concerns in Public Health Perspectives of Bangladesh', *Water Resource Journal*, March, ST/ESCAP/SER.C/196.

Hoque, B.A., A.A. Shafiul., J.T.A. Chowdhury, U.K. Chowdhury, J. Chakrabarty and R.B. Sack (1998). 'Domestic Water and Health Inside a Flood Control, Drainage and Irrigation Project in Bangladesh', *Water Resource Journal*, December, ST/ESCAP/SER.C/199.

Hoque, B.A., R.B. Sack., J.T.A. Chowdhury and A. Nohid (1997). 'Domestic Water and Sanitation in Cyclones and Floods: Priorities and Challenges', *Water Resource Journal*, March, ST/ESCAP/SER.C/192.

Hossain M.V.S and S.T. Naeeni (1973). 'Optimization of Water Distribution Networks', *Water Resources Journal*, United Nation Building, Bangkok, Thailand.

Howarth, R.B. (1997). 'Defining Sustainability: An Overview', *Land Economics*, November, Vol. 73 (4), pp. 445-447.

India Rural Development Report (1999). 'Regional Disparities in Development and Poverty', National Institute of Rural Development, Rajendranagar, Hyderabad.

International Water Resources Association (IWRA) (1982). *Water for Human Consumption*, Tycoly International Publishing Ltd., Dublin.

Iqbal, M. (2000). 'Science and Environment Fortnightly', *Down t Earth*, June 30, p.55.

Jacob, J. (1997). *Economics of Public Water Supply System*, Rawat Publications, Jaipur.

John R.M., D.M. Johnson and R.G. Walsh (1995). 'Valuation Time in Travel Cost Demand Analysis: An Empirical Investigation. *Land Economics*, February, Vol. 71 (1), pp. 96-105.

Jordan, J.L.(1999). 'Externalities, Water Prices and Water Transfers', Economic and Social Commission for Asia and the Pacific, *Water Resource Journal*, ST/ESCAP/SER.C/202/ Sep.

Jyoti, P. and P. Kirit (1999). 'Clean Water Environmental Governance-1', Indira Gandhi Institute of Developmental Research, Bombay.

Kailash (1996). 'Water Crisis in Port – Blair', *Economic and Political Weekly*, August 17, Vol. 31 (33).

Kashyap, S. (999). 'Miracle Man', *Down to Earth*, Vol. 8 (11), October 31.

Khanna, S. (1997). 'Water Weary', *Down to Earth*. Vol. 5 (22), April,15.

Kirit, P., P. Jyoti, V.K. Sharma and J.P. Painuly (1993). 'Natural Resources Accounting: A Framework for India', Indira Gandhi Institute of Development Research, Bombay.

Kishwar, M. (1999). 'Reclaiming Lost Power: Saurashtrians Resolve to Make Their Villages Water Sufficient', Manushi, No.118.

Kothari, A.(2000). 'Where has all the water gone?' *The Hindu*, May 14, (Chennai edition).

Larson, B.A. and E.D. Gnedenko (1999). *Avoiding Health Risks from Drinking Water in Moscow: An Empirical Analysis, Environment and Development Economics*, Cambridge University Press, New York, Vol. 4, pp. 565-581.

Maler, K.G. (1997). 'Environment, Poverty and Economic Growth', Annual World Bank Conference on Development Economics. The International Bank for Reconstruction and Development / The World Bank, pp. 251-276.

Matzger, H. and M. Moench (1994). 'Ground Water Availability for Drinking in Gujarat Quantity, Quality and Health Dimensions', *Economic and Political Weekly*, March 26, Vol. 39 (13), p. 33.

McNeill, D. (1999). 'Water as an Economic Good', *Water Resource Journal*, ST/ESCAP/SER.C/200/ Issue No. 377-8053.

Miller, J.R. (1993). 'On the Economics of Western Local Water Finance: The Central Utah Experience', *Land Economics*, August, Vol. 69 (3), pp. 299-303.

Mishra, M. (1999). 'Charting a New Course', *Down to Earth*, Vol. 8 (6), August 15.

Mishra, S. (1996). 'Safe Drinking Water and Primary Health Services', *Kurukshetra,* Oct.-Nov., Vol. XLV (182).

Moench, M. (1994). 'Approaches to Ground Water Management to Control or Enable?, *Economic and Political Weekly*, September 24, Vol. 29(39).

Mohanty, B. (1992). 'Drinking Water for Growing Cities – Third World Perspective', *Economic and Political Weekly*. Vol. 27 (19), May 9.

Musgrave, A.R. and P.B. Musgrave (1973). *Public finance in theory and practice,* McGraw-Hill Kogakusha Ltd., New Delhi, pp. 80-81.

Nair, R.M. (1998). 'Water: Self help, best help, Survey of Environment', *The Hindu* (Madurai edition).

Narayan, L.R.A. (1999). 'Managing Groundwater", *The Hindu,* June 27.

Narayanamoorthy, A. (1996). 'Electric Pump Set and Ground Water Management, Macro and Micro Evidence of India', *Water Resource Journals*, June, p. 28.

National Sample Survey Organisatiom (NSSO). (1999). *'Drinking Water, Sanitation and Hygiene in India' 54th round*, Department of Statistics, Government of India.

Nerlove, M. (1991). 'Population and the Environment: A parable of Firewood and other tales', *American Journal of Agricultural Economics* 73, pp. 1334-47.

Nieswiadomy, M.L. and D.J. Molina (1989). 'Comparing Residential Water Demand Estimates under Decreasing and Increasing Block Rates Using Household Data'. *Land Economics*, August, Vol. 65 (3), pp. 280-89.

Nieswiadomy, M.L. and D.J. Molina (1991). 'A Note on Price Perception in Water Demand Models'. *Land Economics*, August, Vol. 67 (3), pp. 352-59.

Nitivattananon, V., E.C. Sadowski and R.G. Quimpo (1997). 'Optimization of Water Supply System Operation', Water Resource Journal, Environment and Natural Resources Management Division, United Nation Building, Bangkok, Thailand.

Niyathi, N. (1996). Problems and prospects of planning of rural water supply in Kerala. Proceedings of national seminar on rural water supply and sanitation, pp. 23-24. Thiruvananthapuram: Centre for Development Studies.

Norton, B.G. and M.A. Toman (1997). 'Sustainability: Ecological and Economic Perspectives', *Land Economics*, November, Vol. 73 (4), pp. 553-68.

Pande, G.C. and D.M. Mithani (1990). *Encyclopaedic of Economics*, p.161. Anmor Publication, Ansari Road, New Delhi.

Pathak, M.D. (1999). 'Rural Water Supply/Groundwater Conservation Programmes: Development with the Community', Ashwatha, April-June, Vol. 2(2).

Perry, C.J. R. Michael and D. Seckler (1995). 'Water as an Economic Good: A Solution or a problem', International Irrigation Management Institute, 14 Research Report, pp. 1-16.

Pradeep (1999). 'No Water Where the Oceans Meet', *Down to Earth*, Vol. 8 (5), July.

Pradeep K.P. (1997). 'The effects of safe drinking water and sanitation on Diarrhoeal diseases among the children in rural Orissa', Working paper, No. 277, Thiruvananthapuram: Centre for Development Studies.

Provencher, B. (1993). 'A Private Property Rights to Replenish a Groundwater Aquifer', *Land Economics*, Vol. 69 (4), pp. 325-40.

Pushpangadan, K. and G. Murugan (1994). 'Pricing of Drinking: An Application of case Two-Part Tariff. Working paper, No. 261, Thiruvananthapuram: Centre for Development Studies.

Pushpangadan, K. and G. Murugan (1995). "Cost Efficiency of Water Supply in Kerala," *Productivity*, 36(2), pp. 228-235.

Pushpangadan, K. and G. Murugan (1996). 'Equitable User rates for sustainable rural water supply: An India case study. Proceedings of national seminar on rural water supply and sanitation, pp. 11-14. Thiruvananthapuram: Centre for Development Studies.

Pushpangadan, K. and G. Murugan (1997). 'User Financing and Collective Action Relevance for Sustainable Rural Water Supply in India'. Working Paper No. 274, Thiruvananthapuram: Centre for Development Studies.

Pushpangadan, K. and G. Murugan (1998). 'Pricing with changing welfare criterion: An application of Ransey-Wilson model to urban water supply', Working paper No. 287 Thiruvananthapuram: Centre for Development Studies.

Pushpangadan, K. and G. Murugan and K. Navaneetham (1996). 'Travel Time User Rate and Cost of Supply Drinking Water in Rural Kerala', India, pp.1-18. Working paper No. 266, Thiruvananthapuram: Centre for Development Studies.

Ram, R.N. (1992). 'Drinking Water from SSP Doubtful Claim', *Economic and Political Weekly*, Vol. 27(30), July 25.

Rao, S.R. (1994). 'Urban Water Supply Sector: Some Issues', *Urban India*. Vol. 14(2) July-Dec.

Rathore, M.S. and R.V. Ratna (1996). '*Urban Water Management*', Rawat Publications, Jaipur.

Reddy, R. (1999b). 'Pricing of Rural Drinking Water: A Study of Willingness and Ability to pay in Western India', *Journal of Social and Economic Development*, Jan-June, Vol. 2(1), pp.101-122.

Reddy, V.R. and M.S. Rathore (1993). 'Bias in Social Consumption: A Study of Residential Water in Rajasthan', *Economic and Political Weekly*, August 7-14, Vol. 28, No. 33.

Reddy, R.V. (1999a). 'Quenching the Thirst: The Cost of Water in Fragile Environments', *Development and Change*, Vol. 30(1), pp. 79-113.

Renwick, M.E. and S.O. Archibald (1998). 'Demand Side Management Policies for Residential Water Use: Who Bears the Conservation Burden?' *Land Economics*, August, Vol. 74 (3), pp. 343-59.

Robert, S.J. and W.J. Jeremy (1976). *Village Water Supply Economics and Policy in the Developing World*, Published for the World Bank, The Johns Hopkins University Press, Baltimore and London.

Sachchidananda, (1999). *Social Dimensions of Water Supply and Sanitation in Rural Areas – A Case Study of Bihar,* p. 14, Concept Publishing Company, New Delhi.

Saha, P.K. (1971). 'Self-Financing Urban Water Supply, A Model for Asansol – Durgapur', *Economic and Political Weekly*, Vol. 6(26).

Saleth, R.M. (1994). 'Towards a New Water Institution: Economics, Law, and Policy', *Economic and Political Weekly*, September 24, Vol. 29(39), pp. 147-155.

Sangvai, S. (1994). 'People's Initiative to Solve Water Crisis in Saurashtra', *Economic and Political Weekly*, August 20, Vol. 29(34).

Santhakumar, V. (1998). 'Inefficiency and Institutional Issues in the provision of merit goods: A case study of public water supply in rural Kerala.' Working paper No. 285, pp. 1-34, Centre for Development Studies, Thiruvananthapuram.

Satyan, B. (1996). 'Drinking water supply with respect to people's participation; an experiment of the Thiruvananthapuram District Panchyath' in the proceedings of National Seminar on Rural Water Supply and Sanitation, Centre for Development Studies, Thiruvananthapuram, pp. 85-87.

Schefter, J.E and E.L. David (1985). 'Estimating Residential Water Demand under Multi-Part Tariffs Using Aggregate Data', *Land Economics*, August, Vol. 61 (3), pp. 272-280.

Singh, S.K. (1996). 'Role of Panchayats in Rural Water Supply and Sanitation Programme', *Kurukshetra,* Oct. – Nov., Vol. .XLV (182).

Singh, P. (1999). 'Water of life', *The Economic Times*, 23-29 July.

Sosa, L.Y. (1999). 'Ownership of Water Rights, Water Allocation and Pricing', *Water Resource Journal*, ST/ESCAP/SER.C/203/ Issue No. 377-8053.

Stevens, T.H., N.E. DeCoteau and C.E. Willis (1997). 'Sensitivity of Contingent Valuation to Alternative Payment Schedules', *Land Economics, February,* Vol. 73 (1), pp. 140-148.

Sundaram, K. (2001). Employment and Poverty in 1990's: Further Results from NSSO 55th Round Employment and Unemployment Survey –1999-2000, *Economic and Political Weekly*, Vol. 36(32), August 11-17.

Suresh, V. (2000). 'Managing Water', *New India Digest*, July-August, Vol. 4(77).

Suryanarayanan (1997). 'National Water Policy in India', In Ajit K. Biswas, Cesar Herrera Toledo, Hector Gardenno Velasco, Cecilia Torkyada Quiroze, (ed.) *National Water Plans for Developing Countries*, Oxford University Press, Mumbai.

Sutherland, R.J and G. Walsh (1995). 'Effect of Distance on the Preservation Value', Rural Development and Water Conservation Department and Urban

Development Department, 'Drinking Water Supply Programme – White Paper', Mantralaya, Mumbai.

Terza, J.V. and W.P. Welch (1982). 'Estimating Demand under Block Rates: Electricity and Water', *Land Economics,* May, Vol. 58 (2), pp. 181-188.

The Hindu (1999). 'Drinking water, no longer safe in Delhi', February 22.

The Hindu (1999). 'Unsafe Drinking Water Cripples Villagers', August 15.

The Hindu (2000). 'Farmers Oppose Perambalur Water Supply Schemes', November 14.

Thirlwall, A.P. (1999). '*Growth and Development',* 6th Edition, MacMillan Press Ltd., London.

Thoane, B. (1997). In Karl – Goran Malar *op. cit.*, p. 262.

Travis Katz and Hennifer Sara, (1997): '*Making Rural Water Supply Sustainable: Recommendations from a Global Study',* Washington D.C. – The World Bank.

Turvey, R. (1976). 'Analyzing the Marginal Cost of Water Supply', *Land Economics,* May, Vol. 53 (2), pp. 158-68.

United Nations (1997a). 'Guidelines for Establishment of Pricing Policies and Structures for Urban and Rural Water Supply', *Economic and Social Commission for Asia and the Pacific,* New York, pp. 1-6.

United Nations (1997b). 'United Nations Comprehensive Assessment of the Freshwater Resources of the World', United Nations Dept. of Policy Coordination and Sustainable Development, New York.

United Nations (1998). Economic and Social Commission for Asia and the Pacific, : 'Towards Efficient Water use in Urban Areas in Asia and the Pacific', New York.

Vaidya, C. (1994). 'Willingness to Pay for Urban Water and Sanitation some Methodological Issues', *Urban India,* July- Dec. Vol.14 (2).

Veerashekharappa (2000). 'Reforms in Rural Drinking Water Supply, *Economic and Political Weekly*, February 12, Vol. 34(7), pp. 583-584.

Verma, J. (1999). 'We have enough water. We only need proper water management', *Down to Earth,* Vol. 8(3), June 30.

Vidyasagar, R.R. (1997). 'Water and Sustainable Development: Indian Scenario', *Water Resources Journal,* Environment and Natural Resources Management Division, United Nation Building, Bangkok, ST/ESCAP/SER.C/195/ December.

W.H.O. (1993). 'Guidelines for Drinking Water Quality', W.H.O, Geneva.

Watson, W.D. and R.G. Ridker (1981). 'Revising Water Pollution Standards in an Uncertain World', *Land Economics*, November, Vol. 57 (4), pp. 485-506.

World Bank Water Demand Research Team, (1993). 'The Demand for Water in Rural Areas: Determinants and Policy Implications', The World Bank Observer, Vol. 8(1), January, pp. 47-70.

Yadav, U. (1999). 'Drinking Water for all: A Distant Dream', *Khadigramodyog, the Journal of Rural Economy,* Vol. 44(4).

Index